Rio de Janeiro

Rio de Janeiro

Extreme City

LUIZ EDUARDO SOARES

Translated by Anthony Doyle

ALLEN LANE

an imprint of

PENGUIN BOOKS

ALLEN LANE

UK | USA | Canada | Ireland | Australia
India | New Zealand | South Africa

ALLEN LANE is part of the Penguin Random House group of companies
whose addresses can be found at global.penguinrandomhouse.com

First published in Portuguese under the title *Rio de Janeiro: Histórias de vida e morte* by
Companhia das Letras, Brazil, 2015
This translation first published 2016

002

Set in 12/14.75 pt Bembo Book MT Std by Thomson Digital Pvt Ltd, Noida, Delhi
Printed in Great Britain by Clays Ltd, St Ives plc

A CIP catalogue record for this book is available from the British Library

ISBN: 978–1–846–14802–6

www.greenpenguin.co.uk

Penguin Random House is committed to a
sustainable future for our business, our readers
and our planet. This book is made from Forest
Stewardship Council® certified paper.

Contents

Introduction

The Rio de Janeiro found in tourist brochures is all party, samba, hedonistic sensuality, Carnival and football, set against white beaches and bountiful nature, a place of welcoming camaraderie, harmless roguery, creative improvisation, joy and spontaneity. In short, the marvellous city as sung in prose and verse and sold in package holidays the world over. In 2014, the city hosted the World Cup final and, in 2016, receives athletes from around the globe for the Olympic Games. These mega-events have attracted international attention and added a few more strings not usually associated with the traditional bow of tropical beauty, including wealth, modernity, efficiency, administrative competence and alignment with technological progress. All of these components blend into a solar, vibrant panel that unfortunately eclipses a more sombre, fraught and contradictory reality. The Rio that inhabits the global imagination is one big cliché.

It would be a mistake to deny the existence of many of those qualities, but they in no way annul the underside of the Rio experience, pervaded as it is with violence – much of it perpetrated by the State against the poor – inequality and racism. What seems most interesting and innovative about the present conjuncture in Rio de Janeiro is not just the general abhorrence of the objective hardships affecting millions of its citizens each day, but also of the founding cliché that has quick-dried into an idealized image. The rebellion against platitude has rallied the youth above all, though it has also stoked far wider segments of the population who have realized that the stereotype is not merely a misrepresentation, but actually a handbook for everyday behaviours and perceptions. It is not just a false portrait but is a restrictive model, a straitjacket of identity that constricts other ways of being and feeling.

The old image is gradually crumbling under the weight of society's more lucid and critical apperception. The cliché is in flames and metamorphosis under way. Cities are like snakes that shed their skin.

So from what frame of reference should an author address this process? The first-person singular steps up as the most reasonable and honest perspective, especially when the world shaking and sliding away reverberates not only on substantive levels across public life, but also through so many subjective dimensions of our private lives. It is interesting to see how, in this shift between worlds, subtlety and bombast alternate to the point of overlap, depending on the beholder's sensibility. After all, these distinct, opposing worlds do and will coexist. Purity is a quality of theory, not history, much less histories told from personal standpoints, and so I have allowed myself to adopt this personal perspective with a certain frequency, writing in the first-person singular (and sometimes plural).

Occasionally the clearest mirrors are those further away, so let me begin with a first-person account of an event that occurred in another city. Saturday morning in Jardim

Ângela, one of the most violent neighbourhoods in the world,* on the outskirts of São Paulo. It's midway through 2001. Winter is here, but it's warm inside the packed Santos Mártires parish church. I'm sitting at a table in front of the altar alongside Lula, three colleagues and our host, the Irish priest Jaime Crowe, who arrived in Brazil in 1969 and went on to become an important local human rights leader. Lula is Luiz Inácio da Silva, who in 2003 would take office as President of Brazil, winning re-election for a second term in 2007. A huge crowd, here to see and hear Lula, has gathered outside the church. There isn't enough money to rent a big screen, but the proceedings can be followed over the PA. We're here to gather data for the national security plan we're drafting and we've invited the local populace to come and speak to us about how violence in the area affects their lives.

People take turns at the pulpit to share their harrowing experiences: sons murdered by the police just outside their homes; nephews mowed down by the police in broad daylight; the neighbour's kid, mistaken for a drug dealer, tortured to death by police interrogators; an actual drug dealer, cuffed and unarmed, summarily executed by a police death squad for all to see; the families of witnesses to police brutality subjected to threats and extortion by bent cops, and the countless dozens kidnapped and disappeared, or beaten to death by officers of the law. All the speakers are poor, most are black, and they've all been Brazilian long

---

* According to UN statistics published in 2000. Murder rates in the area stood at just over 116 per 100,000 inhabitants, or 200 per 100,000 if we consider only men aged fifteen to twenty-five.

enough to know what that combination means. The bitter truth they've learned the hard way holds for the slums and shanty towns of São Paulo and Rio de Janeiro, for the ghettoes of all Brazil's major cities and for the lawless wilds of the Amazon, abandoned to the predatory greed of economic interests. As the courage of the first speakers rubs off on the rest, the queue to the pulpit grows and grows. Men and women, old and young, weep and sob their way through heart-rending declarations and leave the pulpit still in tears. Some of them say that they'd been too afraid to tell their stories before, because to denounce police brutality is sheer suicide, but they have decided to do so now because they trust Lula and Father Jaime. They have decided to risk their own necks to ensure that these uniformed assassins don't get away with murder. Their hope is that life will be different under Lula. The stories go on, rolling out their long red rivulet. The crowd listens in heavy silence.

But Lula is showing signs of impatience, shifting in his chair and glancing around. Tapping my arm, he whispers in my ear:

'I can't believe this. It's been over an hour, and no one's said anything about health, education, unemployment. They only want to talk about the police.'

'You know why that is, Lula?' I reply. 'For these people, the police are a question of life or death. Their lives, their children's lives, are in the hands of the police. They never know if their kids are going to make it home in one piece at night: the police are so unpredictable anything could happen. Our democracy will continue to be shitty until the day something radical is done about the police and criminal justice system, and everything else that goes with it — all those issues long ignored by politicians, and which you, too, have not really taken seriously.'

Lula drinks some water and gets up to stretch his legs. I wonder whether I've overdone it a bit. After all, we're comrades — but he's Lula, the presidential candidate. On the other hand, who knows, my little rant might raise his hackles, make him turn finally toward these decisive but invisible issues that lie ever present but just out of sight. My outburst might possibly be the spark that all those lengthy rational expositions could never provide.

After two and a half hours of personal tragedies, Lula addresses the crowd with his customary ardour and charisma. I left the place reinvigorated, hopeful. The dream I nourished was that Lula would be elected and that his presidency, the first leftist government in Brazil's history, would cut the umbilical cord binding the police forces to the government and the other de facto dictatorships that preceded the military coup of 1964. In a sense, the (self-)perception of the police as the repressive arm of the prevailing powers can be traced back four centuries to the arrival of the first slave ships. My dream was that Lula would light the touch-paper for real transformations in public security and the criminal justice system in Brazil.

It didn't happen. Following his election, Lula appointed me his National Secretary for Public Security, but he balked at his commitment. There were priorities that demanded the sacrifice of what on the smorgasbord of political goodies amounted to second-tier concerns, the thankless dirty work of security, criminal justice, the police force and prison system. I was sacked. I became a liability for the government, because I insisted on rubbing its nose in a problematic agenda that the presidency was studiously avoiding. As a nation we paid a high price for this negligence – a price that is particularly exorbitant in Rio de Janeiro, as this book will show.

Politics became a part of my life early on, because I grew up in Rio under Brazil's years of dictatorship. My biography is no more interesting, revealing or important than any other but, like all others, it tells a story. Mine involves the dictatorship, begun by coup d'état in 1964, which took hold within and among all Brazilians, but perhaps us cariocas – inhabitants of Rio – most of all. In no other city did the regime bare its claws so early or so fiercely. I decided to tell Rio's story through my own, because it's the one I know best.

When I went to university in 1972 to study literature, I decided to devote myself to the resistance movement. I felt a need to know society in order to make my engagement more rational so, as a postgraduate, I turned to anthropology and – though aware of its limitations – I began to appreciate the value of the democratic rule of law it had cost my generation many lives to construct. While my anarchist friends read French authors and viewed State institutions as fetters on their desires, obstacles to their liberty, I saw them first and foremost as the restraints which civil society imposes upon the Leviathan: as checks against a totalitarian state.

One question kept surfacing in my mind: when is violence a legitimate tool in resisting oppression, in opposing a dictatorship? At that time – in the 1970s – it was a big issue. I opted for pacific resistance. When, in 1988, Brazil's new

Constitution came into force, the question was reformulated: it was now a matter of reining in the State, its police forces and criminal justice system; of stymieing the arbitrary, brutal and eminently racist traditions of repression that had become entrenched over the centuries and which were newly radicalized during the decades of dictatorship. How do you give the democratic rule of law genuine force in the everyday lives of citizens, especially the most vulnerable? Moreover, how do you do so while striving to curb the rise in criminal violence?

As criminal and police violence spiralled in the 1980s and 1990s, the human rights agenda grew more vocal. No transition from dictatorship to democracy would be complete if the police continued to kill, torture, humiliate and behave arbitrarily. This is the task I have set myself: as an academic – teaching at the Rio de Janeiro State University – and as a civil activist and public administrator. I have held government posts at federal level (during the first year of Lula's first mandate, in 2003), state level (in Rio de Janeiro, from January 1999 to March 2000) and twice at municipal level (in Porto Alegre, Rio Grande do Sul; and Nova Iguaçu, Greater Rio), and I've seen old and new mentalities clash head on.

However self-evident the idea that a democratic police force is an accountable police force might appear, it seems far from obvious to social movements, democratic political parties and wider Brazilian society. The testimonies given on that Saturday morning in Jardim Ângela form a dramatic portrait of the abyss that separates grass-roots realities in Brazil from the political mindset – even among leaders supposedly committed to radically democratic agendas. And nowhere is the matter of police brutality more pressing than in Rio de Janeiro, Brazil's beating heart.

A city sheds its skin like a snake. It changes its colours, tones, sensibilities – all the relationships that define it and bring it to life. But to get to the heart of Rio you first have to strip away the cliché: the image of this city of a thousand charms and unsurpassable beauties, of samba, hedonistic sensuality, Carnival and football, set against white beaches and bountiful nature; with its joyous, partying, fun-loving denizens, known worldwide for their festivity, openness, generosity, musicality and hospitality. It's a cliché with a deep hold and powerful allure. The message it sends out is strong because it's true – but only partially so; and, what's more, the image is all the more treacherous because it serves a function. It succeeds in concealing the darker side of the city. And a cliché designed to eclipse the negative rather than accentuate the positive is a dangerous thing indeed. This book happily declares war on that cliché.

The city of São Sebastião do Rio de Janeiro* was founded in 1565, six decades after the Portuguese colonizers first arrived on the western shores of South America to stake out the territory later known as Brazil. Over five million native indians perished in the ensuing struggle against European invaders and viruses, against which their immune systems had no defence. As such, the first chapter in Brazil's history tells of the genocide of its indigenous tribes. Hardly surprising, then, that a nation born in massacre should, in 1889,

---

* Saint Sebastian is the patron saint of Rio, and his feast day, 20 January, is a municipal holiday.

have become the last in the world to abolish the African slave trade, after 400 years of merciless exploitation. Still less surprising is that today, even as the world's seventh-largest economy, with a population of over 200 million and a GDP in excess of 1.5 trillion dollars, the country remains one of the most violent and socially inequitable in the world, and one of the most racist too.

That said, it is important to stress that not everything about Brazil is cause for shame and indignation. The country managed to re-establish democracy in the late 1980s after twenty years of criminal military dictatorship; today, social movements are alert to the problem of racism and the need to eradicate it; minorities are now consolidating a voice and demanding their rights; and inequality is no longer just part of the landscape but is the subject of fervent debate. It is sadly true that corruption has never been quite as voracious and audacious as it is today – but neither has it been tackled with such resolve, transparency and robustness. Brazil's cultural wealth is as expressive as it is varied, and it runs from mathematics to music, literature to audiovisual production, Amerindian mythology to urban architecture, and the samba-funk of the shanty towns and slums to academic virtuosity. Lastly, Brazil is home to unrivalled environmental riches: to start with, its vast biodiversity. Such is Brazil's ecological importance that the protection of its environment is proving vital to the stability of the global climate. If Brazilian society learns to protect its environment and invest in a low-carbon economy, opting for cleaner, renewable fuels that harness rather than consume natural resources, it will be doing humanity a vital service.

Rio de Janeiro, the country's capital from 1763 to 1960, is Brazil in a nutshell. Today, the city – capital of the state of the same name – is home to a population of 6.5 million. The Greater Rio area accounts for 12.2 million of the state's overall population of 16.5 million. Rio society is growing younger: over a third of the population are aged twenty-four or under with 50.3 per cent aged between twenty-five and fifty-nine. Roughly 200,000 youths between the ages of eighteen and twenty-four – about 27 per cent of the total age group in the city – neither study nor work. The vast majority of these youths live in outlying neighbourhoods. In the Jacarezinho favela, in the north of the city, the figure is closer to 40 per cent.

One statistic plunges us straight into the heart of Rio's darkness. According to the 2010 Census, female cariocas outnumbered males by 53.2 per cent to 46.8 per cent. This difference is not explained by nativity rates or life expectancy, which are within the national norms, but by something else: the staggering number of men – poor black men in particular – who die premature violent deaths each year. In Rio, as nationwide, a young black male is nearly three times more likely to be murdered than his white counterpart.[*]

---

[*] Waiselfisz, Julio Jacobo et al., *Mapa da Violência, 2015* ('Map of Violence, 2015'), based on data from 2012 and 2013, published by Flacso. Cano, Ignacio et al., *Índice de Homicídios na Adolescência, em 2012* ('Teenage Murder Rates in 2012'), a study conducted and published in 2015 by Observatório de Favelas, with support from the Federal Government's Human Rights Department, UNICEF and the State University of Rio de Janeiro's Violence Analysis Laboratory.

Between 2005 and 2014 there were 18,243 homicides in
Rio city. In 2014 alone there were 1,237 murders, a rate of
19.3 per 100,000 inhabitants.* These killings, it is important
to note, were overwhelmingly concentrated in low-income,
low-schooling communities on the fringes of Rio society.
Murder rates in more affluent parts of the city resembled the
European average (3.6 per 100,000 in the middle-class neighbourhoods of Catete, Flamengo and Botafogo, and 3.9 in
Copacabana). In the poorest neighbourhoods, rates hovered
at around 33.9 (in the North Zone) and peaked at 34.6 on the
western fringe.†

In all this, the police have proved part of the problem
rather than the solution. Between 2005 and 2014, 5,132 people were killed in police operations in Rio, equivalent to 28
per cent of the total number of registered homicides. If we
add the police tally to the figure above, the real number of
murder victims in Rio rises to a shocking 23,375 over a ten-
year period. The territorial distribution of the police's use
of lethal force overlaps with the map of homicides: concentrated in underprivileged areas and mostly impacting on the
young black population.

Rio, of course, remains the country's best-known tourist
destination. The city, second only to São Paulo in wealth
generation, is rich, with a GDP in the region of US$80 bil-
lion per annum, with GDP per capita coming in at roughly
US$11,800. The concentration of employment in the
city means that Rio de Janeiro has one of the worst daily

---

*For the sake of comparison, there were 328 murders in New York in
2014. Source: *New York Times*.
† Thanks to Ernesto Salles for bringing these figures to my attention.

commute times in the country, with 28.6 per cent of the population taking over an hour to get from home to workplace. In more distant neighbourhoods like Guaratiba or Santa Cruz, 13 per cent of the population spend over two hours travelling to or from work each day. Traffic is the talk of the town. If you consider visiting Rio, be patient. Our constant traffic jams will not be among the most pleasant moments of your life. It's not chaotic or polluted, but noisy and gridlocked enough to rank among Rio's worst features.

Rio de Janeiro remains deeply unequal. In the first decade of the twenty-first century, while Brazil saw an overall 31 per cent rise in incomes among the poorest fifth of the population, the comparable increase in Rio was 5 per cent. At the same time, while incomes fell by 6.2 per cent among the country's richest fifth over the same period, they grew by 3.3 per cent in Rio de Janeiro.*

André Urani, one of Brazil's leading economists, expressed the magnitude of Brazil's inequalities like no one else, saying that crossing a street in Rio was sometimes like walking from one century into another. Just a few yards could send the clocks back or forward a hundred years. The social abyss is so gaping as to constitute a time lag. Here is some data that gives good measure of the tragedy: in wealthy South Zone neighbourhoods such as Botafogo and Lagoa, a significant portion of the working population (41 per cent and 48 per cent respectively) earn a monthly income upward of five times the minimum monthly wage (R$1,000/+/-$US300 in 2015). In favelas like Rocinha, Jacarezinho and

* The data above comes from the 2013 Human Development Atlas.

Cidade de Deus, only 1 per cent of the population earn that much. In peripheral neighbourhoods like Pavuna and Santa Cruz, only 2 per cent obtain that kind of income.[*]

In the light of these figures, it should come as no surprise that Rio de Janeiro has the second-highest maternal mortality rate of all Brazilian state capitals: 101.4 deaths per 100,000 births. According to official figures, the Brazilian average is 58.1.[†] The state also performs poorly on infant mortality, with 12.7 deaths per 100,000 newborns.

The negative statistics go on, but they don't by any means annul the city's virtues and exuberant beauty, which is the other face of Janus. Tragedy is the flip side, though in my view it's not the hedonism that speaks the loudest.

In the chapters that follow, I will recount stories I witnessed or accompanied over the course of my life and career in Rio; stories that present the city, and indeed Brazil, from angles that – unfortunately – defy the clichés. I will begin with an autobiographical note focused on the embroilments of the public and private, personal feeling and political thought, the national epic and the family tale. It's a tangle that often eludes historical documentation. My biography is no more interesting, revealing or important than any other. However, like all others it serves to illustrate the events that fell within its scope which, in my case, includes the dictatorship installed upon, among and within Brazilians countrywide, and perhaps cariocas most of all, in 1964. In no other city did

[*] Censo 2010/IBGE.
[†] Datasus, 2013.

the military regime bare its claws quite so early or so fiercely. From there, I will visit the dungeons of the dictatorship to describe the trauma and torment of a young woman who dared resist during the implacable 1970s. In 1999, over a decade after the return to democracy, I took a public security post with the Rio de Janeiro state government. I will recount my most striking experiences from this period, involving a community pushed to the brink, in situations that illustrate the nature of relations between the State and society in Rio and Brazil. From the Mangueira shanty town I will skip to another well-known favela, Maré, where, in 2013, I met the leader of a crime faction and was able to see how things look from the other side of the Front. I will then flit back to 2002/2003 for a behind-the-scenes glimpse at Brazilian politics, particularly the seeds of the first major corruption scandal of the Lula government, the beginning of the PT's (Workers' Party) long moral and political decline, and its present, protracted death rattle in the second term of Lula's successor, Dilma Rousseff. This account visits the palaces of power, the power of the police force, and the parallel power of the drug traffickers, and describes one particular criminal's desperate attempt to save himself, in every sense of the word. Another story takes us deep into the criminal and political underworld on a municipal level, where everything seems all the more shocking for being so much the clearer. But Rio de Janeiro is not all violence and betrayal. There is glitz, joy, festivity and even extravagance in the retooling of religion as kitschy showbiz. The city was also the runway for one brilliant economist's forays over the Colombian Amazon, the vast Atlantic and among the streets of England, where he waded deeper into the cocaine trade. Finally, I will look at the largest unplanned street demonstration in Brazilian history, which drew a million people onto the Rio tarmac in June 2013. The narrative offers some flashbacks from the past and says why there is still hope for the future, despite it all.

It's not comfortable showing the world a Rio turned inside out and yet, without the courage to tear up the costume and throw off the mask, there would not be the strength to face the horror and call it by its name. Only thus will this city be able to emerge from its intoxicating, extended childhood. It's more than time to break the spell, shake off the illusion of paradise and take responsibility. The Messiah is not coming. The 'once and future' King Sebastian, our Tropical Arthur, is dead, not sleeping. The sea is stained with blood.

Pedra da Gávea*

I saw Rio de Janeiro for the first time in 1959, when I was five years old and my family moved from the small mountain town of Nova Friburgo, where I was born, to Niterói. I saw Rio from the window of our apartment, which overlooked São Francisco beach. My parents couldn't afford the rent in the better neighbourhoods, so we had to turn to that enchanting slice of shore customarily scorned as a seaside slum. Ours was the only apartment building in the area, which consisted of a smattering of houses, two schools, a barber's shop, a pharmacy and old Horácio's convenience store, where my dad would send me to buy cigarettes or, when his meagre post office clerk's salary allowed, a bottle of soda for Sunday lunch. Out on the headland the historic chapel stood half hidden on a hilltop, while down below nearly a kilometre of white sand cupped a bowl of calm ocean in the arms of the bay. And it was all mine. The adults thought the place sucked because there was nothing in the vicinity and it was far away from the centre, where all the important stuff went on. But what mattered to me was that I had somewhere to play football and a great view

*Pedra da Gávea is an 844-metre-high granite dome in Tijuca Forest, Rio de Janeiro. It is thought to have formed about 600 million years ago. Thanks to its unusual shape, it is sometimes referred to as the 'sleeping giant'.

of the 'Marvellous City', which I could watch light up every evening. With my chin resting on the window sill, I imagined what it must be like over there in that incredible world, home to a place that to me was tinged with myth: the Maracanã football stadium.

Niterói was paradise, with its provincial calm surrounded by Rio's lush landscape. Of course, there is a dose of irony in the description that didn't make sense at the time. The two cities are neighbours separated only by the sea. For anyone over on the beaches of Niterói, the view is picture-postcard Rio: the Corcovado, the Sugarloaf, all the sinuous topography the tourist brochures never tire of showing. On Sunday afternoons, on the other side of that sound, with my portable radio pressed to my ear, I used to see in my mind's eye the games the commentators rendered in quick-fire commentaries. In my own way, from a distance, I too marched up that famous ramp into the world's largest stadium, the sacred cathedral of football.

The beach left deserted on rainy days, the silence of the narrow cobblestone street between my building and the sand, the solitude that only a radio could breach (when my father let me use it) – all of that provoked a curious melancholy, the yearning to live a future that seemed to be taking for ever to arrive.

As the 1960s progressed and the country was plunged into shadow my maternal grandfather thought only of his grandchildren's schooling. Though he still lived in Friburgo, he ended up convincing my parents that they had to move to Rio: he'd give them an apartment there. My dream was about to become a reality. My parents had taken me into

Rio a few times, usually on holiday Sundays, like Easter, when we'd have lunch at my aunt's place in Penha, on the north side, far from the shore. We'd cross the bay on those sluggish old barges. It was beautiful, for sure, but I'd still not been to Copacabana. Most important of all, I hadn't seen Maracanã.

My grandfather was a wily but austere Portuguese who hung around into his hundreds. He was a polyglot and auto-didact who read the greats: Eça de Queirós and Luiz de Camões, Portugal's Shakespeare. The son of a peasant family, he had been a World War One refugee who, among other things, spent a while living homeless, founded a trade union and blazed a trail with all the energy of a stevedore. He ended his days a Salazarist at loving loggerheads with me. A wizard with words, though economical in everything he did, including in speech, my grandfather managed to convince a patrician that the Communist revolution was only weeks away: homes would be seized and opened to poverty-stricken families. The best the owners could hope for was to stay alive, but they could kiss their private property goodbye: it was a notion in the throes of extinction. The patrician could take it or leave it. He settled for a pittance, handed over the keys to his apartment in Laranjeiras and took his family back to Portugal. On 31 March 1964, a month after we bought the apartment, here in Brazil, a military coup ensured the right to property at the expense of freedom and thousands of lives. It is, therefore, to my grandfather and to fear that I owe the apartment my brother and I grew up in and where my mother lives to this day, still lucid and vigilant. Ironically, the fear that had a significant hand in our move into downtown Rio sank its fangs into my generation and poisoned my youth.

Rio de Janeiro, at last. Party time. Wind in my sails. We arrived in Laranjeiras, home to Fluminense Football Club, of which I was and remain a huge fan. My tenth birthday was coming up. I was sure Dad would take me to Maracanã as soon as the apartment was in order and we had settled in. I was introduced to my new school, which had a respectable football pitch with wooden goal posts. It was the real deal, except for a pair of bushy-boughed trees on either side of the halfway line. Nothing to worry a kid who'd grown up playing footie on sloping sands with an oval ball: just another tactical challenge to factor in. Over the five years I studied at nearby Zaccaria, only once did I get carried away with a shimmy out on the left flank and end up bodychecked by a slab of a defender. I came away with all my teeth, just about. The embarrassment hurt more than the impact.

While our trip to Maracanã had to wait for an opening in my father's agenda, Mum undertook to realize another of her first-born's dreams (I have one younger brother). We rode an electric tram to Cinelândia for my first guitar lesson. It was an important victory for me, a positive outcome to a convoluted dispute about proper living.

In 1960 or 1961 — I can't quite remember the date — I had begun to fixate on the guitar, much to my father's annoyance. 'Guitar's for scoundrels, good-for-nothings, layabouts. No son of mine is going to play guitar.' When he got talking like that, there was no point in arguing. The alternative was to enlist my mother's intermediation. The compromise was violin. After all, they were similar in form – but, in his eyes, violin had pedigree. A violinist is an eminently respectable figure. I agreed, but my dalliance with the instrument was brief. I almost drove my family and neighbours crazy, scratching my way up and down scales and stress-testing eardrums. Happily, what I lacked in talent, they lacked in patience. After that, piano seemed a pretty safe bet and, Mum being a piano teacher, we wouldn't have to look elsewhere for tuition. However, the keyboard turned out to be my younger brother's domain and he reigned supreme. He had a talent that would take him places. My obvious but disciplined mediocrity was a humiliation by comparison. As time went on, my sibling rivalry and envy took tangible form in these instruments. After a while, it was time to recognize defeat and withdraw. Thankfully, I could play him off the pitch at football.

Times were changing. We had moved into the most cosmopolitan city in the country, which, though stripped of its capital status in 1960, was still very much the national heart. All of that, and mother's insistence, made my father change his mind and a guitar teacher was hired. He taught me where to put my fingers, how to tune the strings, all the basic notes and seemed to be a master of harmonics – but, alas, my first lesson was also my last. The teacher was an admirer of Lenin, detested the Pope and shocked the hell out of my mother by saying that all churches should be turned into public libraries. He was, in a word, a Communist.

The first days of March 1964. My childhood joy was about to be introduced to violence – right there, on the corner of our street. Maracanã would have to wait. The events of the following months left enduring, indelible marks. Life wasn't going to get back to normal at any time soon. Or, in a sense, ever again.

On 13 March I was in the sitting room of our new apartment, listening to Dad's radio. President João Goulart was addressing a crowd of 300,000 people at a rally outside Brazil Central Station in downtown Rio. He promised basic reforms which would provide quality education, healthcare, land for those who needed it and jobs for all. Moreover, he would do all this within the bounds of the Constitution. The crowd applauded; people also brandished placards demanding these reforms by whatever means, fair or foul. A few days later some sailors mutinied against their appalling working conditions and managed to open a direct line of negotiations with Jango, as Goulart was commonly known, a move which enraged the stuffed shirts of the military top brass. The resulting unrest had society on the edge of its seat, nerves frayed.

I had turned ten the day before this rally, and though I didn't really understand what was going on I felt plugged into the world. Politics seemed to sweep people into a fervour, just like in the stands of Maracanã. I was made of the same stuff as that moment in history – I don't know what that means exactly, but it was true: it seemed to awaken me, change me in some indefinable way. I recall to this day the president's voice, his southern drawl, the way the last words of each sentence seemed to trail off. Why was I glued to the radio on that 13 March? Partly to be at my father's side, certainly. But also to try to decipher the mystery of life, among other things.

Less than a week later, on 19 March, a crowd of much the same size took to the streets of São Paulo under banners that read: 'Yes to social justice. No to Communism' and 'Reform, but only within the Constitution'. Churches tolled their bells as the march got under way. The movement was orchestrated by Catholic women's groups and received the full support of the Governor of São Paulo, Ademar de Barros, whose wife led the rally.

What I didn't know was this. In the intervening days left-ist leaders, like Leonel Brizola[*] and Luiz Carlos Prestes, the Secretary-General of the underground Brazilian Communist Party,[†] had fired up all engines. Even moderate politicians were fanning the flames. The Communists themselves were in the minority. They didn't have the manpower to start a revolution. Brizola's pro-Goulart militias, the so-called 'groups of eleven', weren't going anywhere fast, and the Peasant Leagues, under Fransisco Julião, were strong, but limited to the north of the country. Indeed, the president welcomed this pressure from the Left, because it helped counter the even greater pressure that was now coming from the Right, especially from Magalhães Pinto, Governor of the influential state of Minas Gerais, and from the incendiary Carlos Lacerda, Governor of the state of Guanabara – which basically corresponded to the city of Rio de Janeiro. This radicalization on either side allowed Goulart to pitch

---

[*] Lionel Brizola (1922–2004), twice Governor of Rio de Janeiro, was Goulart's brother-in-law.

[†] Although banned, the Communist Party existed and was tolerated; its leaders were known, they negotiated with leaders of other parties and were respected as real players.

his tent at the centre, occupying the political middle ground and presenting himself as the man of reason. A former Labour Minister for President Getúlio Vargas, Goulart was a moderate social democrat, a man of the centre-left with ties to the unions. He wanted to steer the ship with a steady hand, avoiding stormier waters and consolidating social conquests within a democratic context. He had stable institutions and the military to back him up. However, the CIA financed elections through the Social Research and Study Centre and used its propaganda machine to spread fear of Communism and warn against an imminent Red Revolution. The scaremongering strengthened the Right. The little anecdotes of my childhood bear witness to the efficiency of this paranoid marketing, and the unwitting but disastrous collaboration of the leftist leadership. Goulart was in danger of losing the run of this polarization, which threatened to annul the centre and leave the situation at the mercy of the gravitational pull of the stronger pole. The one with the weapons.

When push came to shove on 31 March 1964, and the Right moved against the Constitution to depose the president, it didn't have the military might to back it up. On the other hand, the Left proved incapable of rallying society against the threat. In the meantime, the US Navy launched its Operation Brother Sam, deploying its Caribbean fleet to the Brazilian coast in support of the Right. João Goulart decided to leave the country in April to avoid a bloody civil war he couldn't win. He died in exile on 6 December 1976.

The same day, a Tuesday, late afternoon. My father came to pick me up from school with my maternal grandmother.

Bad sign, especially judging from their faces. Stranger still was the fact that loads of other parents had decided to do exactly the same thing. Rua Catete was like a car park, full of Gordinis, Dauphines, DKVs, Beetles and Aero Willyses. Whatever it was, it wasn't restricted to our family. The adults' talk on the short journey home was worrying. A bomb was about to go off. A disaster. A hecatomb. Even more disturbingly, in my presence they tried to disguise their conversation, which just made matters worse, sending my imagination into overdrive. I didn't sleep a wink that night, I remember. As the hours passed, my sense of malaise grew and grew. And even if I hadn't been worried sick, who could possibly get some shuteye with the grumble of tanks chewing up the asphalt? How could I get off to sleep with Grandma praying her rosary up and down the hall all night?

I felt cracked down the middle. I didn't want Goulart to lose. The stuff he'd said, and that those on his side were saying, resonated with what I'd come to value myself. And the people I heard speaking ill of him all seemed more fully rounded versions of what was worst in my dad. As for Grandma's praying, I didn't like that either. I was angry at being shooed out of the sitting room time and again. I was furious at having taken a beating I didn't deserve. I thought it was wrong that there had to be time for this and time for that, things the kids couldn't hear or know, that my haircut always had to be the same crew cut, clippers set to number one, that I had to go to Mass every Sunday, which was interminable and in Latin, and that I was expected to take the class medal every year, top spot, no matter what, and that the one time I came home with an 8.5 out of ten my mother burst into tears. The Mass was fake, mind-numbingly so; the medals were just tin junk that served no other purpose than to please the family and make us feel superior to all the others, but I knew full well that if it hadn't been for my grandfather, not only would I not have been in that school, I wouldn't even have been in Rio de Janeiro, and that it was all just a big lie. I didn't want to be with them, but they were my family.

I finally did doze off, but my sleep was brief. At about 5 a.m. my father came in and woke me and my brother. His voice was so different when he spoke that we didn't even grumble. I jumped out of bed and ran to the window. In the half-darkness I could see the tank parked in the street outside our building, its muzzle trained on us. It's hard to describe the shock. I guess it's how people feel during an armed robbery. Except that in a robbery you know what the thief wants and you just hand it over — your watch, your wallet — but staring at that tank, I didn't know what I was supposed to give up. Only later did I learn that what we were being told to surrender was our freedom, a certain something that adults had, and which must have been great. Years after those events I read about freedom in books and gleaned the concept of it at least, and I tried to exercise it on a subjective level. Real liberty would only come in 1985, when citizenship was allowed to creep out of the closet. In 1988, with the promulgation of a democratic Constitution, freedom became a universal right and a public experience.

The tank was aiming at my window because the building we lived in on Rua das Laranjeiras sat in between two key government buildings: Laranjeiras, where the president

stayed when in Rio, and Guanabara, home to the governor.
By March 1964 the two were sworn enemies. Lacerda, the
governor, was the civil arm of the coup. He was waiting for
troops to arrive from Minas Gerais so he could besiege
Goulart. As for the military, it wasn't clear exactly who was
with whom, but in those days not much seemed obvious. At
times like these, predictions are confirmed more by belief
than by actual events. It's a sense of opportunity that prevails,
because opportunity always roots for the winning side.
When the possible is as good as probable, it pretty soon
becomes reality. It's the gravitational pull of power. The tank
was parked on the corner of Gago Coutinho and Laranjeiras:
its target was Lacerda at the Guanabara Palace. In order to hit
it, the tank would have to send a volley over our nine-storey
building. Our apartment was on the eighth floor – hence the
impression that it was taking aim at my bedroom.

We rushed down to the garage. There was a little garden
in front of the main entrance and it was now home to a new
form of flora, the camouflaged uniforms of soldiers flattening
the plants. Camouflage, my father explained – incrongru-
ously, in the circumstances – was supposed to make people
look like vegetation. He asked the soldiers' permission to
leave the building and drove out slowly, waving his white
handkerchief at either end of the divided street. On the
right-hand side was a wall of sandbags providing cover for
the president's men, whose automatic rifles and machine
guns could be seen poking over the barricade. They were
arranged in formation with their backs to the tank. On the
left, the coup's troops were like a mirror image of those on
the other side – which was only natural, seeing as they'd

been trained at the same academies, by the same instructors, wore the same uniforms and wielded the same weapons. They, too, were crouched behind sandbags.

To be honest, I only know they were sandbags because my father said so. He also told me about the weapons, although by this time I was so worked up that the details of the military positions were pretty much lost on me. My father, a good driver, slalomed around the obstacles with ease, but his movements were slow and deliberate so as not to spook the adrenaline-charged soldiers. My grandma and mum were frozen with panic.

As soon as we were out on the open road, my father slammed the pedal to the metal. It was the only ride up to Novo Friburgo I can remember when my mother didn't complain about the speed. We got there in under three hours, record time. En route, the radio kept us informed of which states had so far adhered to the coup – it was on that trip that I learned the meaning of the verb 'adhere'. The house of cards came tumbling down over the next twenty-four hours. There were murders on that 1 April, though little is said about them to this day. By the morning of 2 April the coup had been consolidated. It was a little after midnight when the President of the Senate, Auro de Moura Andrade, broke with protocol and declared the presidency vacant, despite the fact that Goulart himself was still on Brazilian soil and in full possession of his constitutional powers. At 3.45 a.m. on 2 April, Moura Andrade transferred the presidency of the republic to the Speaker of the House, Ranieri Mazzilli, who, in turn, nine days later, relinquished the post to Castelo Branco, a right-wing pro-American Marshal who was regarded as honest and even moderate when compared with his successors. In that respect the historians are right when they say that it was not entirely a military coup d'état, but a civil-military coup. When Andrade transferred the presidency to Mazzilli he did so in the company of the President of the Federal Supreme Court, Alvaro Ribeiro da Costa.

The road through the Mar Mountains, which run south to the state of Santa Catarina, is winding, and I always got car-sick and we would have to pull over. Not this time. It was a straight run. My brother was thirsty, my grandma needed the toilet, I badly needed some fresh air, my mother, as always, wanted nothing but to cater to all our needs, and my father just drove and drove, eyes on the road, in silence: we lost radio reception as soon as we reached the mountains. We drove into Novo Friburgo with an immense sense of relief. But when we got to my grandfather's house, Dad couldn't park outside because the place was chock-full with military jeeps. We'd barely clambered out of the car when one of our uncles sped past us in a military flak jacket and a semi-automatic on his hip. He was in a hurry and didn't stop to greet us. He just waved, pulled on a helmet, jumped into a jeep and signalled for the troops to move out. It seems my uncle was the head of that particular snake. The whole detail rattled off in a cloud of exhaust fumes. My grandfather explained that our uncle was going to a meeting with the commander of the 4th Army, stationed in Minas Gerais.

We spent the whole afternoon in the garage, listening to the radio. I don't know why on earth the men figured they had to huddle up in the garage, but that's how it was. The radio waves had a hard time climbing the mountains and many a sentence was cut short by crackle. One thing that was crystal-clear to me, and which I remember to this day, was the voice of Lacerda, the Governor of Rio, speaking from his bunker in Guanabara Palace. He was barking through loudspeakers at the palace and you could hear his words over the radio: 'The Palace is under attack. I am here to kill and to die . . . Admiral Aragão,[*] monstrous murderer, don't come close, or I'll kill you with my own pistol, you scum, you bandit, you traitor. Your time has come.' The game was up by the end of that afternoon. We went into the sitting room for tea, where my grandfather turned on the television: a rare occurrence in his spartan and ascetic world, where no jokes, sodas or other such excesses were permitted, and where never a swear-word was heard, nor a pronoun misplaced, nor a verb conjugated in the wrong tense or person.

We watched as victory was declared and flags waved on the wind. The coup had taken power. The atmosphere in the house was jubilant, or as close to euphoric as my grandfather's austere presence would allow. I neither shared nor fully understood the sentiment. Muted, confused, shaken by contradictory emotions that resisted words, I had neither the vocabulary nor the arguments to process those inner antagonisms. Given this, it seemed reasonable to celebrate. They all seemed happy, so whatever had transpired must have been good, and I trusted my parents. And yet something seemed wrong. There were family conflicts between the adults, though no one ever spoke about them openly.

[*]Rear-Admiral Cândido Aragão, who remained loyal to Goulart and took up positions outside Guanabara Palace.

On that day, as at all other family get-togethers, a big lie held sway. My uncles never said as much, but I knew they didn't appreciate my father's lack of ambition. I'd overheard comments at Christmas gatherings and on birthdays, when I'd eavesdrop while apparently playing. Their criticisms were always muttered (I realized early on that most important information usually is) and invariably attributed our family's poverty to a blinkered civil service mindset, an engrained torpor that showed none of the entrepreneurial spirit my grandfather and his sons so highly prized. They'd been against their sister's marriage to this 'paper pusher'. That's what they called him. They didn't like my father, but kept up appearances at the expense of sincerity. The extremely authoritarian manner in which one of these uncles brought up his kids disgusted me: they weren't even allowed to whistle. In the totalitarian kingdom that was my uncle's house, censorship kept a tight hold on all channels of communication. So I was a dangerous agent provocateur, a Che Guevara in short trousers. Hardly surprising, then, that I was barred from this uncle's house. All of that gave me the niggling feeling that there was something farcical about the joy on that 1 April. I wanted no part of it.

What, however, I did want – and I wanted it a lot – was to join the crowd in the stands of Maracanã. Finally, in the autumn of that same year, 1964, I convinced my dad to take me to the Flamengo v. Fluminense derby.* The date,

---

*Flamengo claims to be the most popular football club in the world, with 40 million fans. Fluminense is one of the oldest and most traditional clubs in Brazil and is located in Laranjeiras, my neighbourhood.

18 October, is engrained in my memory. Known as the Fla-Flu, these derbies were always a big deal, but this clash of titans in particular was considered unmissable. According to official figures, there were 136,000 ticket holders in the stands that day, and 150,000 in total, including guests, staff and the press. I was so excited about finally going to Maracanã that, the night before, I developed a fever, something to which I was prone: my nerves ran roughshod over my body. Of course I hid the fact from my mum, or there'd have been no Maracanã for me. It would have given my dad the perfect reason to back out. That afternoon only fell short of perfect because Flamengo managed to even the score in the last minute of injury time: three-all. It was a dream game, with the lead changing hands twice. We opened the scoring, then Flamengo pulled one back and scored another to make it two-one. In the second half we scored two to go ahead. It looked like we were on course for a memorable victory, until Flamengo were awarded a penalty in injury time. But the Fla-Flu is like that, unpredictable from beginning to end, full of rivalry and dramatic twists of fate. That's what makes it the derby to end all derbies, the greatest epic in Rio football.

My idol, the writer Nelson Rodrigues, a true Flu fanatic, once wrote that the first Fla-Flu, a cosmic phenomenon, was played ten minutes before the dawn of time. I couldn't have hoped to break my Maracanã duck in a better way, with a better game. It wasn't just the match, an epic, but the thrill of the stadium itself. We parked a good distance off and walked the rest of the way, my dad's hand holding mine. The closer we got, the larger it loomed. I didn't know what

moved me the most: that vast monument of stone and steel,
bigger than anything I'd ever seen, bigger than I'd imagined
it from photos and films; the profusion of Fluminense
tricolours and Flamengo's black-and-red stripes; or the
increasingly intense cacophony of out-of-tune voices. Then
again, maybe it wasn't any of that; maybe it was just the realization of something imagined countless times over on the
window sill of our old São Francisco apartment: a boy's
dream come true, walking toward a stadium with his dad.
There was no place for mum there, or my brother, who was
too young for such an adventure. Back then football was a
man's thing. I looked up at my dad, and held his hand tight
so as not to get lost. When we scored, he hugged me. Not
even politics can separate a pair of true Flu fans.

But there are so many games, so many walks among
crowds, flags, words between father and son, pauses, lulls,
coffees at the sitting-room table, gestures left unmade, forgotten afternoons, dusks of fading Sundays, the ashes of
things that pass us by. Ashes that end up blown into a corner
of the room, where they go unnoticed. I guess that's why,
from that point on, things went downhill. Maybe if it
weren't for that, or some mistake of mine or my dad's, none
of what happened next need have. But there's no point
denying that it did.

However confused my feelings may have been at first,
they eventually began to side against the military regime. It
got to a point where, two years after the coup, I no longer
felt any inner contradiction whatsoever. All doubt had been
dissolved by a growing antagonism toward my father. In
life, changes occur imperceptibly, especially when you're

going through the biggest change of all: adolescence. All of a sudden you're not what you were and not yet what you will be. And you never saw any of it coming. All the subtle, daily mutations went on right beneath your nose and you never noticed. Then, out of the blue, you're spinning in mid-air, and you've no way of knowing if the springboard has given you the distance to clear the edge of the swimming pool. That limbo is shit. There, a swear-word. I first swore at fifteen: a late developer in that regard. On that score at least I was true to my father and grandfather. They both detested foul language — that's what they called it. At twelve it was still a no-no and I respected that. It was one thing my dad and his father-in-law shared: a distaste for vulgarity and a love of words. Both self-educated, they revered language. My father's dictionaries were the only books we had at home until I had enough cash to start adding my own. The shelves of my grandfather's bookcases bent under the weight of his opulent grammars and dictionaries. I doubt this account would ever have been written had I not inherited that obsession.

I said that change tends to happen on the quiet, without our noticing it, but sometimes, I suppose, that wasn't exactly how it went at my house. Sometimes change wasn't something grasped with hindsight; it came with a date and a time. In the first days of August 1966 my mother and father, my grandmother, my brother and I were having lunch. I was twelve, and I'd just got back from holidays in Espírito Santo — a small state close to Rio, poorer than Rio but full of natural beauty — where I'd met a student activist who must have been sixteen or seventeen. We'd spoken on the

steps of the church where I was waiting for my grandfather
to come and pick me up. We talked politics, as everybody
tended to do at the time. I confessed to my socialist leanings.
He congratulated me, said it was the only ideology worth
having, but corrected me on one point: the ideas I'd described
to him weren't socialist, but Communist. When I returned
home, as my father had been the first to know of my socialist
faith, I figured it was only right that, as we sat down to
lunch, I set him straight too.

'Remember those ideas you said were socialist when we
spoke that day while playing football in the corridor in
Niteroi? Well,' I continued, 'they're actually Communist.'

The explosion knocked me for six. He must have forgotten all about that conversation five years earlier – he slammed
the table with such force and yelled so loudly that that is the
only way to explain his reaction. My grandmother burst
into tears. I was sent straight to the back room for the rest of
the day. In my exile at the other end of the apartment I
could still hear my grandmother's lamentations and my
father's growling. Luckily for me, I'd been sitting at the
opposite end of the table. Mum sneaked in to visit me later,
with the rest of my reheated lunch, and tried to make me see
my father's point of view. But I figured I'd understood that
perfectly well on my own. I decided not to say anything. I
resembled him in that, at least. Silence was my war strategy.
If he wanted a fight, he'd get one. We took our vows of
silence toward each other. Against each other. We didn't
speak for nigh on a year, which was a pity, because quite
apart from the atmosphere around the house, any future
trips to Maracanã went down the drain.

Looking back at this episode today, I guess, deep down, our whole relationship was a minefield. Maybe, saying what I did, that was exactly what I wanted: to trip the wire, blow into pieces what was already in tatters, just to see what would happen. Perhaps the shock would give us both a chance to make a new start? Between a child and his cause there's always a father and a mother and the vicissitudes of the family tangle. But instead of jolting things back to life that landmine blocked the channels of dialogue and affection with rubble. Mum was the go-between, and we observed our truce armed to the teeth. Harmony would only be restored decades later.

I left home early and married too early, at eighteen, less than a year after starting university. Not long before meeting my first wife, I experienced my second and most serious family quake, the one that really sent me packing. The scene I describe above gives a good measure of the knot politics and family formed in my life. Maybe my personal tangle wasn't an isolated affair – it may well have been the lot of my generation, with political repression and tyranny seeping into our families' private lives. There, in those events, the template was forged for the ferocious Rio that would evolve, the city where police militias storm favelas, where a racism never acknowledged as such always points the finger at the same colour, a place where vice became just a part of the fabric, where the poor refused to stop popping up and debunking the myth, and where the nouveaux riches harbour shiny dreams of Miami. Back when I was only eighteen Rio had already seen its halcyon days. The decades that followed would be marked by its decadence. The best way you could describe Rio throughout my youth and much of my adult life was to ignore the present and try to recover a still-recent past, however idealized that might have been. But at least there was football and music. That, though, is another story altogether.

I got home in time to have dinner with my parents and my brother. I never spoke about myself or what I did when I wasn't home. But that evening, try as I might, I couldn't help myself. I had to get it off my chest. It had been one of the worst days of my life. M.T. had disappeared. The police had taken her. She was a student leader at PUC, the university I studied at. The student movement, like the union movement, was banned, but we still met and tried to hold out. M.T. was beautiful, gentle, but firm. She seemed so fragile. I liked her a lot. It was 1972. The dictatorship was jabbing its bloody talons into any nook or cranny where some semblance of independent, intelligent life, some measure of indignation, still lingered. Social inequality had reached monumental levels, salaries evaporated against rising prices, censorship was total and international denunciations of the state's systematic use of torture forced the regime to tighten the tourniquet of repression, torture and murder. And now M.T. was gone. I and others involved in student politics went to see everyone we could. The university showed solidarity. The rector and directors contacted the authorities and followed up every possible lead. If we could at least discover where they were holding her, then the regime wouldn't be able to deny that they had her. Securing some recognition of a detainee's whereabouts was a major step toward keeping that person alive. If M.T. was in custody, then she was alive when she got there and her safety was now the responsibility of the State. When they wanted someone dead they did it there and then, and put it down to resisted arrest, suicide or attempted escape. One way or another we had to make it as difficult as possible for the authorities. While the university did its part, we contacted as many public personalities and high-profile figures as we could. Our last visit was the most important: we managed to get an emergency audience with an eminent Catholic bishop.

After trying every possible avenue, there was still no sign of M.T. I got home in a state, imagining the worst. But I tried not to say anything, and I was succeeding until my father turned on the TV. He liked to watch Globo news over dinner. It was the most popular news broadcast in the country, but it was also a mouthpiece for the regime, so I usually left the room when it came on. That night, however, it was the last straw. Something snapped. I accosted my father.

'How can you sit there and watch those lies? A friend of mine was snatched today. She's being tortured this very minute, as we eat. No one knows if she'll make it through the night.'

My father slammed his fist on the table:

'Don't be fooled by that Communist propaganda, boy.'

I shot back:

'So torture is just something made up by the Communists?'

'And isn't it?', he replied.

Whatever strength had been holding all the pieces together inside me dissipated on the spot. The parts of what

I had come to recognize as me, myself and I flew out of orbit and gravity couldn't claw them back. My hand on one side, reason on the other, hatred frothing in between, my mind a swirl of debris circling my livid body, I picked up a plate and hurled it at my father's head. Years afterwards the dent in the wall marked the spot where the projectile had smashed into pieces, without actually hitting my father, physically at least. I imagine he came out of the duel as dead as I did.

M.T. survived that hellish night and the others that followed. She was brutally tortured and, once released, went into exile. When she finally came back to Brazil she resumed her life with the same integrity as always, and with the admiration of her friends, although far from Rio and from politics. But the hell is still there, somewhere. There is nothing that can disinfect it, eradicate it.

I needed time and courage to apologize to my father. And when, several years later, I did, he took the opportunity to apologize for breaking my guitar. It was a toy guitar he had smashed on the floor when one day, aged five, I refused to brush my teeth. I loved that guitar, which, as a gift from the rich side of the family, was far too expensive to replace. So, tit-for-tat, a plate for a guitar: we were quits. The country also needed time and courage to return to democracy. Like society, my father changed with the years. He opened his mind, went to work for the Brazilian Bar Association, which played a pivotal role in resisting the dictatorship, and where he was surrounded by people of another order, better informed and more liberal. Ironically, fate saw fit to deposit my father in the very institution that did the most to denounce the regime's use of torture. When he retired, he was a different man. As was I.

While I was writing this book my father was nearing his end, my mother at his bedside day and night. For nearly three years I divided my time between the book and him. During the last few months, which he spent in hospital, I visited him daily. The hospital is located in Tijuca, in the north of the city. From my house the shortest route is also the most scenic: the upper Tijuca road, which runs through powerful, exuberant Atlantic forest in a part of the city far removed from Rio's trademark shore. The forest Rio, with its lush smells, deep colours, scant traffic and few people, its provincial squares, milder climate, rustling leaves, gurgling streams and birdsong, is another place entirely. On that last night I made my way back home after a forty-eight-hour bedside vigil. I needed to rest. Not long after I'd arrived back, my wife called to say it was time. I jumped back into my shoes, headed robotically for the car and looked up at the Pedra da Gávea, absolute in its majesty, as I drove through Tijuca Forest. I knew then that the next time I drove along that road nothing would be the same, not the colours, the birds, the sounds, the weather, not myself, not the past or the future and not this book. Nothing would be the same, even if the Pedra da Gávea continued steadfast in its eternal commitment to its own stone truth, its incorruptible and inexhaustible mineral resolve.

No Ordinary Woman

It's 13 August 1970. Nine o'clock at night. Brazil, under dictatorial rule since 1964, has found itself immersed in the gloom of obscurantism, political persecution and censorship since 13 December 1968, when a coup within a coup tightened the military grip. Dulce and Alexandre had only been living together for a couple of days. Despite their relationship, safety had to be their foremost concern. Nomadism was tiring, but it was necessary. Each move required careful assessment of the risks and alternatives involved. Tension set the tone. A pleasant, homely existence was impossible, for all the cosiness of their modest but well-located apartment in the bucolically named neighbourhood of Jardim Botânico (the Botanical Gardens), on the south side of town. Both from Pernambuco, they'd met and fallen in love in Recife. Now in Rio, leading the solitary existence a life in hiding entails, each was really all the other had. Going underground had been vital to their safety, even though they were no longer politically active: most of the militants had either been locked up or killed, and the left-wing organizations effectively decimated. The most they could do now was stay alive.

Dulce's life had been interwoven with politics from a young age, so much so that leaving her hometown had become an absolute necessity. In Alexandre's case life was only partly clandestine, and fitted well with his academic activities. He was writing his doctoral thesis at the National Institute of Pure and Applied Mathematics (IMPA) under his real name. The IMPA was an academic institute of international repute, a sort of refuge for exceptional talents – an island of excellence shielded from the persecutory gaze of the dictatorship by the abstract nature of its subject of study. He had fled Recife soon after the coup in 1964 and studied mechanical engineering in the Rio countryside.

Nine-thirty. The street is quiet. The only sound is from the neighbour's TV. So when they hear footsteps in the hallway stop outside their door, it sends a shiver down their spines. It isn't normal, but then it might just be a neighbour wanting to borrow something. It couldn't be anyone coming in from the street because the front door is kept locked and there's no doorman. Before thoughts of this nature have time to form properly, twenty men armed with shotguns, machine guns and handguns storm into the flat. The couple have no guns and no chance of escape.

Dulcinha was fifteen and living in Recife when her world started to crumble. On the morning of 31 March 1964, as her father walked her to school, they came upon a neighbour shaving in a mirror propped against a pot of lather on the coping of his front garden wall. He smiled, bid father and daughter good morning, then wiped his face clean with a towel before justifying his unflustered mien: 'General Justino is on our side.' The man's word carried weight, and his ally, Justino Alves Bastos, commander of the 4th Army, had the troops, weapons and ammunition to back it up. The neighbour in question was

Pelópidas da Silveira, Vice-Governor of the state of Pernambuco. A former mayor of Recife, he went down in history as a modernizer and democrat. During the elections of 1962 he supported the reformist leader Miguel Arraes and helped him get elected Governor of Pernambuco.

The vice-governor's calm defused the intoxicating atmosphere of rumour and ill omen. Nevertheless, the tension was rising across the city and festering in the mangroves. Dulcinha, her siblings, her parents and those relatives on the side of Governor Arraes found themselves immersed in a toxic brew. The anxiety wore on until the radio and telephone calls dashed whatever hopes still lingered. Night fell. Luiz Pandolfi and Eurico Chaves Filho, her father and her uncle, couldn't shield her from the scene. The image would come to encapsulate a whole period of Brazil's history and sucked the girl into the folds of its darkness. Two men started a bonfire in the garden and fed it with Dulce's father's entire library – his pride and joy. The flames spewed fiery snatches of book pages. While legal culture smouldered and literature turned to ash, the flames across the dark town, in the eyes of the young girl, flickered like votive candles for a world now lying in state. Luiz Pandolfi was a labour lawyer, university lecturer and literary critic. Eurico Chaves Filho was a labour court judge, an active participant in the community and a close collaborator with the Arraes government.

In the small hours of 1 April 1964, anyone vaguely connected with the Arraes government or with social movements became vulnerable. Books were taken as incontrovertible evidence of crime. The junta raided homes at random, and whatever meaning the notion of home once had was eroded in inverse proportion to the mounting attacks on privacy. When the dictatorship consolidated its grip on power, which it did before long, the brunt of repression shifted not only onto supporters of the deposed government, but onto all critics of the new regime. Books had to disappear, and any letters, documents, journals, papers or other traces of ideas sympathetic to social reform became incendiary. Prudence recommended lowering one's voice and one's profile, as pretty much anyone could be an informer. On that night of 31 March 1964, as she watched the bonfire burn, Dulce witnessed the Brazilian political tragedy unfold in its most didactic form – the graphic brutality would begin the following day.

On 1 April the coup was already a reality. The new regime, with tentacles in each state, was organizing fast. For the defenders of the constitutional law which the army was trampling underfoot, the only thing greater than the uncertainty was the certainty of defeat. The first lists began to emerge of those to be purged from political life, expelled from the civil service and from university posts, and have their passports cancelled: Luiz Pandolfi and Eurico Chaves Filho were among them. In the middle of the afternoon a ruckus aroused Dulce's tremulous curiosity, and she ran out to the corner where Guedes Street met the asphalted avenue. It was an uproar of shouting and imprecations. She tried to squirm her way through the crowd to see what was going on, but she wasn't strong enough. She wanted to know what all the cursing was about, the clanking chains and snapping leather straps. Gregório Bezerra, arms tied, feet burnt by acid, was being pulled and at times dragged down a Polish

Corridor behind a police car, bound for the prison. Grit and all sorts of shards stuck into the soles of his bare feet in such quantity, and so deeply, that his daughter would still be plucking them out with tweezers on cell visits six months later. A member of the Brazilian Communist Party and of peasant background, Gregório was imprisoned until September 1969, when his name made the list of political prisoners exchanged for the American Ambassador, Charles Burke Elbrick, and was able to go into exile.

Dulce arrived home shaking and confused. The coup d'état had embedded itself in the girl's spirit and that of the woman she would become, binding them both to a single history, for ever. For Dulce, as for many of her generation, politics would be not just an activity or interest, but a way of relating to oneself and to others, of making sense of life.

August 13 1970 – the beginning of this story is no longer important. Neither memory nor dream can overcome the fear. Twenty armed secret service policemen raid Alexandre and Dulce's apartment. In theory, their prodigious capacity to inspire terror renders actual physical violence unnecessary, but that doesn't stop them employing it anyway. They bear down with the force of an invading army, smashing all obstacles before them, turning the whole place inside out and making it crystal-clear that the only force limiting their actions is their own will.

The inspection focuses at length on evidence of the more serious types of crime. First, Alexandre's papers, replete with unfathomable formulae, most likely encrypted plans for attacks on the nerve centre of power. In reality they're draft chapters for his doctoral thesis. He tries to explain, deny, consider – all in vain. The commander is convinced that interrogation will extract the truth like a tumour. Without an anaesthetic. The second item of evidence is a bunch of keys on the sitting-room table. Why so many keys? The officers reckon they've found a treasure map that will lead them to the hideaways of subversive cells. The leader of the operation beams triumphantly, ignoring Dulce's explanation that they're just copies for the door downstairs and to the apartment. The third piece of damning evidence is a letter from Dulce's mother, Carmen, in which she wrote: 'If you need anything, dear, remember your cousins. That's what family is for, after all, right? Money, shelter, if in need, don't hesitate to call them. R. lives in Copacabana, in DF five-hundred and X, apartment XX (she wrote the numbers). Lurdinha, remember her? She always sends her best. She says she'd like you to visit her in Rio when you get back from Chile, so you can catch up. She lives in Botafogo, XXXX Street.' Her doting mother gave her the addresses of relatives so she would feel more secure and less alone in any eventual hour of need. But her concern for her daughter's welfare led her to censor her own words, inventing a code of abbreviations. Carmen's wily imagination went no further, but it was her attempts to convey information without being specific that caught the police's attention and suggested that there was more to it than that. There wasn't, but it got the mentioned relatives arrested anyway.

One particular episode injected a note of comedy into the tragedy. Cousin R. was having a party with some friends when the special ops unit stormed his apartment. He was hauled off along with all his guests. A social get-together was mistaken for a political assembly disguised by music, dance and drinks. As guests arrived and rang the doorbell, oblivious to the trap they were about to fall into, they were asked to confirm that they'd been invited by the owner of the house. That way no one could claim to have got the address wrong or not to know the chief suspect, the ring-leader of the supposed assembly.

Dulce is twenty-one. The political line pursued by her organization, Aliança Libertadora Nacional (National Liberation Alliance), had suffered something of a reality check, leading Dulce and some of her comrades to question it. The State's power was overwhelming. Everything you tried to build up to counter it was dwarfed out of existence, made to look fragile and vulnerable, almost puerile. The dictatorship squashed all opposition like a bug. The belief that some Quixotic tilting would serve to inspire the oppressed to rise up against it, like the spark that sets the bush ablaze, wasn't borne out by what they saw in the streets, the squares, in the fields, in the censored and co-opted press. Routines ground on, one week rolled into the next, and fear drove everything forward like tank tracks powered by toothed sprockets.

'Whatever you have to do, do it fast, so you can get back to normal as quickly as possible,' said Henry Kissinger, then US Secretary of State, to the Argentine Foreign Minister, César Augusto Guzzetti, in June 1976.* Kissinger's warning

---

*This information comes from the 3,700 hours of secret recordings made by President Richard Nixon, as the journalist Dorrit Harazim divulged in the article 'Na roda-viva da história', published in *O Globo* newspaper on 10 August 2014.

sounded more like a carte blanche, or even an order. He was eager to wrap things up before an incumbent Jimmy Carter took office on 20 January 1977 and to forestall the impact of a new law passed through the US Congress that would suspend all aid to nations guilty of human rights abuses. Quick action had to be taken before the new legislation came into effect. That 'action' was the extermination of a generation, dumped into the ocean from airplanes with rocks to weigh the bodies down; it was the ruthless extirpation of every last trace of opposition to a despotic regime.

It was different in Brazil. When the Brazilian dictatorship was in full stride, between 1969 and 1974, there was no need to hurry. The torturers had all the time in the world to sink the blade of terror into their victims' flesh, ample time to tweak the instruments of torment, angle the electric probe into inflamed orifices, tear the body apart, instil panic, play with death. Except, that is, during the first twenty-four hours of detainment, or the forty-eight hours after that. Maybe even seventy-two. When it came to the first couple of days, the order was to be professionally cruel and fast, applying the maximum amount of pain to extract information with a two- or three-day expiry date at most. 'When is the next meeting? Where? Who are you to meet with? Give me the addresses of the safe houses you and your comrades use.' Unless a confession was obtained fast, word would spread to the rest of the group, the safe houses would be vacated and the cells disbanded.

The secret lay in gauging this fleeting, variable, idiosyncratic window of opportunity; in sensing a person's pain threshold. The measure of a torturer's competence lay in his ability to calibrate torment. Imprudence kills the goose that

lays the golden eggs, as the popular saying goes. If you rush to
the well, you might break your pail. The torture team and
their superior officers don't want to break the pail, at least not
until they are sure there's nothing more it can draw. What's the
use of a dead goose? What good is a broken pail? They yield
neither golden eggs nor information. The more haste, the less
speed. You can't gather intelligence from a dead subversive.

The brute batters, the troglodyte throttles, the butcher
pushes his quarry to the brink, but a taste for violence in all
its varied forms is not all it takes to make a good torturer, a
real expert in extreme interrogation. It's a trade that requires
self-control, the ability to keep the inner killer on a leash
measured with mathematical precision. And yet a sadistic
vocation is a must, as without its gusto a talent for calculation
is of little use. The Brazilian dictatorship trained innumerable torturers, recruited from the ranks of the police, the
army, air force and navy. Men – there are no records of any
women – with blood in their eyes and on their hands; men
who took pride in their work and were loyal to the State,
many of them decorated by generals. Some of these men are
still alive today. They drag their past behind them like a ball
and chain, most of them reacting with scorn to the incessant
denunciations. But the pathology is institutionalized. The
armed forces pretend it never happened. Torturers of every
rank have been left in peace to grow old among grandchildren and great-grandchildren over Sunday lunch. Dis-
tracted, they ebb into senility, that melancholy of tardy
innocence; decrepitude in the service of historical amnesia.

Dulce wanted to believe they weren't going to kill her.
The family would soon realize something was wrong and

would come looking. Besides, the arrest of her cousins, under such pathetic circumstances, would throw up nothing but dead ends; she alone had ties to a subversive organization. Alexandre's connections with the Brazilian Communist Party, the reason he'd fled from Recife in 1964, had been severed after countless disagreements and disappointments. Why would the torturers kill a girl from Pernambuco who had no real role to speak of in an organization that was wasting away anyway? Back in Recife she'd been a leader, helped recruit loads of new members, but her involvement had been scaled back because of over-exposure. Her staying in Recife had become dangerous not only for her, but also for the ALN (Aliança Libertadora Nacional). It was imperative that she move to a larger city where nobody knew her – or almost nobody. Rio de Janeiro won out against São Paulo because Alexandre was there. And because she had always loved Rio.

Her passion for the city was nothing new. In December 1963, instead of the traditional debutante's ball when she turned fifteen – an eagerly awaited rite of passage for most girls, usually ending with a waltz with one's dad – the family decided that a Rio cruise would be much more fun. Boarding the ship with Dulce, bound for the nation's former capital, were her parents, grandmother, a cousin and her three brothers. The city was a dream, a perfect blend of fantasy, exuberant landscape and seductive novelties – a kiss, a beer, her first piss-up, a sense of freedom. Ipanema was a vision of paradise, and its licentious aura seemed to warrant a bikini, something that would have been out of the question in stuffy old Pernambuco. While the adults took in the museums and tourist sights, the kids hit the beach and the bars.

Dulce's second trip to Rio was also for fun, in 1967 along with a group of fellow students. Her third time there, in 1969, was on a difficult mission. In February 1970, unable to stay in Recife any longer, Rio was the natural choice.

Yes, it was an important thought to keep in mind at 9.30 p.m. on that 13 August 1970: they weren't going to kill her. She said it to herself over and over as she was led away with a sack over her head and cuffs on her wrists, threats seething in her ears. She insisted on the reasoning: she was no use to them dead. For long hours, deep into the night, she locked herself inside a state of mind that allowed no hesitation and remained absolutely steadfast. She would say nothing, let nothing slip, her abductors would get nothing out of her. She knew the worst thing would be to give information in trickles. Offering information in snatches would only encourage them to keep on turning the screw, because it would mean it was working and that there was more to come if they persisted and intensified the torment. That's the prisoner's lot. Dulce felt guilty about getting Alexandre arrested, and the chance that her cousins might suffer the same fate. Dulce swore to herself that never again would anyone have to pay such a high price because of a political persuasion that was hers and hers alone. She thought of her parents and family back in Recife. Perhaps the mixture of fear and guilt had caused a sort of paralysis, a short circuit, because, paradoxically, it steeled her.

They had reached what seemed to be the limit. The shocks wracked her, but she kept her mouth shut until the spasms and the electric charge had passed. They saw they'd have to change method, and decided to try truth serum. She was taken down from the rack and felt her joints buckle beneath her. It was impossible to stand. They flung her into the so-called 'dragon's chair', a metal armchair hooked to a dynamo. A few minutes later a doctor came in and betrayed no hesitation whatsoever as to the procedure. Phlegmatic and precise, he located the vein and injected the oily liquid. Dulce didn't lose her mind, but she did feel herself begin to drift as her perceptions disconnected. The doctor left as abruptly as he had entered. Dulce would see him again many more times.

The good cop/bad cop routine was already a cliché, so Dulce, still doped, wasn't surprised when she was led into another room and allowed to sit down. There she was spoken to with civility and politeness, almost friendliness, by an agent she had not seen in the purple torture room. Dawn was breaking on 14 August. She had spent hours on end in the purple room, where, between bouts of fainting and panic, she'd lost all notion of time. The room, painted to disturb, was located in the basement of the barracks on Barão de Mesquita Street in the middle-class Tijuca neighbourhood in Rio's South Zone. Dulce had been taken from her apartment to Doi-Codi,* the Military Police's intelligence ops and internal defence agency, where she was isolated from the other prisoners.

Doi-Codi was an embassy of hell on Earth for all who knew of its existence. It was the secret service wing in

---

*Destacamento de Operações de Informações do Centro de Operações de Defesa Interna, an organization subordinated to the Brazilian Army during the dictatorship.

charge of investigating political crimes, expert in employing
the orthodox methodology of the Brazilian State: technically applied violence. Until the end of the nineteenth
century the victims had been slaves, but after abolition in
1888 its most frequent visitors were the black poor. Finally,
from the coup of 1964 until the end of the dictatorship, the
targets of State violence tended to be opponents of the military regime, which brought the middle tiers of society
within its brutal range. With re-democratization history
returned to its normal course and, despite significant social
changes, the cruelty once again trained its sights on the
black poor from the slums and shanty towns. The benefits
of rule of law had not yet trickled down to the base of the
social pyramid.

Over the course of the dictatorship, its novelty was not
limited simply to broadening the range of State-sponsored
violence. Another very serious development was a clear
break with tradition: instead of delegating the dirty work
to the police force, the military were now ready and willing to take political repression into their own hands. That
is not to say that the police weren't involved, working
alongside the military and acting on their orders. In the
Doi-Codi dungeon, Dulce herself saw shields and rings
belonging to the death squad, the dreaded *scuderie* Le Cocq,
a group of policemen specially trained to conduct extra-
judicial executions, among other activities. The promiscuity
between law and crime, the cops and the cons, so typical of
Brazil and of Rio in particular, ballooned during the military regime, which pulled out all the stops on political
repression. The dictatorship's legacy to a democratic Brazil

was the galvanization of criminal police militias,* which gradually peeled away from other institutions, though without ever really abandoning them, and went from plying rough justice to involvement in professional crime, particularly illegal gambling rackets and the drugs and arms trades.

The soft-spoken man in the second room was tall and strong, and he told Dulce that the worst was behind her now, that there would be no more torture. All she had to do was tell him where and when the next rendezvous would be, give him the addresses of the safe houses in use and the names of the people she reported to, and list the names of the activists she knew in Recife and Rio. There would be some further questioning later, but nothing important. For now, all she had to do was answer the questions he put to her, and it would all be over. Dulce showed him her burnt and bleeding lips, her swollen, frazzled tongue, and whispered with the little voice she could muster that she was in no condition to talk. She could barely get the words out, because her mouth was seared like a gaping wound. The agent then showed her a document and asked her to sign it. It was nothing, he said, just stuff they already knew. There was nothing in it that would incriminate anyone or compromise her before her former comrades, marking her as a rat. It was just paperwork,

* The militias are the fourth faction on the Rio crimescape. These heavily armed bands of retired, discharged and active servicemen from the police forces, fire brigade, prison system and security corps began to form in the 1990s to run the drug lords out of the favelas and seize control of their racketeering and protection schemes.

bureaucracy, red tape to show that the agents had done their job. The man admitted that, in the light of his vast experience, and having heard how she'd handled herself under torture, it seemed pretty clear to him that she wasn't going to give up the goods. So it was just a formality, nothing more. He set the typewritten statement before her and showed her where to sign. There was nothing of any value in it, he assured her. She could read it and see. The large man shuffled the pages before Dulce's face, as if to prove what he'd said. Sign here.

She showed him her hands, which were disfigured by deep gouges, especially on the fingers they'd coiled the electric wire around when they weren't delivering shocks to her vagina, nipples, lips, tongue, ear lobes and little toes, which had been practically scorched off by the charge. Her wrists, ankles and knees were also severely injured after hours on the 'macaw's perch', which was basically a *parrilla*, a spit-like iron bar the prisoner was hung over by the back of the knees, with their wrists bound to their ankles behind them. The bar was then raised onto stumps, leaving the detainee hanging head-down, naked, so he or she could be subjected to a range of different torments. Worse than the dragon's chair, another apparatus used to administer electric shocks, the 'macaw's perch' came with an additional dose of humiliation, especially for women exposed in this manner before a group of men. Such intense voltage running through the body also caused incontinence. It was a torture designed for maximum physical agony and moral degradation. From time to time, either to bring her to after passing out, or because she refused point-blank to answer any of their questions, Dulce had buckets of ice-cold water thrown over her as she hung from that obscene bar. What followed were the worst moments of agony, because the water served as a conductor and heightened the severity of the shocks. Dulce understood there and then the real meaning of the expression 'to see stars', only in this case the sparks were quite real. Her pale skin scintillated.

Sign here, the man insisted, with a tremor in his voice that betrayed some roil of emotion below the surface. Dulce showed him her hands again and tried to look as defiant as her injured face would allow. A few seconds ticked by, an interval too short to let tensions come to a natural head, decoding those undertones. So Dulce didn't really know what was happening when the gentle giant suddenly hurled his two-metre frame and hundred-odd kilos in her direction, knocking her debilitated body to the floor, arms still cuffed behind her back. Lying helpless on the tiles, she felt the unbridled force of the agent's kicks to her legs, womb, face and breasts, until the last waves of consciousness broke into foam. For as long as she had been able to process what he was shouting at her as he laid into her, all she had gathered was that he was going to kill her and every single subversive he got his hands on – or his feet to. His hatred had got the better of him. His fury had possessed him, blown the charade. It was as if his violence had shaken free of him and was lashing out like the still-wagging tail of a dead animal. Dulce was bombarded by flashes of lucidity, and in one such glimpse between blackouts she saw the other agents dragging the mastodon off her, shouting that she couldn't die, that they needed her alive.

When the beating stopped, Dulce couldn't walk. She was deposited in a tiny dark room, four metres square, while the agents debated what to do with her. This bizarre little place was at the same basement level as the torture room, and was used as a holding cell while some other crew was working a detainee or the purple room was being hosed down. Two particular feelings dragged Dulce's will in opposing directions. If they weren't going to kill her, they couldn't go on torturing her either. That brought relief, a glimmer of hope, a gulp of oxygen amid the stench of scorched flesh, a tinge of respite from the pain. On the other hand was a terror that made her shiver: she couldn't feel or move the left side of her body. After they'd slung her into that claustrophobic cubicle she'd caught some snatches of their exchanges: they were discussing whether or not to admit her to the military hospital. For Dulce, transfer was the best option, though she realized she wouldn't be safe there either; she knew of many people who'd been tortured and killed on the hospital premises. But at least the chances of recovery and a little respite were better there than in the Doi-Codi dungeon. What was more, news of her capture would be more likely to leak from the hospital, and the more people who knew of her whereabouts, the less likely they were to execute her.

She had just seen first-hand that tensions were running high among the torturers, so an order to keep her alive was no guarantee they actually would. There were bouts of uncontrollable fury, lines were being crossed that could have led to accidents, miscalculations. And hatred wasn't the only thing the torturers and their victims had in common – there was the exhaustion too. The exhaustion of a whole night spent in that chamber of horrors. It was nowhere near as bad as it was for the detainees, for obvious reasons, but it had to take its toll nonetheless. It had to get to you. Some of the torturers came across as stone-cold, professional purveyors of violence who betrayed no sign whatsoever of inner life. But those were the minority. Many of the thugs seemed to become emotionally invested in the production of pain, whether through enjoyment or rage. Perhaps there was even a sliver of moral conscience, a niggle of guilt or shame, which they had to crush out of existence. It was a vicious cycle: hurt and dissolve the hurt, intensify the brutality until no trace of the torturer was mirrored in the eyes of the victim's pummelled body.

None of this occurred to Dulce, though. She couldn't think of anything except the paralysis down the left side of her face and body – arm, leg, hand, foot. Though she knew that the agents would do everything they could to terrify her, that they would lie, she almost believed them when they said she'd never recover, never be able to bear children, never walk again, that her life was definitively and irremediably ruined. That's what they said to her as they applied the electric shocks. And their prognosis was confirmed when she asked for medical assistance because she couldn't feel her left side.

Dulce concluded that there was method in the torturers' savagery. The madman, the psycho, the sadist, whichever they were, or whatever role they played – there was always discipline in the torments they meted out, an ability to scale the pain and modulate the effects. With the exception of the odd temper tantrum by some stressed-out, temperamental mule, they knew how to vary the intensity and the quality of the suffering they inflicted. Jocular hostility, for example, was a method employed to cause the deepest possible impact. The shocks were classified according to the part of the body the electrodes were attached to, the length of contact and the voltage applied: higher, lower, constant, intermittent, progressive, irregular, cadenced with peaks and sudden breaks. Each onslaught was preceded by a title: *trip to Russia*, *trip to China*, and longest, strongest and therefore worst of all, *trip to Cuba*.

In the end, they decided not to transfer Dulce to the military hospital. They improvised a medical ward on one of the upper floors, and she was kept there for about a week, on meds, smeared with ointments and hooked to a drip. The most she could do now was keep her sanity. She had to concentrate on something, but there wasn't much she could do chained to a bunk. Every day they made a point of reminding her that she'd be going back to the purple room as soon as she was fit enough. The fear of going mad inspired some odd pastimes, such as counting the number of cracks on the ceiling and the number of dash pebbles in the wall. Keeping her synapses busy helped kill idle time, the cradle of nightmares. The following words were daubed on one of the cell walls: 'Here a mother can't hear her child cry.' With nothing else to focus on, no matter how contrived, she couldn't shake the memory of the pain and that diabolical phrase, which evoked the human being's absolute solitude before the unthinkable, before a reality so traumatic it was impossible to assimilate, comprehend or control. Dulce shuddered not at death, but at the horror; not at the end, but at what seemed to have none. She decided not to give in. She would exercise her mind and renew her vow to keep silent. They would not get what they wanted. She could not defeat death, but she would not allow them to defeat life.

The day dawned when she was considered fit enough to return. The time had come to subject her to new takes on cruelty. After one bout of torture, she was dragged to a tiny cell. She hadn't been in there for long when the door opened again and an alligator was thrown inside. It was about one and a half metres long and probably well fed, as it didn't attack her. It just crawled over her body, nothing more. There wasn't anything she could do, so she surrendered to the reptile's promiscuous proximity, which proved more frightening than actually dangerous.

After a few days Dulce was transferred to a collective cell. The advantage there was the solidarity and assistance given by the older, more experienced political prisoners. Never had friendship, empathy and compassion struck her as so marvellously key to the survival of body and soul. She even prayed with the religious among them, though she was not a believer herself. Belief was irrelevant. Invoking powers, whether real or not, did her good. She soon understood that it brought them together, and that their unity was the deepest source of strength they had, affording consolation and hope.

At any moment, morning, noon or night, a soldier could turn up and take one of them away. And such removals were never for any other purpose than torture, and they knew it. So the sound of footsteps, the clank of the lock and the sight of the door opening to reveal the figure of a guard not

holding a tray of cabbage – the only food they were given
was cabbage – signalled the worst. If the guard came in
without a tray, someone was taken for torture. It made everyone recoil. In fact, the torture started there and then, with
the guard staring hard at each of them in turn, as if unsure
whom to pick, sneering at the fear his perverse mind game
spread through the cell and savouring the pleasure of lord-
ing it over those terror-stricken women. Finally, after some
eeny-meeny-miney, his pointed finger would settle on *mo*
while the others screamed out murderer, coward. It was all
they could do.

The chosen prisoner was cuffed and hooded and led off
to the purple room. Between the cell and the torture chamber the prisoners were at the guard's mercy. He would trip
them, tell them to watch out for steps that weren't there,
bash their heads off the wall and generally take sadistic
pleasure out of ferrying his quarry into hell. At night,
higher-ranking officers would visit the cells in the company
of dogs every bit as fierce as their handlers. 'This one tripped
and fell on her way to confession, isn't that right, sister?' The
guard's joke would continue for the benefit of the visitors,
while the dogs strained at the leash. 'This other one fell off
her bike, and this one got slapped around so bad by her
hubby that we had to take her in before he finished her off,
right slag. See what you get for sleeping around?' The superior officers would smirk and only rarely intervene, usually
with some brief lecture exalting order, progress, patria,
family, property, decorum and the regime.

Dulce was about to complete her first month at Doi-Codi
when she was taken back to the purple room for an unusual

experiment. Visits to the torture chamber had been fewer that last week, which instilled some hope that perhaps the worst had passed. Hence her despair when the guard opened the door and pointed at her. On that morning there were more than the usual crew of four. Many more. Dulce heard the murmur in advance, but it was only when they pulled the hood off that she saw all those unknown men staring at her as the agents stripped her and strung her to the macaw's perch. The official in charge of proceedings addressed the group, explaining the kind of damage the position could inflict, such as bone friction, torn muscle, ripped skin, pinched nerves, causing varying degrees of pain. Panic and terror could be dialled up or down with methodical tweaking, toying with expectations and breaking the will and self-esteem through degradation and fear. He followed up the theory with a practical demonstration, telling his assistant to increase or decrease the voltage as he moved the electrodes about her body. Next, he demonstrated how results could be maximized by drenching the victim with ice-cold water, and how untimely death could be forestalled by avoiding the left side of the body, so as not to overburden the heart. He also gave some practical tips on how to occupy the intervals between shock cycles by beating the soles of the victim's feet and other sensitive areas, so as to undermine resistance. The violent shocks, the series of beatings, the neutral language in which he explained each sadistic detail of what he was about to do and the hellish atmosphere of the place heightened the horror and burst through all physical and mental limits. There was a good chance the victim would choke on her own vomit and pass out.

Back in her cell, her fellow prisoners huddled around her and embraced her as she sobbed. She was visited by a doctor, the same one who had administered the truth serum on the first day and had overseen her treatment during her spell in the makeshift ward. He examined her, with a soldier looking on, and then announced his diagnosis, or rather sentence: she can take more. She's in bad shape, but she's good to go. So two soldiers came into the cell and hauled her off for the second part of the lesson. Her cellmates echoed her own cries of no, no, murderers, she'll die, it'll kill her, you cowards.

This time she was taken out into the yard, where she was tied to a post. The officer in charge dispensed with the hood so she would be able to see the gun. She'd been sentenced to death, he said. The students gathered around, enthralled. The hood was pulled over her head and the darkness exacerbated the fear. She felt the gun barrel press against her skull as the master-torturer bandied on about what happened to prisoners who refused to collaborate and the importance of eliminating these traitors. He said that any hesitation in carrying out such an order was cause for court martial, so, as a soldier, he had to execute the terrorist, and he would do it out of love for Brazil. The gun barrel pressed hard into her temple, and she could hear his finger slowly press the trigger. Click. The noise defused the tension, temporarily at least. Dulce was sure they did not actually intend to kill her, the execution was just a pantomime, but accidents do happen. Intentions can change on their way into action. No matter how cold the instructor was, he could not disguise the hatred that was pushing at the thin membrane of control. Each simulation drove all the air from her lungs and made her almost faint. She had survived, again, but could only relax when she was back in her cell and in the arms of her cellmates.

Two days later they came for her at night. Dulce was sure there could be no more surprises in store. She was wrong. They led her into the purple room and told her to wait, on her feet, for the interrogating officer. She tried to empty her mind, focus on her breathing. She had heard that meditation helps dissolve despair. Finally, her torturer entered the room, looked her up and down like a butcher examining a slab of meat and informed her that, tonight, the shocks would either make her talk or be the end of her. He sat down at the desk and started reading and rubber-stamping documents, as if he were snowed under with paperwork. After a while he stood up and made as if he was about to prepare for the torture session, only to leave the room, saying he'd be back in a minute. Dulce lost all sense of time. As the night wore on, her legs grew weak and her feet went numb. The man eventually returned and sat back down at the desk. He spent the next ten minutes or so shuffling through the papers, then got up and circled her. He walked over to the *parrilla* and started getting it ready. Dulce, still alert, still standing, reckoned the time had come and felt her blood freeze in her veins. But her torturer stopped and turned to her: not tonight, too busy. But I'll deal with you soon enough.

The sadistic charade was played out a few more times, until he finally decided to put an end to his perverted little game of not tonight, but tomorrow . . . The farce was reprised a couple of times. They'd come for her in the middle of the night and take her away. It would have been a relief were it not for the fact that the staged scenes were interspersed with very real bouts of excruciation. This macabre play-acting was a particularly cruel form of psychological torture. The fear was constant, and not even night brought any respite.

For the duration of his daughter's imprisonment in Rio de Janeiro, completely incommunicado, Luiz Pandolfi did not rest for a minute. He rallied his contacts, hired the best lawyer, Dr Heleno Fragoso, a man with expertise in defending political prisoners, and started trying to find out what could be done to shorten and alleviate Dulce's suffering. He soon discovered there wasn't much he could do, other than hope and pray that Dr Fragoso would manage to find some loophole or file some sort of plea. The very least he hoped for was official proof that she was still alive and in detention: any such recognition from the military would have made it nigh impossible for her to disappear. It was an important step. But Fragoso went one better than that.

After her third month in confinement, having had no contact with the outside world and weighing only forty kilos, Dulce was removed from her cell and hooded once more. She feared the worst. They put her in the back of a police van and took her somewhere. She was ushered, cuffed and blindfolded, down some strange corridors and into an empty room, where they took off the hood and ordered her to stand and wait. A door opened, and in walked her father. It was one of those indescribable moments in life. An endless hug, as the months of defensive recoil slowly unwound. But there was little time and so much to say. She felt a need to spill out the truth in a torrential stream, but her father didn't want to hear it, and she understood that it would have made no difference anyway. Holding her in his arms, he could feel it all in the emaciated frame to which his daughter had been reduced, hearing her cry on his shoulder, fragile as a child of war or famine. Luiz was devastated by his impotence. As soon as they said goodbye, he rejoined his brother-in-law Mario, who lived in Rio and was waiting for him outside in the street, and asked him to take him straight to the nearest cardiac hospital. He could feel her pain in every organ of his body.

Other moments that would mark Dulce's life and change the meaning of things, turning reality inside out and shredding long-held theories, were three visits made to her cell. The first: a soldier opened the door and asked Dulce if she'd like to write home. She hesitated, figuring it was probably a trick, but she couldn't resist, and accepted the paper and pencil that were offered to her. She wrote her letter and gave it to the young guard. She learned a few months later that he actually sent it, and her family received it. The following week another young soldier came into the cell, but instead of taking her out he walked over to her and gave her a portable radio, out of the blue. For fifteen minutes she was able to listen to the news, to music, hear human voices from outside the walls of her confinement. It was a chink in the lead plaque of hours and days. Of course, she had to keep the volume to a barely audible minimum: if the young soldier had been caught, he would have come in for some severe punishment. A few days later the same guard allowed her briefly to visit

Alexandre through the door of his cell. They could exchange
only a few words, and were unable to touch or to kiss, but it
was more than Dulce could have dreamed of.

The mere thought of this act of genuine compassion
moves Dulce to this day. It goes some way toward counter-
ing what she experienced of evil in its purest form. She saw
humanity in its extremes, and it was enough to dismantle
and renew all notions of utopia. Dulce raises a coffee cup
sitting beside the tape recorder and smiles with the levity of
one who still believes. She takes a deep breath, so as not to
suffocate, sets the cup back down on its saucer and finds herself without a voice to continue. Her eyes well.

In the 1970s, the Left was divided on how to deal with
informers. Some defended capital punishment, the famous
'justice killings', for those who betrayed their own organization by giving up contacts or the names of comrades. The
verb 'betray' carried the secondary connotation of inability
to hold out under torture. The purpose of these justice killings, of which there were only two cases, seemed to be to
provide further motivation for prisoners not to break under
torture rather than to punish those who had. The logic they
were designed to inculcate was more or less the following:
I'm dead one way or another – the torturers will kill me if I
don't talk, and my comrades will kill me if I do, so I might
as well take the path of honour and loyalty to the cause.
Dulce never subscribed to this violent autophagy. The time
she spent in the purple room, even though she was one of
those who did resist, refused to inform and yet lived to tell
the tale, made her more tolerant of those who weren't so
strong. Nobody should be blamed for being a victim, she'd

say. It's not the victim who makes a confession, it's the torture.

Dulce oscillated between both poles: mortal hatred of the snitch, and forgiveness. One day, while she was hanging from the macaw's perch, a well-dressed man was led into the purple room and showed no hesitation in pointing straight at her and giving her codename and details of her activities and contacts within the organization. He was a member of her group, with whom she had shared numerous responsibilities in the past. But there he was, dispassionate, completely indifferent to the humiliating conditions in which he now encountered his former comrade.

The rage stung like the electric shocks. His shameless pusillanimity hurt her more than the interrogators' fists. It gnawed at her like it did when her tormenters sat there eating burgers while she was tortured — and that was a common occurrence. It would be years before she was even able to look at fast food again. In her memory, the nausea ended up serving as a well of terror, a substitute for an image so terrible it had to be eliminated at all costs.

Months later, during the first session of her trial, after her detention had been formally admitted and the torture had ended, she found herself in his presence again. They were both handcuffed and he turned to her and nodded some tenuous greeting, which she repelled in disgust by looking away. These appearances before the military court were the only chance she had to denounce the torture she'd been subjected to while in custody, and she spared no detail in describing it. Nobody was under any illusions as to that window of freedom, which evoked justice without exercising or respecting it, although everything was duly recorded. Even if it counted for nothing with regard to her own defence, maybe it would come to some good in the future, if preserved in the regime's bureaucracy. The Brazilian dictatorship maintained certain formalities that other criminal regimes throughout Latin America – namely Argentina, Chile and Uruguay – had dispensed with summarily; formalities that were a hollow mimicry of democratic institutionalism. Even so, there may have been some relative importance in the stenography, some record of events to which the regime would never officially admit.

So Dulce told everything as it was. Then came her informant's turn. He confirmed his confession and denied that he had suffered any mistreatment. The prosecutor, who knew whom he was dealing with, confidently asked the man what had happened to his right hand. Dulce craned her neck to see. The man displayed his crippled limb, which he had kept concealed up to that point, and said that the injury had been sustained in a car crash prior to his imprisonment. Dulce hadn't noticed it before. His hand was mutilated, lined with deep scars and seemingly paralysed, mangled into a monstrous hook. Another prisoner sitting beside Dulce whispered something like 'Did you hear what they did to him?', and it all suddenly became clear. That man had been utterly destroyed. When he'd entered the purple room he probably wasn't well dressed, much less dispassionate. He had merely been clothed, which was an exorbitant luxury for someone hanging naked from a *parrilla*, exposed to voyeuristic inspection. It no longer made sense for her to loathe or blame him. Loathsome was the dictatorship's apparatus of cruelty. That's what Dulce told me. She had forgiven him. At the end of the court session she made a point of passing close enough to him to say, in a murmur, that she bore him no ill-will, that it was all OK, that he shouldn't feel guilty.

There's a huge difference between a comrade breaking under torture and an infiltrator who wins trust only to betray it. While Dulce was in jail, her father needed a certificate of clearance from the local ordinance department on some property he owned in Boa Viagem, on the Pernambucan coast. His son Roberto was entrusted with the task and headed for the Navy office in charge of such matters in Recife. He went over to the counter, explained what he needed and was told to go to the second door on the right and ask for Captain Roberto. He did as he was told and was asked to wait. After a while he was called inside: 'How can I help you?' Roberto Pandolfi was so shocked by who he saw that it was all he could do to mutter the name: 'Captain Roberto?' The officer sat up in his chair and blurted angrily: 'What are you doing here?' Dulce's brother gave no answer. He turned around and left the building, seething with fear and hate. Captain Roberto was known to him and his family as Antonio, his younger brother's private tutor, a regular visitor to the Pandolfi house in the months leading up to Dulce's imprisonment.

'Antonio' had gradually won over Luiz Pandolfi, presenting himself as a left-wing sympathizer and constantly asking after Dulce, away studying in Chile. He became something of a family friend, and Luiz made a point of giving him a lift whenever the lessons ended late. He'd declined the offer at first, but eventually accepted out of politeness. However, he never let Luiz drive him home, saying that he lived too far away and that a lift to the bus terminal would do nicely, as there was a direct line he could take from there without having to make two other changes. And so things continued for months on end. Shortly after Dulce was arrested, Antonio made some excuse and stopped giving lessons. They hadn't heard from him since. Only now, in the entrails of a bureaucratic maze, had they discovered his true identity, and it came as a major shock to the whole family, already rocked by recent events.

The realization of having lived with the enemy is a powerful sensation. It throws open the fragility of one's home, one's family, and injects the venom of groundlessness and guilt. It's as if reality were shaken up, causing a sort of vertigo that undermines all certainty. The enemy had not only made it through the door, he'd sat with you on the sofa, sat at your table over dinner, shared stories from a false past and touched the emotions of the family. It was like a magnet pressed to a compass. If Antonio was Captain Roberto, then anything was possible. Nothing causes more insecurity than the sense that the reality you and your loved ones had believed to be true was actually false.

Dulce spent forty-five days at the Department of Public and Social Order, DOPS, a political repression unit under the Rio de Janeiro State Security Secretariat. Given the solidarity and camaraderie of her cellmates and the absence of torture, threats and sadistic late-night visits by authorities and their canine entourages, DOPS was like heaven on earth.

Amid all the twists and turns that bind Dulce's story to the history of the nation, one figure stands out. A woman named Laura. Laura was a prostitute and, as prostitutes do, she spent the night with a man, just another in a long line of clients. She didn't know who he was, where he was going, what he did for a living or how old he was, whether he was married, single or widowed, if he had kids, if he was happy. Laura didn't even know his nationality as he had a funny accent, but then hookers don't ask to see their clients' passports. She never saw him again. Then one day she was arrested. It was no big deal, prostitutes were often taken in for questioning. They'd probably just hold her for a few hours and let her go. But this time was different, and she was scared. There were a lot of cops, and not just the civilian kind, but Military Police too, and soldiers. They turned up in vans and cars and took her away with a hood over her head. Weeks later she wound up in a Doi-Codi cell with Dulce. Laura was going to be let out soon, and they didn't want her to be a complete basket case on release. She was too shaken up simply to be let back out into society. They'd tortured her with their customary ferocity. The client with the strange accent was a wanted militant with the Uruguayan Tupamaros. Dulce would never forget the fear she saw in Laura's eyes and her incessant questioning. The woman simply could not understand what had happened to her. She'd been manhandled by the police before, but she'd never imagined anything like what she'd just been put through. She wanted to know, she needed to know, she begged Dulce to explain it to her: 'Who are you people? What did you do? What crime did you commit that was so terrible? Why do they hate you so much? Why so much hate? How can there be so much hate?'

On 8 December 1970, news reached Dulce that the Swiss
Ambassador, Giovanni Enrico Bucher, had been kidnapped
in Catete, Rio, by a group led by the Communist Carlos
Lamarca, and that Dulce's name was on the list of political
prisoners the governor was to release if he wanted there to
be a happy ending. She received the news with mixed feelings. It would be great to get out of jail, but she'd have to
enjoy her liberty in exile. There was no way of knowing
when democracy would be reinstated in Brazil, or when
she'd be able to come back to see friends and family, speak
her own language, breathe Brazilian culture, resume her
relationship with Alexandre, restart her career and return to
politics. Exile was the price of her freedom, which was
something of a paradox: freedom came with territorial limitations. On the other hand, if she remained in jail there was
always the chance she'd be released before long. The horror
was over. Maybe they would just let her go. Her cellmates
encouraged her to opt for immediate release, even if that
meant exile. The logic was clear: what sort of security could
she possibly expect in a dictatorial regime's holding cell?
There was no assurance the torture wouldn't resume, if only
as revenge for the ambassador's abduction. In fact, holding
out made no sense. So Dulce prepared to say goodbye. Little
by little hope gave way to anguish, as the negotiations
between the government and the political group responsible
for the kidnapping proved protracted and fraught. It was
only on 13 January 1971 that the seventy released prisoners
embarked for Chile. That morning some soldiers came for
her and took her for the customary medical. The marks of
torture were still there for all to see. She was loaded into a

police van and taken way. The van drove and drove for over an hour. Dulce couldn't see outside, so she had no idea where she was when it finally parked.

It didn't take long for her to understand that she was being transferred to solitary confinement at the Talavera Bruce women's prison, in the hottest part of Rio, Bangu. Sunk in that West Zone Rio valley, cell temperatures hit 50 degrees Celsius in summer. Dulce panicked, yelled, begged, demanded some explanation. Instead of freedom, she'd been transferred to another version of hell. The conditions were infinitely worse than she'd grown used to at DOPS. Instead of contact with her fellow prisoners, to whom she'd attributed the restoration of her health and sanity, the bases upon which she'd begun to plan for the future, she found herself consigned to utter claustrophobia and uncertainty. Her insistence eventually yielded answers: this was her lot, no mistake, no misunderstanding. She would not be going into exile. She was here to stay. Talavera Bruce was her new address, and there was no date of release. That would be decided by the authorities. Her term? Years, maybe decades, maybe life. Dulce eventually understood: her scars meant it was impossible for her to leave the country because they were incontrovertible proof of torture and thus of the criminal nature of the Brazilian dictatorship. She would have to remain in Brazil.

At the prison her world was limited to that tiny, suffocating space with a concrete bunk and mattress, seatless toilet, tall sink and a green iron door with a peephole. The toilet didn't flush from inside the cell, so the guards had to be called to flush it from the outside. After a while she was allowed to receive visitors, like all the other inmates. Yard time and the end of solitary confinement finally afforded some contact with other political prisoners, who were kept apart. She spent six months in that claustrophobic bunker. There was no torture, other than the isolation and deplorable conditions. The total lack of any prospects was exasperating. She received no information about her fate, how long she would be kept there or what would come afterwards. That February she married Alexandre. It was the only way he would be allowed to visit. Her relatives up in Pernambuco sent treats, sweets and cake to the newlyweds through her mother. A judge officiated at the ceremony and Dulce was immediately escorted back to her cell. There was no celebration, much less any conjugal visits, the later invention of a restored democracy. Some of her fellow prisoners managed to convince one of the wardens to place a man-sized collage on her bunk, made out of newspaper.

In June 1971 Dulce was transferred to the Bom Pastor prison, located in a convent in Recife. People queued up to visit her, and she celebrated her return to her hometown as a gift of destiny. The bars on the windows were more like domestic security grids, and the treatment was civil. It was a sort of reconditioning for freedom, which finally came on 14 December 1971, her birthday. A storyline that contrived such a coincidence would be dismissed as unbelievable. Dulce returned to Rio de Janeiro, where she lives to this day, to get back to her studies and her former plans. There was still a long way to go between her release and her present standing as one of the nation's leading historians.

Mangueira

Inspector Frazão comes blustering into my office early one Monday morning.

'Sorry, I don't have an appointment, Mr Secretary, but this is an emergency.'

Police and journalists have a habit of dropping the prefix when addressing the Under-Secretary for Security for the state of Rio de Janeiro. In return, in everyday contact, all Civil Police inspectors — first, second or third class — are simply inspectors and Military Police lieutenant-colonels all colonels.* It's 1999 and Frazão is a permanent candidate for the job of Chief Inspector. Tough and experienced, he's risen through the ranks and is now in charge of the most important criminal investigations sector.

I shake his clammy hand. He's overweight and flushed, the colour of a lit cigarette end in the dark. The sweat rolls down his neck. Unbuttoned shirt and thick gold chain tended to be the trademark garb of the racketeer and bent cop, but Frazão was an exception. He preferred low-profile shirts, fully buttoned, covering up the chain. This particular

---

* In Brazil the work of the police is split: the Military Police undertake patrolling and preventative tasks, whereas the Civil Police are in charge of investigation. Each state has both Military and Civil Police forces. The Federal Police, however, are responsible for the whole range of duties.

shirt is cream, light and stuck to his sweat-soaked torso. He's not one for the exotic rings that replaced gold teeth in the repertoire of Rio underworld extravagances. His mind elsewhere, Frazão is breathing like an animal on its way to the slaughterhouse. He adjusts his Glock, his eternal companion, holstered on his belt behind his back, and makes no attempt to conceal his distress. He sits down and stares at the bulletin board to his left, which I use to track project progress. It's an instinctive movement, an automatic impulse to avoid eye contact. It's not projects he has on his mind. Our meeting is delicate. We're not friends, nor really even collaborators. He's facing accusations before international human rights forums for which I was a consultant before joining the government. The awkwardness is mutual. We act as if there were no corpses piled up between us on the office floor, but the atmosphere is unbreathable.

'I've come straight from the hospital.'

For the first time, he focuses on me.

'I had some sort of seizure.'

He speaks with some difficulty. Perhaps for physical reasons.

'I haven't slept.'

That explains the bags under his eyes and the pasty skin.

'I spent the whole night talking them out of it. Until five in the morning. I thought it wasn't gonna work. You have no idea. You haven't the foggiest. When these guys pop, there's no controlling them. No one can. You messed with a real hornet's nest, Mr Secretary. If you want to criticize, then criticize. You want to punish, then punish. No problem. No problem at all. But you can't badmouth the force in public.'

There's no pause. Frazão is on a roll.

'You can't do that, you can't go saying the police were wrong; stating in public that the police were in the wrong. If they feel disrespected, they stop. If the government takes the police to task, then it loses all authority. But worse than sitting back is when they decide to get stuck in and put things to rights. When my people decide to act, Mr Secretary, a lot of scumbags end up six feet under.'

The scene springs to mind: an opera singer in the church, seething, spitting a threat into an enemy's ear.

'They wanted to whack a dozen or so from the shanty town and leave the bodies at your door, and at the governor's door. Twelve or thirteen, at least. And they said that would be letting them off lightly.'

The arteries pop in his neck. His accelerated heartbeat rubs off on me. The circle closes.

'I managed to hold them back this time, but I won't be able to rein them in next time. There can't be a next time.'

The inspector moves another piece in a game of chess that had begun three days earlier.

Of course, I am that under-secretary, and I wasn't thinking about any of this on that Friday morning, 14 May 1999. I was in the middle of a makeshift platform, surrounded by authorities gathered to celebrate the bestowal of public honours on some elderly citizens for their unparalleled moral and material support for the Copacabana police battalion. The initiative was that of Colonel Mello, highly regarded by the members of the neighbourhood clubs and charities. He'd been commended by them and was returning the compliment. The exchange of minor tributes was a pastime for the elderly, a touching moment for the families and a source of exasperation for me. There I was, standing to attention beside the Military Police Commissioner, Sérgio da Cruz, as the police brass band belted out the national anthem. Why do the police have a brass band? It's because the average solemnity loses the run of itself without a soundtrack to peg the dramaturgy to the roles and protagonists. I'm one of them, suit and tie consigning me to ceremonial formality for over two hours now — much of which has been spent under the scorching Rio sun — when I have so many other things to do. I've been in the job for four and a half months, and I've set myself the mission of changing the world — or at least the perverse world of policing scandalously marred by racism, misogyny, homophobia and class bias. Brazil shifted from a dictatorship to a democracy with the promulgation of the 1988 Constitution, but the legacy of history based on authoritarianism and slavery cannot be legislated out of existence. Especially in such a sensitive area, where the State bares its claws more ostensibly, authorizing men and women who grew up in a tradition of war against the enemy within to 'compel compliance'. Oblivious to any such political musings, the Copacabana police chief reads out a speech laced with poetic citations in praise of the honourees. The commissioner says a few words and then it's my turn. I thank, I applaud, I congratulate. The rhythm slows, and I sit back down. Next up is the spokesman for the group of honourees, chosen for being the eldest among them — no small feat in that company.

Copacabana is a senescent neighbourhood, with the highest population of old-age pensioners in the country. Plus tourists, of course. It's a place known for its music, vintage feel, shopping and hectic traffic. Perhaps the image most frequently associated with Rio de Janeiro worldwide is that sweeping arc, mirrored by the undulating flagstones of the promenade, running between the Sugarloaf and the wet rocks of Forte at the far end.

My cellphone vibrates in my breast pocket. Discreetly, I take it out and slide it down to my knee. I excuse myself to the two colonels with a subtle hand gesture and withdraw. I reckon they'll deduce that I wouldn't do such a disservice as to slip away in the middle of a speech like that unless it was really urgent. And the urgency in this case is the governor. He asks me where I am; says that the Mangueira community has come down from the shanty town and taken over the avenue below. Thousands of people are crowding the asphalt and they're on the warpath. Something not very clear, but obviously very serious, has happened, that's all we know. The Secretary for Security for Rio, Colonel of the Military Police Josias Quintal, is somewhere in the countryside and it will take him a while to get back, so I'm in charge. He tells me to get over there immediately, and to contact the commissioner. My heart is pounding and I barely have the breath to reassure him. My voice runs ahead of my reason and I say something more or less like this: 'He's here with me. We'll go there together, straight away.' As I scurry back to the platform to call out the commissioner, it occurs to me that I have no training whatsoever in handling an infuriated crowd.

My attention wanders. I set myself on autopilot: apologies, brief justifications, the walk over to the commissioner's car – which is better equipped than mine, and bullet-proofed to boot. We leave a trail of perplexity and disappointment behind us. We sit in the back seat, with a bodyguard up front beside the driver, as protocol dictates. The second car, also bullet-proofed, carries four more bodyguards and a driver, and it remains in constant radio contact with us on a special frequency. Another radio in the first car is tuned into the regular Military Police frequency, so we can follow events as they unfold and glean some idea of what happened up in Mangueira, which goes more or less like this: some Civil Police raided the shanty town late last night and a youth from the community was shot dead. We still don't know what the mission was.

In Brazil, the Civil Police and Military Police serve very different functions, the former investigative and the latter combative. So, assuming each institution's responsibilities were respected, the Civil Police could only have gone into Mangueira to conduct an investigation – either that or they were there for personal reasons, perfidious or otherwise. Conducting an investigation at night sounds highly unlikely, as there'd be no eluding the drug gangs and their scouts. Sometimes Civil Police are sent into shanty towns to make an arrest, but there was no way they were executing a warrant in the middle of the night in an area ruled by drug lords and armed gangs. Unless they were infiltrators and their cover had been blown – but that was even less likely. Brazilian law does not look favourably on the practice, because the promiscuity between the police and the criminals is notorious enough already and undercover operations tend to contaminate attempts to combat corruption.

So before talking to the chief of the Civil Police and those involved to hear their version of events, I come to the conclusion that the institutional boundaries must have been ignored yet again and that the Civil Police ran an incursion into the favela to seize arms and drugs. There'd be nothing new in that. The two institutions are constantly competing and they waste a lot of their energy trying to undermine each other. However, launching an operation like that at night was strange and suspect, to say the least. The department's policy prohibits armed incursions, because the risks to the community far outweigh the possible benefits. So I call the chief of the Civil Police. He doesn't know what went on either. It looks absurd, and that's exactly what it is. The Security Department has no control over its police forces; even the police commanders have no control over them. They're not so much institutions as archipelagos of relatively autonomous units, each with its own remit and appetites. This is what makes building the conditions for governability such a pressing and challenging task.

The advantage of police cars is their ability to blow through bottlenecks, run red lights and basically work traffic miracles. I ask the ever-discreet Colonel Cruz for his opinion, but he's at as much of a loss as I am. Word arrives that the riot police are at the scene. They've beaten us to it. Far from bringing relief, the news makes me even more apprehensive. Tropa de Choque (literally, Clash Squad): what was one to expect from a battalion whose very name spoke its vocation? The car's blackened windows stain the Rio cityscape with an eerie, sombre pall. I prepare for the unexpected, a contradiction in terms, but apt when it

comes to thousands of people pouring down from the hill-
side slums. The scene stoked the imagination of the romantic
revolutionaries of the 1960s every bit as much as it distilled
conservative middle-class fear. The pop music of the day
used and abused the image, woven into the most varied
plots. It was basically hackneyed to death.

The avenue that skirts the foot of Mangueira is an important thoroughfare. It connects the North Zone to downtown
Rio, a decadent suburb and the heart of the city, the seat of
its public institutions – a throwback to Rio's heyday as the
national capital. The Mangueira shanty town is in the general vicinity of Maracanã Stadium and the Rio de Janeiro
State University. It lends its name to one of the oldest and
best-loved Carnival samba schools, and has inspired dozens
upon dozens of songs that form part of the rich heritage of
Brazilian popular music. In other words, that 14 May would
be no ordinary day, just as Mangueira was no ordinary
neighbourhood.

The car leaves us just metres away from the riot police's
rearguard. Stealing between soldiers, I can just about make
out a slab of deserted avenue and a human mass condensed
behind some imaginary line 150 to 200 metres away from the
police barricade. The riot police await their orders, protected
by their shields, helmets, bullet-proof vests and firearms. I
have to act quickly to prevent fear from taking over on
either side and triggering a tragedy. We're briefed by the riot
police commander. Nothing we don't already know. I notice
the briefing is directed exclusively to Colonel Cruz. It's as if
I don't exist. The riot police commander is ignoring me.
The notion of civilian leadership doesn't compute with the

military mindset, and there's a lot behind that – most of the history of power in Brazil, in fact. There would be no sense in my pretending to be in command and start yelling orders. It would be pathetic and inefficient. I tell Colonel Cruz that under no circumstances is he to authorize the use of weapons or an advance on the crowd. No matter what happens, he has to keep his men in strictly defensive formation. No matter what, Colonel. I had to be not only emphatic but also redundant, repeating myself, to compensate for the ambiguity of my role. I'm not afraid of the crowd on the other side. I'm afraid of what the riot police will do if let off the leash. I fear their atavistic commitment to violence. I fear the automatisms racism can produce.

I move through row after row of riot police. I don't know how many of them there are – fifty, sixty, a hundred. I see soldiers from different battalions, all led by Choque. And other garrisons are arriving. I move beyond the front line. I'm standing in the empty avenue. Colonel Cruz accompanies me. Just a few steps into no man's land and I realize that the commissioner's presence is probably unwise. There are two sides to the ambiguity: it reduces my authority before the troops, but it might boost my chances of dialogue with the community. I ask the colonel to hang back, saying that I need him there, ahead of his troops, to prevent any rash decisions. He understands. No questions asked. He withdraws and I press ahead, alone. I know they're watching me, at least those on the front line. I can't get a sense of the numbers. A thousand? Three thousand? Five thousand? It's impossible to compute. I can hear the voices, the shouting, the volcanic Babel. I decide to keep my tie and suit jacket on.

No more farce. These people have had an overdose of hypocrisy over a lifetime. I am there to represent the State. The
suit is my uniform. I try to clear my head. The avenue is
strewn with the symbols of hate: smoke grenades, sticks,
stones. It's a long walk. The voices grow louder. Individuals
begin to emerge from the multitude.

I can finally discern the faces of men, women, children,
and the crowd begins to make sense. It's as stimulating as it
is intimidating. I am an extension of the police. I'm part of
what has incited this revolt, this rage, this despair and indignation. People surround me on all sides, but only the children touch me. They seek physical contact, even if they say
nothing. They all look as dazed and confused as I do. I walk
into the thick of the crowd, as if wading into the sea. There's
no empty space, unless I create it with my movements, only
to have it filled by a frenzy of legs and arms, pushing and
shoving. They don't lay a finger on me, but I'm completely
engulfed.

What follows is frankly unreal – a scene I wouldn't believe
myself if I read it in a book. The crowd falls into circles
around me, as if some theatre director had arranged them to
evoke a Greek choir. These rings form, like ripples around a
stone thrown into the water, growing larger and wider the
further out they are. The inner ring is all children. It's the
kids who hemmed me in, besieging me the very moment I
crossed their lines. These children are sobbing, shouting,
vying for my attention, tugging me by the hand and pinning
me in a wheel, growing tighter, as if it were a group hug,
cathartic and reparative. I can only decipher snatches of
what they say to me. The sentences come out jumbled and

gurgled. Each girl, each boy, flings in my direction a fragment of the story, bellowing at me to make themselves heard with all their might, speaking with their whole bodies, buckling over, as if nothing in the world were more important right then than making me understand.

And what I understood is this: a teenager was shot dead by the police in an alley, and there were witnesses. This teen was a lot of things, dear things, to different people: a schoolmate, a friend, a brother, a relative, a neighbour, someone's nephew, someone's grandson, someone's son. He was executed. And they – the kids – are very sad and very angry, and scared too, very scared.

The children are then replaced by the women of all ages, some as young as in their teens. It's the same drama, different cast. They're crying and desperate; shouting over each other, always a squall. They don't touch me, but they fight for every bit of space to get their words across to me. The story told by the children is retold in greater detail. Looking them in the eye, I listen attentively, but I can only do this one person at a time, which frustrates the others. They can see the communication is breaking down, and their attempts to overcome the obstacles just add to the anguish and the noise. The choir is not in synch. Or maybe it is, if we consider that the meaning they want to convey is incommunicability itself. This, collectively, is what we're grappling with: the impossibility of communication between society and the State; the community and the police. However, I am convinced that what we experienced there was a collective unconscious outburst, unbeknownst to any of us, myself included. The emotions shared in such torrential outpouring shed a great deal of light on incommunicability and, in so doing, become forms of communication themselves. The choir of so many dissonant voices helped open windows of communication by creating a shared language beyond words. It is incredible that such events occur without anyone organizing or orchestrating them, just the pure power of collective intelligence, that which the anthropologists call culture.

After the women come the men. The crowd falls silent. The narrative is the same as the women's and the children's, but it's audible and clear. And they add an explanation. The youth was executed by Civil Police who had invaded the shanty town in order to extort money out of the drug traffickers. His murder was a reprisal for the breakdown of negotiations on a raise in their pay-off, the cash bribes they received to turn a blind eye. The kid was unarmed, the men stress. He had nothing to do with the situation.

It's rare to come across anyone willing to risk life and limb by testifying against the police. Especially when you consider that there is zero chance any investigation will find against the officers, no matter what evidence is given. There's also little chance the crime scene will be investigated, because that would suppose there was a crime. When an on-duty policeman shoots and kills someone, it goes on record as use of lethal force in response to an act of resistance. In other words, the victim got himself killed by posing a threat to the physical integrity of officers and civilians. To fit that particular bill, the cops chosen for operations inside shanty towns often carry what's called a candle kit: a second weapon to be placed in the hand of the corpse, among other items to be planted as forged evidence.

I look at the people around me, and when the men finally hush the crowd I say something more or less like this: It's hard to believe, but we can do things differently. What happened last night shouldn't have happened, and can't keep on happening. The best thing we can do to put an end to all these barbaric deaths is to respond clearly and immediately, today, now. The government on one side and you on the other. I'll need your help to do that. I'll order a crime scene investigation, but the witnesses have to play their part. I'll guarantee their safety.

Various voices hurl questions at me simultaneously. Going to the police station to make a deposition against police officers is suicide. No one will go. I insist. I'll be with them the whole time and I'll take their statements personally, along with the chief of the Civil Police, whom I trust entirely.

Suddenly everyone around me starts shouting, as if a bomb full of voices has just gone off. I don't know what's happening. No one responds to my proposal; it's as if I've disappeared. The men who were talking with me are all looking in the same direction now, and they're echoing the shouts from further off. Innumerable arms are raised, all pointing at the same person or thing. The younger ones start jumping up and down, trying to get a better view. My first impression is that some imminent threat has caused the group to disperse, but the fact that they are all running in the same direction puts paid to that theory. I just stand there, perplexed and immobile, until it dawns on me that all I can do is run as well, follow the throng. Drifting away from the mêlée, I get a better view of what's going on: two men are fleeing as fast as their legs can carry them, one lugging an unwieldy camera. They don't look like pros. Stones and blocks of wood hurtle over my head. The fleeing pair are the target. The stronger, younger men rush off in hot pursuit as the two make for the line of riot police. The avenue is on two levels, with four lanes apiece. The pair escape down the lower level. The space is clear, but the quicker of the protesters take up strategic positions from which to hurl their missiles. Bystanders could get caught in the hail of rocks. I keep running with the stampede, yelling at them to stop, stop throwing stones, let the guys escape. The riot police adopt attack formation. I leave the pursuit and muster what energy remains to get myself into a position from which I can be heard by the squad. There's no time to dial the commissioner's number, and I don't have a radio, so everything I do is improvised. Running and shouting are mutually exclusive actions. I slow down and start opening and crossing my arms over my head, ordering them to hold fire, hold their positions, the men will get away, they won't be caught or hurt. That's how I see it. They'll more than likely emerge unscathed from that Stone Age storm. I try to shout at the protesters; I try hand signals, but I don't know how to make them. How do you shout in gestures? The best I can do is a grotesque excuse for a negative: no, no, stop. Don't throw any more stones. Leave the two men alone. Come back. Let's continue our talk. The guys with the camera disappear among the rows of riot police and I turn my back on the squad and try to communicate with the crowd, which has spilled over onto both levels of the avenue, losing density in the process. The running has given way to collective hesitation: what to do now, where to go? I try to communicate through gestures. I point back toward where we were before the hunt for the cameraman and his friend began. I start moving in that direction myself, signalling for them to follow me, take my lead.

I must admit, by this stage I'm seething. I'm ready to explode like the crowd of protesters just moments before. I'm filled with hate for those idiots who almost lit the fuse. The imbeciles who waved their camera around with all the subtlety of a flag or sub-machine gun. A video camera that must weigh about seven kilos and was probably last used by some secret agent in *The Pink Panther*. They wanted to film the protesters, especially those who were talking to me. That much was clear. The people of Mangueira can spot their kind a mile away. Especially when the Sherlock and Watson in question slink away from the ranks and start filming people with their suitcase-sized camera. I later discover that the pathetic P-2 (that's the name given to the Military Police's secret service team and its members) took up position under a tree on the island that separates the two levels of the avenue. Sticking out like a sore thumb, they were quickly identified – with no need for further proof – as infiltrators planted there to identify the cops' potential accusers. These two morons were acting against everything I'd been trying to achieve. They ruined my credibility, or at least could have done. I honestly don't understand how the episode didn't leave me totally demoralized before the crowd and torpedo my negotiations. I was now out on a limb, my chances of staying safe inversely proportional to the likelihood of my being hit by a rock in freefall. But I escaped the worst – perhaps because the crowd noted my own indignation at this turn of events, or because they knew there was no way I would put my own neck on the line like that just to net some footage of the ringleaders.

The crowd retreats in waves back to where the negotiations started. I repeat my proposal. The same group of men are standing around me, and they repeat their response. There's no point in vouching for their safety. Who would be dumb enough to believe that anyone could protect a slum dweller from police reprisal? Who provides witness protection? The police. It doesn't add up. Not in Brazil, at least, and especially not in Rio de Janeiro. It would be naive to think otherwise. And they're right, I can only agree. Their arguments are compelling. I reformulate my proposal. Two hours from now I'll go up to the shanty town with the chief of the Civil Police to take the witness statements myself. Any house or community centre could be used as a makeshift police station. It could be a place of their choosing. Absolute confidentiality guaranteed.

They exchange glances, quickly deliberate and accept my offer. The only condition I want to put to them is that they clear the avenue. The city has to get back to work. I'm just about to say this to them when another unexpected event interrupts our conversation. Like a peal of thunder, the roar of a police chopper descends upon us, turning the situation on its head.

Without warning, the Civil Police helicopter starts hovering low over the crowd. It's unlike anything I've experienced before. I don't know what sort of buzz this gives the crew, especially the shooter hanging out of the left-hand side from a safety harness, wielding his machine gun. I suppose it must give them some perverse pleasure, because he's laughing his head off as he pretends to open fire on the mass down below. He makes no attempt to conceal his glee, and the exercise in humiliation works. The machine and its addendum – the laughing gunman acting out an aerial massacre – are designed to intimidate. Especially when they ascend and descend above the heads of the crowd, the roar of the blades drowning out all other sound. The aerial performance sends out a viral message of fear. If I had to sum up the experience in a single word I would say impotence. These sinister fly-overs, followed by the degrading mockery of laughter and massacre, are an affront even to the coolest of mortals. The cynicism of the State and the hostility of the police exhibited in the sordid play-acting of a sniper are just the continuation of the nocturnal assassinations by other means.

Though intimidated like everyone else, I channel my strongest emotion into an immediate response to this arbitrary act of aggression. The feeling of impotence has to be annihilated by some urgent assertion of authority. I call the chief of the Civil Police, to whose orders the chopper responds: I've never spoken to my friend, Inspector Carlos Alberto D'Oliveira, in such terms before. I've never given him an order, much less barked one at him. But I've no alternative now: 'Send the chopper flying over Mangueira back to base immediately and have the sniper arrested on the spot for abuse of power, breach of decorum and the code of ethics, and for threatening the Under-Secretary for Security for the state of Rio de Janeiro and four thousand, nine hundred and

ninety-nine other people as well.' Carlos Alberto barely has
the time to say that he is as surprised as I am, that he didn't
order any fly-over. I hang up and see the quizzical looks on
the faces of those who heard what I just said. In less than a
minute, the chopper pulls a risky manoeuvre and flies off at
full speed. The group around me watch the effect of my
phone call. There's a sort of incredulity in the air. The spokes-
men for the protesters seem more convinced now that I have
some power and that my proposal should be taken seriously.

At around 3.30 p.m., at the Olympic Vila in Mangueira, I
accompany the deputy chief of the Civil Police, Martha
Rocha, and a handful of aides as statements are taken from
the witnesses and their families. The victim's name is Alex
dos Santos. He was fourteen years of age.

That night, on my way home, at around ten o'clock, with
my cellphone battery running low, I take a call from the
Military Police Commissioner. Bad news: a killing in the
Coroa shanty town. Another teenager. Another police killing, except this time they're Military Police. Colonel Cruz,
probably fearing another Mangueira event, which would
leave his institution high and dry, tells me that it actually
looks like the cops are telling the truth about this one. The
soldiers in question came to the police station of their own
accord and handed in the weapon found on the deceased – a
Glock pistol. Everything points to legitimate use of lethal
force. The commissioner concludes: I know my men.
There's no way they would hand in a Glock if it was just a
cover-up. They love that gun, it's expensive as hell.

I don't argue with my friend, Sérgio da Cruz. He's a serious man and I wouldn't confront him simply because I

disagreed with his interpretation of events. But the fact is, I know of dozens of situations in which a Glock has been the perfect ruse, precisely because it incites this kind of reasoning.

In the last few seconds before my phone goes dead, the colonel tells me that residents of Coroa and the family and friends of the dead youth are on their way to the first Military Police battalion, where the boy's killers are stationed. The Coroa community is an enclave between the city centre and the Santa Teresa and Rio Comprido neighbourhoods. Its location is strategic, because it sits over the Santa Barbara tunnel, which connects with the South Zone, the most affluent part of the city. It's an important factor to consider when gauging the possible impact of a demonstration in that region.

I give up on some R&R and head for the battalion, where the protesters have gathered. I invite them in, but I'm stopped at the door. The guards don't recognize me and call the battalion commander, creating an awkward situation for all concerned. In this atmosphere of misunderstandings, an emergency meeting gets under way in the reception wing. Between sobs, and backed up by residents' association reps, the relatives, neighbours and friends of Rodrigo Marques da Silva tell us that the boy was fifteen, the best student in his class, liked by all and incapable of carrying a gun or of any involvement in drug trafficking. The whole favela knew him and could vouch, collectively and individually, for his conduct and personality. Many people witnessed the crime and were willing to testify. In an atmosphere of utter commotion, the people from the community accused the police of cold-blooded murder. With an added touch of brutality, the murderers kicked the boy's mother away from her son's body, grabbed the corpse by the arm and dragged it through the shanty town, brazenly parading their victim for all to see, totally assured of impunity. Rodrigo was helping some friends and neighbours draw up the table for the local football championship when they heard gunfire and made a run for it. It was the cops, who'd entered the shanty town, once again, to renegotiate their pay-offs. Rodrigo was unlucky enough to be seen running and was shot in the back.

After the events of earlier that day I'd figured I'd exhausted my stock of revulsion. Not so. I propose the same course of action. I promise to go to the Coroa shanty town with them and start taking their statements, with the help of some police officers in whom I have complete trust. Carlos Alberto is already committed to the Mangueira investigation, so I have to decentralize. The number of cases is multiplying, but it is imperative that I keep track of each and every one. The secretariat and the state government have to issue a strong and clear response. Two incidents on the same day show that we're not dealing with exceptional, isolated events here. This is the routine of pain and iniquity of Rio de Janeiro. The victims are always poor and almost always black. What does that say about this city – about this country?

What follows are two dramatic days during which the future of Rio hangs in the balance, the near future at least, in one of the most important stamping grounds for black youths from the most underprivileged neighbourhoods. For every step forward there's a step backward: growing pressure on Carlos Alberto, reprisal attacks by drug gangs, oscillations in the media, the two parties vying for public opinion as leverage for a political victory. One side presents itself as counter-establishment, breaking from tradition, while the other defends the conventional political modus operandi and the decades-old forms of dealing with the shanty towns and outlying slums. Let me explain.

It's Saturday, 15 May and we're back in Mangueira, early, to continue the work. Carlos Alberto warns me of an insurrection under way in the Civil Police. He understands my position, agrees with my ideas, but reckons that the powers that be inside the force won't stand for it. He feels pretty sure he'll be removed from his post and that I won't be able to hold on much longer either. And that's just on the political front. He'd rather not speculate on the dangers we face personally.

The governor calls me during a radio interview and puts me on air. He reiterates his commitment to putting an end to police violence and says that these cases are exemplary; that they'll serve as models for a new approach from the Security Department, the police and the government. Live on air, the governor announces that he'll be visiting the community that very morning. The hustle of media and politicians, especially of the opportunistic variety, will transform Mangueira into the stage for a grand event. Before Anthony Garotinho – having taken the nickname *garotinho*, 'little boy', as a surname – no governor had ever gone up to a shanty town to ask the forgiveness of a family and community hurt by State brutality. Nothing can erase the boldness of that act: not the fact that he was a politician 'with an expiry date' – as Marcos Sá Corrêa, one of Brazil's foremost journalists, used to say – nor the fact that his later political life took him in such different directions.

The reaction of disgruntled police did not take long in coming. They weren't used to being contested, evaluated, criticized or investigated. Curiously, hard as it is to believe, their backlash received some inadvertent help from the drug lords. For the drugs and arms traffickers, hostile relations between the police and the community worked in their favour. Pay-offs are a lot less expensive and dangerous than a more competent police force that has the respect of the community. Grassroots hatred of the police made the armed presence of criminal factions less humiliating, repugnant or scary. In short, it made it more tolerable. As people living in areas under drug lord control will often say, the situation may be deplorable and perilous, but at least the 'movement' is more predictable than the police, with their sudden armed raids and episodic visits for the most varied reasons. There's nothing so terrifying as an unpredictable power, because unpredictability makes it impossible to adopt a survival strategy and turns the dial of insecurity up to the maximum.

That afternoon I stop by the cemetery to pay my respects to Rodrigo and his family and then climb Coroa, as arranged, where I start taking witness statements. The testimony is compelling. The ballistics and CSI will be inconclusive, as always, because the perpetrators tampered with the crime scene before leaving, making a full technical investigation impossible. The ballistics would be definitive were it not for the fact that many police officers carry private weapons in these cases. Weapons that later disappear. The guns handed in for examination are their police-issue handguns. The Glock did not belong to the victim. My scepticism was correct, and Colonel Cruz wrong.

I come down from the favela and find the mouth of the Santa Barbara tunnel blocked by crates. I personally remove the obstacles, take the tunnel and call some people from my team who are still up in the shanty town. They consult with Rodrigo's family, who deny that they have anything to do with it. The news spreads through the favela: the traffickers are behind the attempted blockade. I head for Ipanema, where I'm to give a live TV interview on the latest developments. It's important to win over public opinion in favour of legality and against police brutality. I'm worried, despite the fact that the news from Coroa says that all is calm. Rodrigo's family recognize our efforts, and this is respected by their friends and family.

During the interview I receive some disastrous news. The road below Coroa has been blockaded again, only this time some buses have been stopped inside the tunnel, emptied of passengers and set on fire. War is declared between the Coroa drug gang and the police. Paradoxically, it's a war that will strengthen the Military Police and, by association, the Civil Police as well, because its first casualty will be the city itself. In the light of recent events, strengthening the police at this point plays straight into the hands of those sectors most resistant to change, those who defend violent repression and who are all too eager to discredit our critical approach. That evening the governor is bombarded by visits and telephone calls from old-school police and their political allies. The conservative Tropa de Choque, on the pretext of helping the governor restore order, calls for my head and that of Carlos Alberto.

One day he would tell me all about this, and I'd ask him: Governor, what order was there to restore?

Two days later, Inspector Frazão comes into my office, on the verge of a stroke after a sleepless night spent convincing his cops not to raid the shanty town and whack a dozen or so slum kids so they could deposit their corpses on my doorstep, and that of the governor. He says:

'You can't ever pull something like this again, ever, or I won't be able to answer for my men. If you want to criticize, then criticize. You want to punish, then punish. No problem. But do it on the quiet, discreetly, confidentially. You don't wash this sort of dirty linen in public. If you try, you'll end up tarnishing the organization. And these guys won't take that lightly. I can't let that happen. It's the image of police authority that's in play here, Mr Secretary. You know the Military Police don't have any juridical authority as such. In the legal sense of the word, that authority lies with the Civil Police. In truth, we are the only police force. It's inadmissible that you or anyone else should sully our name.'

When the blood boils words can get out of line, and I can't give myself the luxury of worsening the situation through a lack of self-control. So I outsource my response to an imaginary character who represents me in more intense moments. This character keeps his calm, speaks quietly and carefully. He never gives in to the inflamed rhetoric of the human rights defender parked on his shoulder, speaking into his ear.

Sweetly, my voice says to Inspector Frazão that opinion polls show that the two police institutions in Rio de Janeiro do not have a good image, in fact they have a deplorable image. If it's the image that worries him, then the best way to improve it is to recognize the problems and act transparently to rectify them and rebuild lost trust. Public criticism, recognition of the mistakes made, an apology and commitment to change will do the institution's image a lot more good than the same old mantras no one believes in any more.

'Take the case of the helicopter, Mr Secretary. There was no error.'

I can't disguise my perplexity. He continues:

'There wasn't. Technically, the sniper with the gun made no mistake. He did what he's supposed to do. An excellent professional.'

Proper police practice involves laughing your heart out while simulating a massacre? It involves a helicopter hovering only metres above people's heads? Toward what end? To disperse the crowd? Frighten people? What if there was someone armed down there, a hothead, say, and he takes a pop at the sniper, whose body is halfway outside the chopper? Regardless of whether he hits him or not, what would the response be? To open fire on someone mixed into a crowd of thousands? What consequences could we expect from that? What could possibly justify an action involving that level of risk for the protesters? Would this technical resource be employed in a wealthy neighbourhood? Would a student rally from some elite university receive the same treatment? Or does the technique vary depending on skin colour, social class and postcode?

'Well if you want to discuss ideology . . .'

'It's not about practice or ideology, Inspector, it's about good sense and the facts. Let me tell you something, Inspector Frazão' – and here I pulled the rope a little tighter – 'I'll take the liberty of offering my opinion. As I see it, technically speaking, you should have arrested these policemen who threatened to kill a dozen or so people in different shanty towns. You did everything you could to dissuade them, you spent the night convincing them not to kill innocent people at random just to get back at me and the governor. And for that I will be eternally grateful. It was a noble gesture, but, technically, you should have put them under arrest.'

The conversation does not end well for either of us. It is a no-win discussion for both. The ambiguities and contradictions would keep us wrapped in tension right up to the dénouement. The gang of cops that almost drove Inspector Frazão to a heart attack on the night of 16/17 May 1999 could well have been the same gang that carried out the same threat some months later. There's no way of knowing for sure.

Carlos Alberto D'Oliveira was removed from his post on 13 December 1999. I followed, on 17 March 2000.

Linha Vermelha[*]

Six o'clock in the afternoon, a hot Monday, the wind bending umbrellas on Venezuela Avenue, downtown Rio, one of the rare references to any of our South American neighbours. The new-money apartment buildings and condos of Barra da Tijuca, in the West Zone, prefer to be called *Pigalle*, *Villa Toscana*, *Residence du Soleil*, *Palace des Princes*, *Versailles*, while the malls are unabashedly anglophone: *Downtown*, *New York City Center*, *Fashion Mall*.

From Venezuela Avenue I reach Rodrigues Alves. Five minutes later I'm on Rio Branco, heading out of Mauá Square, where the sailors keep their historically austere, pissed-off pose and the bawling is as incessant as a parade of fanatics. Cigarette flare, moustaches, suit jackets.

The old square is holding out despite the jousting between the developers, the owners of the surviving townhouses and the environmentalists. It's a hub of urban decadence and the ham-fisted hurry of renewal. In the small hours, the homeless and the illegal immigrants bed down in crumbling squats.

Mauá Square opens onto the quay's horrendous corridor of warehouses, darkened by an overpass marked for

[*]Literally 'Red Line', an inter-municipal expressway in Rio, and one of the city's main arteries.

demolition. Inaugurated in 2013, the Rio Museum of Art, white as a blue whale, looms on the mutant cityscape like a prophecy or essential declaration on something important but forgotten.

Rio folk don't tend to have much patience for concepts. All we know of ourselves is what our mirrors – TV and cellphone screens – and the exhibitionist contortions of the native aesthetic decide we need to know. Even so, here we are less resigned than the average Brazilian, perhaps because of centuries of inequality and hypocrisy from the racist elites entrenched in our democracy, debasing worthy institutions and the very idea of equality proclaimed with such pomp and ceremony in the Constitution of 1988. The masses submerge into an ocean of Pentecostal evangelism, hot for baptism, solidarity and belonging, peace, spiritual redemption and a set of values that justifies capitalism, that authorizes happiness in this world, not the next, and that supplies them with the password and the dictionary. The working class want the misleading language of the markets translated for them because it's the key to what they call reality, the language their kids are acquiring and which their grandchildren will surely speak. They have to be polyglots; they don't want to lose Portuguese or the tradition that goes with it, and they dream of navigating the new world with their moral compass tucked safely under their arms. They want to learn to read the primer of profit, of initiative, of entrepreneurship and risk without losing compassion, the treasure bequeathed by their forebears. Twenty-first-century Brazil is fast and strange, but attractive – 'Just look what happened with the neighbours, here in the favela: they've come up in the world, travelled by plane, and the youngest has just started university, who'd ever have said? And all so fast.'

The leftist ideologues lost all hope in redemptive dialectics when President Lula surrendered to the limits of institutional politics, caught between the globalized economy and the sham symbolism of a myth that once deserved a noble name: 'sovereignty' – back when google was just onomatopoeia and the animals still spoke.

In Rio, you just get on with it. Pragmatism is the common sense of the realist. Routine is measured out in strides, sleepless nights and sweltering heat, with music, beer, unending commutes on packed trains and buses, effusive greetings, prayers, shows of affection and an incredible dose of violence, a lot of it coming from the police, whose murderous brutality is a match for the Praetorian Guard of any of the world's bloodiest dictators. But the carioca gets on with life with an even more incredible dose of humour and fair play. Rather than despair when the electricity goes down and the air chokes up, we dance, sing, beat the drum and the gods wake us from the nightmare. And then, if only for a few hours, everything seems possible again, and we're devilishly happy.

Six in the afternoon, Monday, Venezuela Avenue. I check the address, walk through the tinted electronic doors and hand my ID to the girl at the reception desk. She turns her camera on me, tells me to take off my glasses and asks me where I'm going. She calls up to the law firm on the twentieth floor, hands me an ID badge without looking up from her desk and calls the next in line. The security is more lax here than at the place I've just come from. Most of all, the building lacks the rites of security. In the favela, the shanty town, there was liturgy in abundance. And security too.

Four and a half hours before heading up to the twentieth floor to fulfil a promise made earlier that day to a complete stranger, I arrived, punctually, at the designated spot. I sat down at a table in the food court in a mall in the city's North Zone. The place has been thriving ever since higher wages and unlimited access to credit made the average Joe's consumer dreams come true. The intellectuals scoff at the illusions capitalism builds into the junk it sells. But the poor know the difference that air conditioning and a microwave can make in the life of a family spanning three generations that puts in twelve-hour days only to pile up at night to sleep in two suffocating rooms. They take pride and pleasure in savouring the comforts (or fetishes) that were once the preserve of their 'betters'.

I'm dressed as arranged: green T-shirt, jeans and grey sneakers. The intermediary behind the whole labyrinthine arrangement is an ex-neighbour of a former student of mine, who grew up in one of the favelas in the Maré Complex. Green was my choice. The only non-negotiable rule was that red was out. In the communities under *Terceiro Comando* (Third Command) control, red, the colour of the enemy, is strictly prohibited. The *Comando Vermelho* (Red Command) was the pioneer of organized crime in Rio de Janeiro, and it ruled supreme from the 1970s up until its first rival faction, the Third Command, emerged out of disputes over the growing drugs market. The dynamics of the conflict ended up spawning a third faction, the *Amigos dos Amigos* (Friends of Friends), known as the ADA.

I'm approached by a man in his mid-thirties. He doesn't hesitate. I get the impression he knows me, which makes the whole wardrobe thing seem a bit irrelevant. He checks my name, mentions his old neighbour, saying they'd grown up together, then explains to me that his part will be to take me to the gas station at the mouth of the favela, where I'll be met by another middleman. He asks if I'm OK with that; if we can proceed. I pay for my coffee and we head for his car.

We arrive at the gas station ahead of time, but the look-out who is to signal to my new handler is already there. My student's ex-neighbour tells me to wait in his car while he checks that everything is OK. He goes over to a kid in shades leaning against a motorbike, who then revs off into the favela without any attempt at discretion. A few minutes later a modest car pulls out of the shanty town, flashes its headlights and parks alongside the gas station. The guy from the mall comes back and asks me to follow him. We walk over to the car and he tells the driver who I am and asks if the boss is expecting me. Assured that all is set, he says goodbye and leaves. I say hello to the driver, whose name is never given, slide into the passenger seat, and off we go. I figure he knows no more than I do about what lies ahead. He was probably just told to pick me up and take me to the boss, no questions asked. We drive in silence. The less I say the better; the less exposed I'll be to error, especially when I have no idea what might constitute an error in this context.

However swift and easy things have been so far, this part of the trip is slow-going and more difficult. It took me an hour to get from my house to the mall, and a half an hour from there to the gas station, with only the traffic to contend with. But inside the favela, we're stopped at least ten times. At each checkpoint the car is searched, though with us still inside. The open windows mean each spot check is brief. Even so, the constant pull-overs are exasperating. The sentries are shirtless kids in Bermuda shorts and flip-flops mounted on motorbikes or sitting at drug-decked stalls, some packing handguns, others semi-automatic rifles. The drill is the same at each checkpoint, no frills, no farce. I'm an outsider in my host's empire, and my driver intones the same mantra: 'The prof's here to see the man.' The sentry signals to someone. They don't always understand each other. The communication is cautious but incompetent. Why keep repeating the same explanation? I notice that either my driver is lost or he's going around in circles. We drive past the same place more than once. I don't say anything. I've been here before, at debates arranged by local NGOs, and while I don't know the territory all that well, it's familiar enough for me to see there's something theatrical in all this. Only one hypothesis strikes me as plausible: they want to make sure I'm alone. Finally, an hour after entering the favela, we reach a square full of foot soldiers. I thank the driver and switch off my cellphone. I instructed my wife that if I hadn't returned or sent word by 10 p.m. she was to call my former student and a friend of mine, a community leader. I close the car door, say goodbye to the driver and wait. The men are watching me. I nod by way of greeting.

A young man leaves the group and approaches. He shakes my hand, but doesn't introduce himself, and points toward a car. We get in and he turns the key.

The young man I'm sitting beside is public enemy number one. His sole priority right now is staying alive. His eyes dart about, like the feelers of some insect with a very short lifespan and very fast legs. Of all my meetings with major figures from the Rio underworld, this is the most unpredictable. I'm not there to interview the drug lord, I've been granted no such privilege. He has no time to waste on self-promotion. Ever since the feared and famous drug baron Márcio José Sabino Pereira, aka the Mathematician, was executed by a helicopter sniper during a police invasion of Vila Aliança on 11 May 2012, my interlocutor has found himself at the helm of Third Command outfits citywide. His readiness transmits confidence, and makes me nervous. Zealously protecting his own life, he can guarantee my safety – but to what extent can a criminal faction guarantee anything in a state policed by 55,000 officers? How many of those would be deployed in a final offensive against Maré? After all, it would not be long before the media announced the recapture of the complex from the hands of the traffickers.

I observe him in profile, but I have to be careful, with one eye on my interlocutor and the other on the narrow streets rolling before us. In the sprawl of a horizontal shanty town like this, the dirt roads are not so much winding and steep as perpendicular, which means there could be anything around each corner. I redouble my attention after the first few

sudden jerks this way or that, making me reel in my seat.
Where is he taking me? Neither of us is wearing a seatbelt.
We could run into a police patrol at any time, so we need all
the mobility the vehicle, our synapses and physical fitness can
afford. He says not to worry, there's nothing to fear. So why
the pistol on the dashboard? What's with the car on our tail
carrying a crew of five armed men with grenades and machine
guns? Why the bellicose cortège on this sunny afternoon?
The men are tooled up; streets are gonna burn: is that the
message they're sending out to the community? But I don't
ask. I'm there to listen. After all, he requested this meeting.

To put me at ease, he expounds his practical philosophy:
*If you want peace, prepare for war. It's better to be loved than feared,
but fear is more efficient, so long as it doesn't feed hatred, a wellspring
of betrayal.* That's not true, he doesn't say any of that. Rather
he speaks about life and the extremes he's been forced to,
which reminds me of Machiavelli. I get the impression that,
reflecting upon his own experience, he learned the Florentine
master's lessons on political anatomy at a young age. He tells
me the Third Command is ready for whatever comes. There,
at their home base at least, there's no lack of discipline,
ammunition and planning. Steering wheel in his left hand,
walkie-talkie in his right, he gives me a demonstration of
how it all works as he calls his crew:

'Listen up. All good in the area?'

A metallic voice responds in military tone, but street
speak:

'Aight, man. All cool.'

He looks at me, proud. I get the feeling there's something playful in the whole performance. It's as if he's

trying to catch some hint of fascination in me. The boy smiles from under the character's armour. The radio check is an operation he'll repeat a few more times after that. As we drive, he cranes his neck this way or that to look in on the various posts, as if inspecting his troops. There are sixteen control posts dotted across the territory, all just a radio call away, each on its own frequency. The 'falcons' are on permanent lookout. The analogy to the world's smallest bird of prey is an apt one: in trafficking, the younger crew sits watch, and alertness is not always the only skill they need. It's a job that requires a deft hand with a firearm too.

'Any strange, and the boys call it in,' he says. 'We've got total security.'

In fact, none of this military-grade control over strategic points of the favela might even be necessary. He tells me he's got cops in his pocket from every battalion in town, including Bope,* Choque and CORE, the elite units of the Military and Civil Police. What he knows about police corruption is enough to keep him alive or get him killed, depending on the perspective. I presume the authorities don't rock the boat much. After all, he's an inexhaustible source of money and he's hardly going to rat on his uniformed accomplices. They don't come cheap, but they guarantee business stability and a steady flow of revenue, either by turning a blind

---

*Bope, Batalhão de Operações Policiais Especiais (Special Ops Battalion), is an elite military police squad widely feared by Rio's crime lords but generally respected by the population as the least corruptible branch of the city's police force.

eye or by tipping him off about police raids or possible attacks by the Red Command or ADA, the rival factions.

Yet, though I trust my interlocutor's security system, every now and then my attention drifts. Where exactly is he taking me? I gradually become convinced we're not going anywhere at all. For some reason, he thinks it's safer to talk in transit. Maybe he's afraid he'll be ambushed if we stay in one place. I could be a Trojan horse, an agent on a mission to pinpoint his whereabouts. But that makes no sense. If he asked to meet me, it's because he knows my background, at least well enough to deduce that double-dealing is not my style. I start thinking that this aimless, pointless jaunt is a pretty good metaphor, but then a sudden swerve around a dog injects a rush of adrenalin and I snap back.

'I'm exhausted. I couldn't sleep last night. Times have been tough.'

He says a police invasion is imminent. The cops on his payroll have informed him that a major onslaught is planned to recapture the complex and set up a UPP, a Police Pacification Unit.

The Police Pacification Units are a State government programme that has proved extremely popular among the middle class and enjoyed a honeymoon period among the residents of the favelas, until they realized that it was six of one, half a dozen of the other, which was only to be expected, seeing as there was no police reform to go with it. While there are hundreds of favelas in Rio, UPPs were established in only a few dozen located in the so-called Olympic belt, in other words close to wealthy neighbourhoods and near regions where the Olympic Games will be held in 2016. The Maré Complex consists of seventeen favelas with a combined population of 140,000. It's located along an expressway linking the international airport to all the city's main zones. That's why the government decided to extend its UPP programme to include the complex. The Maré has been under drug lord control for years, carved into three by the city's main factions, the Red Command, ADA and Third Command. As these three factions are sworn enemies, instead of a tri-border region at the heart of the complex there's a war-torn Gaza Strip, one of the most violent flashpoints in Rio.

The police function as a sort of fourth faction, because they respect the law about as much as the drug dealers do. Worse, they treat the locals as if they were the enemy. Certain corrupt cells within the police force oscillate between business and confrontation. Of the two options, alliance or war, the latter tends to be used as a bargaining chip to drive up the price of police collusion. But armed conflict is just one string to a whole bow of promiscuous tactics. War is a part of the business, but for the police war is business by another means. The list of services rendered by the corrupt cops includes nightly rentals of the armoured cars used to storm the shanty towns, the famous *caveirão* (skulltruck), an imposing symbol of police brutality. Designed to protect the police, all too often it's used to humiliate the locals with insults blared over the loudspeakers, peppered with random gunfire that spreads panic and chalks up a toll of innocent victims. Rental of a *caveirão* costs about 30,000 dollars a night. Another common and lucrative service is the arrest of leaders of rival factions, which opens a window of opportunity to seize the enemy's territory and its captive markets. A variant on this is the seizure of drugs and weapons to be sold back to their owners or on to their opponents. But make no mistake: there are good, honest police in Rio too, worthy men and women who put their lives on the line to do their constitutional duty despite their miserable salaries.* These people are severely compromised by their criminal colleagues, who are not only corrupt but carry out extra-judicial executions, practise torture and make reckless raids on shanty towns, disrespecting the rights of citizens and putting the lives of the poor and vulnerable at risk. A long-standing characteristic of Brazil in general and Rio in particular is that State-sponsored police violence is always perpetrated against the poor and, more often than not, the black poor. Between 2003 and 2014, 10,699 people were killed by police in the state of Rio de Janeiro. Racism is endemic to the criminal justice system.

'I see no way out.'

He leans forward and slows down:

'Things have turned bad. They're gonna come in here after me. I got too big. After they killed the Mathematician, the heat turned on me. I know too much.'

He has a point. Alive or behind bars, he poses a serious threat to the police hierarchy. His memory is an explosive archive of institutional rot in Rio. I hadn't thought of it that way, but it's true. I start to believe the police would do whatever it took to get rid of him before the UPP was set

---

*The starting salary for Military and Civil Police in Rio is roughly 30,000 reais per annum (approximately US$12,000).

up. There's a considerable price on my interlocutor's head precisely because of the fear he inspires, and corrupt cops are old hands at spring-cleaning potential witnesses. The stories would make you squirm. I ask if maybe I could help in any way. He shakes his head. I'm not sure whether the gesture means no or I don't know. I tell him I'll do all I can to prevent any further loss of life, his or that of the people of Maré – after all, a precision hit was unlikely, one that would surgically remove the leader without causing any collateral damage. Sitting beside him in that car, it's as if we've become brothers.

However hard I try not to think about the possibility of my outing with the favela's owner – that's what they call the drug lords in Rio's shanty towns – coinciding with the expected police invasion, I don't always succeed. Wouldn't he be better off going south, I ask. Why not disappear?

'That's what I should do, but I can't. I did for a bit, but I came back. I've too many responsibilities here. The community needs me. I have a family, a mother, a small son, my buddies. I can't just leave everyone behind.'

You feel responsible for the community?

'Sure. If the cops came in here and just fucked us up, that'd be one thing, war is war. I feel the loss of a buddy, sure, but I know it goes with the territory. But coming in here and abusing the community is something else entirely, I can't accept that. And that's what they do. They're cowards. They kill innocent people. They don't care.'

But the cops only invade because you guys are here. You put the community at risk. He disagrees. If his crew weren't there, someone else's would be, and the cops would keep on doing the same thing. This hypothetical other outfit probably wouldn't respect the community the way he does, or says he does. I don't believe it, it doesn't fit what I've been told by people who live here. Yet one thing is true: there are more violent gangs out there, and things could get worse in the absence of my interlocutor and his group.

'And another thing, man: if I turned myself in, do you really think they'd let me stand trial, get put away, do my time? If they got their hands on me I'd be dead sharpish.'

He's right, but I don't say it. He asks me what I think of Afro-Reggae, a successful NGO that helps kids mixed up with the drug business make a clean break, with job opportunities and legal aid. I speak enthusiastically about the project, but he cuts me off:

'I've been hearing stuff.'

What stuff?

'Stuff,' he says. 'I don't know. I don't trust them.'

He wants to know what I think about the organization's director. I speak highly of José Junior and he changes the subject. A few weeks later the reasons for his reticence were made clear: Red Command leaders locked up in a maximum-security prison were planning to execute Junior. Thankfully, the plot was discovered and thwarted. He wants to avoid further conflict with the rival faction. It's enough having the police bearing down on him.

'I tried to reach an agreement with the other side.'

I note a certain reluctance to mention the enemy by name. The other side?

'The Red Command.'

'Right.'

'They didn't want to know.'

'Are you going to try again?'

'It's the only way, there's no other.'

'What about the ADA?'

'I want to talk to them too.'

I ask him why it's so difficult for the three factions to reach an accord.

'Too much history. People and history.'

I think I understand: the decision makers on all three sides are enmeshed in a web of hate. A spiral of tit-for-tat. On the other hand, the market is divided geographically, so any dispute over customers would be easy enough to iron out.

'It'll happen someday, that's the reality.'

I glean that he sees the truce as a tactical retreat, imposed by a correlation of forces. The movement – that's what they call the drug business – is in crisis. But to what extent have they brought this on themselves?

'I don't think the way you organize yourselves and conduct business works any more. There's no future in it. Think about it; everyone says you're smart, that you like to read and write. Nobody can run such a tight ship for this long and earn the respect of the community without having some virtues. You're not just feared. I don't sense any hatred when people talk about you here, even when they are against what you do and want the trafficking to stop. I get the feeling the majority wouldn't want to see you dead. They want to be rid of the movement, but they'd prefer to see you get on with your life.'

He says he knows that, and yes, he likes to read, but he doesn't write well. He asks if I'd like to write his story. He says he's read two of my books and seen the films *Elite Squad* 1 and 2,[*] which he loved.

'My life would make a film. A day in my life would make a book and a movie. If you hung around here for a few days, you could write your third book and make a third film afterwards.'

He seems to daydream as we speak. After some moments I feel as if we're not really having a conversation at all; that it's just a series of declarations punctuated by silences and my interventions. It's as if I wasn't even there, or was only sporadically, to authorize him to go on thinking out loud. One thing that contributes to that sense of strangeness is the fact that we're both facing ahead, rather than each other, even if I keep glancing back and forth between him and the street. As he's the one driving, he turns toward me less often. I get back to the subject.

'Don't you think the movement's seen its day; I mean, things like having to maintain a private army, train soldiers, enforce discipline, keep morale high despite all the risks and losses, the hardships, persecutions, despite the angst-ridden, futureless lives, it's unsustainable. You spend a fortune on weapons and bent cops, but you don't sleep right, you can barely enjoy the money you make, and many of you are dead by thirty. Most, in fact. What for?'

'I'm exhausted, man. And on top of that I've caught one hell of a cold.'

---

[*] Directed by José Padilha.

I'm not surprised, I say. I want to stick to my line of reasoning, but he points to a beautiful girl walking toward us on the left. She stops when she sees the car, and he slows down.

'My girl. I'm just gonna pull up to pick up some meds. She bought them for me.'

The car stops, he lowers the window and introduces me to his wife.

'A friend.'

We exchange a brief and friendly greeting, then she hands him the medicine and hits him with a barrage of clinical recommendations: 'You have to rest, take the meds, drink lots of water.' He opens the bag and rummages through the boxes of pills until he finds the one he wants. He thanks her, blows a kiss, then he raises the window and we're off again.

'She brought you a whole pharmacy.'

'She looks after me'.

Amid so many problems at least there's some recompense, a special woman. He smiles out of the corner of his mouth.

'You think it's right to ban drugs and criminalize those who deal them?'

'No, I think it's wrong, an act of hypocrisy that has disastrous effects for all concerned. I think drugs should be legalized, like alcohol and cigarettes, which are worse and kill more people. But I also think it's totally wrong the way you guys operate outside the law and use violence to do it. That's not a good way to go about changing the law. And the violence is absurd.'

'You think *we're* violent?'

'Yes, you are, and so are the police. Even though it's illegal, there are far less destructive ways of dealing drugs. Less

destructive for you, too. Getting armed to the teeth, raising an army, seizing control of a favela and exposing the
population to daily risk, it's madness. You could live anywhere and deal to whoever wanted to buy, no guns needed,
just circulating in the city, like they do in Europe and the
US. It'd be cheaper for you and there'd be much less
violence.'

'That'll happen'.

'You said two things are going to happen: a truce between
the factions and a change in the way the movement operates.
If that's true, then the UPP will speed the process up. The
establishment of the UPP is an opportunity for the drug
business to modernize, abandon the territorial dominance
model and give up the guns and the violence. There's more:
negotiating an agreement with your rivals, unifying, is an
opportunity too, not to get out of the business, but to
change the way it's done, right?'

He doesn't answer. A thought dawns on me and it makes
me want to laugh: the government's biggest ever anti-
trafficking programme will actually speed up trafficking's
modernization, rendering it even more lucrative and
attractive, giving it a new lease of life and making it
stronger, economically more rational. Moreover, the UPP
is driving the factions together when their division is,
indirectly, part of the authorities' containment strategy,
and a good source of kickbacks to supplement the cops'
lousy salaries. I savour the irony in silence, but then he
brings me back to reality:

'I've committed crimes, but not everything they accuse
me of.'

I ask if he has a lawyer, but instead of answering he proclaims his innocence on most of the charges the police and press have lodged against him.

'I never killed anyone.'

'But you welcome the police with a hail of bullets.'

'The police come in shooting.'

'So how do you know you haven't killed anyone?'

He reiterates his innocence and I repeat my first question.

'I had a lawyer, but not any more.'

There it is, my chance to contribute to his safety and to create an honourable and legal way out of the corner he finds himself in, waiting for the inevitable night after night. I propose arranging a lawyer for him. I'd be prepared to scout for a good professional who'd be willing to put their credibility on the line, for free, in order to cut a deal that would make it worth my interlocutor's while to turn himself in, saving his own life and defusing a powder keg of permanent danger to the community in the process. It's a good action, but a risky and uncertain one. I'm sure I could find a lawyer who'd be willing to help.

'Would you turn yourself in, if you could count on the representation of a respected and experienced professional? I mean a lawyer who could separate the wheat from the chaff, the false accusations from the crimes you really committed, and for which you would have to take full responsibility, doing whatever time you were given. You'd make a balanced, fair sacrifice, paying for what you did, not what you didn't do. It would be one way of not sharing the Mathematician's fate, and saving your men's skins in the process. Would you be willing to turn yourself in to the authorities?'

He repeats the prognosis:

'They'd whack me on the spot, man.'

His voice is like a bucket of cold water. I feel my optimism was off-tone, detached from the reality of things. It occurs to me that maybe I'm too old for such romanticism. I'm embarrassed and afraid he's going to take me for an idiot – naive, pathetic, over the hill – or a manipulator on autopilot who's playing him for a fool. My speculations are interrupted by a last-gasp hypothesis that comes out of nowhere.

'Look, I've had an idea. Imagine this, in all the papers, the world over, front-page, and on every news broadcast, all over the internet: you, kneeling at the feet of Pope Francis. There he is, blessing the young man who only hours before was seen as the most dangerous drug lord in Rio de Janeiro. You repent, decide to turn yourself in, and the upper echelons of the Church would commit to negotiating with the State and judiciary to ensure your rights were respected in full.'

'That would take a miracle,' he says with a half-smile.

'The Pope works miracles,' I reply.

'A prisoner's rights respected in Brazil? That would be something, for sure.'

'It's a miracle a public blessing from the Pope might well be able to pull off. A magnanimous gesture, unprecedented, broadcast live on transnational networks. It would be as if you were protected by a sacred mantle. The eyes of the world would make you untouchable, armour-plated against any attack the police might dare to make. Your survival and physical integrity would become a matter of State. It would be world news: the most wanted drug lord in Rio turns himself in to the Pope. Can you imagine that? The Pope will be arriving in Rio in a little over a month. You know that. You must have heard. The press talk about nothing else. It'll be the biggest event of the year, even bigger than the Confederations Cup. He'll be here for World Youth Day. He's going to celebrate Mass for millions of people. People from all over. The world's press will be descending on Rio.'

'It's complicated.'

'I know, of course it's complicated, but not impossible. I have contacts in the Church. Who knows? I could try, if you like. You'd leave here and go into hiding, accompanied by priests and bishops. They'd make sure you've severed all contact with the movement and a lawyer would take care of the legal aspects of your surrender, but you'd have to be serious about starting afresh, after paying your dues, of course. And this would also help you get the lightest possible sentence and make your return to society that much easier afterwards. You'd have more opportunities and there'd be less discrimination.'

'I'm not ready for that.'

'Think about it. A negotiated settlement, with legal guidance and Church mediation, ensuring that you, your family and your crew escape death or torture.'

'There's no way, man. I'm not ready for that. I've got a wife, a kid, family, friends, I play my footie at the weekend.'

I see I've let my imagination, overly fertile at the best of times, run away with me.

'Complicated.'

Along the way he points toward the pavement, at the people walking, standing and chatting, coming and going from stores and houses. There's not a hint of uneasiness. The locals are unfazed by the unmistakable presence of the most powerful man in the 'hood. He passes like a ghost rattling its ball and heavy chains. Two dark cars: ours with air conditioning and tinted windows, which make it hard to tell who's inside; the other, his security detail, windows open, gun barrels sticking out like a lethal pincushion. We roll slowly past each block.

'We'd better turn back. It's not safe to go beyond this point at the moment.'

He mutters something into the radio and the security car overtakes us and blocks the incessant flow of motorbikes, bicycles and vans spewing from the narrow alley ahead. He makes a deft turn, aided by the hydraulic steering, and lowers the window. The sound rushes in: a cacophony of barking dogs, loudspeakers announcing sales and discounts, community radio stations offering legal aid for couples in crisis, kids running after a ball, favela funk belting out of a doorless van, the metallic urgency of faith in loud renditions of psalms, summoning believers to a marathon of prayer. 'Accept Jesus,' exhorts an imperious voice. Tonight, the pastor promises to drive the demons from the souls of those possessed by Umbanda spirits.* The car reverses slowly

---

*Like Candomblé, an Afro-Brazilian religious tradition.

toward a wall on the other side of the street, stopping just short of a tangle of wires drawn between a roof, a lamp post and a hole halfway up the façade of a cyber café. The narrowness of the street asks a lot of the driver. We stop. He greets someone by name, waves to a group playing Subbuteo on a green table top at the door of a bar, and signals to a middle-aged man. It's a precise sign, or so I presume. The man responds with an equally exact gesture which my interlocutor understands, but I don't. The smell of grill fat wafts from a blue stall framed with rings of smoke that keep the flies away and dissolve into the air and the dust. Two motorbikes pull away at speed, after making due reverences to the boss: one is carrying two armed men, the other a couple. The woman riding pillion is a brash display of thigh, while the man, semi-automatic resting on his lap, shows her off like a trophy. A cheap choreography of the same old Latin machismo. My interlocutor raises the window with a push of a button. We're back on our way. I can't make out whether the fast-departing bikes and the exchange back there with the group hold any particular significance. I say something, anything, to feign some serenity, but he sits there in silence, a little tenser than before, or maybe the buzz of the atmosphere has just heightened my sensitivity. I can't help but reflect on the daily routine of war, the extreme hardship, life on tenterhooks. I ask myself to what extent the horror recedes, dissolved by routine. I should be thinking about the kids lying face-down on the school playground, hiding under their desks, trembling to the sound of gunfire, haunted by the memory of so many corpses, trails of blood, bullet holes in lamp posts and walls, the horror stories the neighbours tell and which they're now starting to experience for themselves. I should be thinking of all that, and of the families torn apart by urban warfare, but I'm not; I'm thinking of myself.

He distracts me with praise for his regime:

'Look around you. The people here are at ease, they feel safe with me around. I look after them, they don't need a UPP, the cops, none of that. We keep them safe. It's the police that bring the fear, the violence, the insecurity. The people here have only fear and anger for the cops. Ask anybody. They'll all say the same thing. The community prefers us.'

He insists on the benefits his command provides.

'No, we both know that's not true. Where you have guns and someone willing to use them, what you've got is not security, it's not safety. People might feel defended, but they won't feel safe, and they know they're not. They accept it because they've no choice. Just as you can't turn yourself in to the police and the courts, they can't go to the police or the courts for help. No one – neither you nor they – trusts the institutions. Let me level with you: in your case, like so many others, I'd prefer to see a solution geared toward life, not vengeance. What they call retributive criminal justice is just state-sponsored revenge. I'd love to be able to say to you: the past is the past, let's build the future. Start your life from scratch, far from crime. Carry with you the memory of all the good things, the friendship, loyalty, courage, leadership, that aggregating ability, the energy and initiative, the entrepreneurship. But leave the rest behind.'

'You proposed amnesty.'

He knows. I want to ask who told him, but I just confirm it. It was in 1999, when I was Under-Secretary for Security for the state of Rio de Janeiro. It was a scandal, though some people understood my argument and supported it. The idea was to open a window of opportunity for people involved in crime to abandon ship before it was too late. It would be a way of recovering thousands of youths who'd become embroiled in drugs and arms trafficking and didn't know how to step back, because surrender would be suicide, and betrayal a death sentence. It would be a way of getting these kids out of crime before it became all they knew how to do. Society could only win by that. Such a bold move would probably extricate far more people from crime than years of policing – at less cost and with lower risk – and more sustainably, too, as there'd be less chance of a relapse. On average, each prisoner costs the State nearly US$1,000 a month. The money saved could be channelled into providing food, education and housing to those on the programme (and their families), far away from their old stamping grounds. Two years of support and job placement could easily be funded with the savings on prisons and police and judicial procedures. If the aim is to bring down crime and violence, then why not? We'd be giving these kids a second chance to respect life and other people's rights, while building a society that doesn't invest in order to punish, but to ensure equal opportunities, that constitutional pillar long ignored by the State. In other words, society would be giving itself the chance to be less unjust.

'I heard about amnesty. That's why I wanted to talk to you.'

It wasn't easy explaining that the proposal was done and dusted.

Whenever someone balks at amnesty and comes out with the wise consideration that 'it's a controversial idea', I always give the same reply: 'Yes, it is – immensely controversial. If you can come up with a better idea I'll be glad to support it. If your suggestion is to reform the public security and criminal justice systems, then I'm all for it, and it will probably come in time, when the country becomes more democratic and true to its Constitution. However, while the historical process follows its twisted and unpredictable course, what will become of the thousands of youths inducted into crime thanks to a lack of institutionalized escape routes, capable of ensuring their rights and demanding that they fulfil their obligations?'

End of the line. Up ahead I see the square we left from. He breaks the silence:

'So you mean there's no chance of amnesty?'

Rather than answer, I insist for the umpteenth time, risking insult:

'Let me find you a lawyer. Wouldn't it be worthwhile to sit down with a professional and weigh up all the accusations against you and draw up a defence strategy? In the meantime, I could talk to some entities and try to find a secure way for you to hand yourself in.'

'There's no way, man. Not for me,' he says one last time.

We sit in silence for a while, but it's not the end of our conversation. For no apparent reason, he changes his mind:

'Find the lawyer.'

Pleased, as if I'd managed to help in some way, I ask if he would agree to a meeting outside the favela. As things stand,

I can't imagine any of the lawyers whose names spring to mind agreeing to take the trip I've just finished. Not out of fear, but a sense of responsibility. Alright, maybe a little fear, too, why not?

He parks the car.

'I don't know you well enough to take that risk. I need time. Leaving here is too dangerous.'

I want to wish him well, him and his family, and say that hopefully the day will come when he has the courage to give himself up and reinvent himself, but I don't say anything. I'm sure he can glean those sentiments from the very fact that I'm there at all.

The closing scene of our meeting spits acid in my eyes: twenty to thirty men celebrating the arrival of a shipment of weapons, gleefully pulling firearms out of the crates. One of these, little more than a boy, though strong, raises a machine gun over his head, triumphantly saluting his boss as he steps out of the car and walks toward the group. Another seems blind to everything else around him, as if lost in ecstasy. He arranges himself around the weapon, plotting his body on its new axis. Celebrating wildly, the soldiers of the Third Command are oblivious to my presence. With no goodbyes, I withdraw. A description comes to mind for what I've just seen, a testosterone-fuelled ritual in which the adepts gnash their teeth and growl.

The car that brought me here is waiting for me. It drops me off at a meeting point, a bar with a strange name on the corner of a lane with no name, where another car stands waiting to take me on the second leg of my return to a drop-off point outside the shanty town, at the Federal University of Rio de Janeiro, near Ilha do Governador. It's five in the afternoon. I tell the driver of the third car that I have to go downtown. I call a friend and ask him to receive me at his office after work. He's one of the best lawyers in the country. He knows I wouldn't contact him like this unless it was serious and urgent. I confirm the address and note it on my cellphone. The driver says something, but I can't concentrate enough to listen. We drive along the Linha Vermelha, an emblem of the city and fitting title for this chapter. As we hug the fringe of Maré, caught in a bottleneck, my chest tightens. I feel ashamed of my country.*

---

*The man I visited in Maré that day was arrested in 2014. Twenty federal agents raided an apartment far from the favela and found him alone inside. He did not resist arrest.

Gunfire at Night

Luiz Inácio da Silva, better known as Lula, one of eleven children born to a peasant family from the state of Pernambuco, left the north-eastern backlands as a child to look for work in São Paulo. He rose to prominence in the city's industrial belt in the late 1970s, toward the end of the dictatorship, as a charismatic union leader with no traditional party or ideological ties. A realist, Lula's negotiation skills, radical rhetoric and ability to rally the masses secured a number of union triumphs. In 1980, at the age of thirty-five, he created the Partido dos Trabalhadores (Workers' Party) – PT – which was ideologically averse to coalitions or concessions. In 2002 Lula launched his fourth bid for the presidency. By this stage, not only had PT grown to become the largest party in the country, it also had the deepest-running connections with grassroots social movements. Stung by its past defeats and intent on finally taking power, PT changed tack, formed an alliance with the Liberal Party and drafted a 'Letter to the Brazilian People', in which it committed itself to respecting the market and adhering to the overarching economic policy set by the outgoing Fernando Henrique Cardoso administration, which had contained inflation and stabilized the economy. The party also pledged to tackle social inequality. Both promises were kept.

In 2001 I joined the party and helped draw up the public security chapter of the government's master plan. One of the aims was to change the status of the National Security Department, which was given the responsibility for security policy but not the power to follow it through. Unfortunately, this institutional contradiction continues to pose a major problem today. On 1 January 2003 Lula assumed the presidency of the republic and I was appointed National Secretary for Public Security. I moved into a hotel in the capital, Brasília, a two-hour flight north-west, but returned to Rio whenever I could.

One month later, the doorman at the apartment block my parents had lived in since the 1960s in the leafy Laranjeiras neighbourhood of Rio – the building I'd grown up in and where I still stayed whenever in town – heard a car pull up in the middle of the normally sleepy street. Stirred from the torpor of a sweltering summer night, he got up, rounded the desk in the reception area and went out, over to the railings that looked out across the garden.

Nothing ever happened in that part of town, especially at night. Even during the rockiest patches of Rio's history, in the 1980s and 1990s, when economic decline and social crisis fuelled a whorl of urban violence, Laranjeiras had remained more or less immune.

Oblivious to the imprudence of his curiosity, the doorman angled for a closer look. The car outside in the street didn't park or drive away. It just sat there, engine running. Lovebirds kissing goodnight behind the blackened glass? Not likely. The no-frills vehicle resembled an unmarked police car, hardly a fitting setting for a late-night romantic dalliance. As the doorman craned his neck, a man got out of the passenger side, leaving the door wide open, and backed his way into the middle of the empty street, where he stopped and scoped out the building. At pretty much the same time, two other men got out of the back of the car and flanked him.

The doorman froze. He sensed something was about to happen – something momentous, perhaps the sort of thing that would make the grandchildren gasp one day. The three drew their weapons and opened fire. Living to tell the tale was beginning to look optimistic. Diving to the floor, the doorman barely saw the three gunmen as they sprayed the building, shattering windows across all nine floors, then jumped back into the car and sped away with a screech of tyres. For the doorman, languorous summer had plunged to Ice Age night in the emptying of a gun's magazine.

In Brasília, the phone call from my mother woke me at 3 a.m., before my aides, the police or the press came on the scene. It didn't take long for me to realize what had happened. The bullets were a message aimed at me. Let me rewind a little in order to explain.

Just as my work with the government was beginning to get into gear, I was contacted by some Highway Police from Rio de Janeiro. They said they needed to talk to me in private. The conversation was short and to the point. They were anxious, and though I suspected their intentions at first, it soon became clear that these were honourable men concerned for the integrity of their institution and their own careers. Corrupt cops don't just harm society, they also impair the honest police officers only trying to do their jobs, forcing them to become accessories by omission or unwilling accomplices in their schemes. These men trusted me enough to risk giving me some very serious information about their superintendent, the chief of the Rio division of the Highway Police. The story they told me was staggering, and it involved the receipt of stolen goods, adulteration of fuel, handling contraband and other crimes, all orchestrated by the superintendent himself. They had documental proof of the whole scheme, and its architecture was truly impressive. There were photos of a warehouse with tanker trucks driving in and out with adulterated gasoline, and photos of road block operations on the federal highways criss-crossing Rio state that were manipulated to give cover to stolen cargo. The trucks carrying the contraband would be told to wait at a gas station just over state lines in São Paulo until the coast was clear. Once over the border in Rio, they were home and dry.

I asked them to recommend two colleagues who would be able to accompany me immediately to Brasília, then called the Director-General of the Federal Highway Police Department – the national commander of the institution, to whom all twenty-six superintendents report – and invited him to a meeting at my office in the federal district. We took the first available shuttle flight and were there within two hours.

The meeting was tense, and the director-general took some convincing. He was sarcastic, and dismissive both of the accusations and the evidence that supported them. We had never been on the best of terms, though we'd been cordial enough as protocol required. He knew that I'd been against his appointment by the Justice Minister who, in this case, was acting on a recommendation from the Government Chief of Staff. It had all come down to some old-school back-scratching: the Federal Government would accept the referral from a southern governor in return for congressional support. In my view this should have been a technical appointment, not a political one.

During the director-general's candidacy, I had gone to visit him in his home state. I wanted to hear his thoughts on his institution. What was his evaluation of it? What were his plans for it? What was his reading of the national public security crisis and what significant changes did he feel the Highway Police could make? The then candidate had absolutely nothing to say, and he didn't have to. An affable guy who had the governor's trust and a good nose for politics didn't need to waste his time on things like planning and performance.

Before long, the meeting started chasing its tail. The director-general, rebutting my arguments and waving away the evidence I produced, was clearly reluctant to initiate any action against his corrupt colleagues. I knew I had to take a heavier line. I demanded that the Superintendent of the Rio de Janeiro Highway Police step down pending further inquiry. Even if it was all just a mistake, a misunderstanding, or even a frame-up, the fact was that he could not continue to occupy a position of trust and responsibility with such serious accusations hanging over his head. It was only when I threatened to take the matter directly to the president that the director-general gave in. I was bluffing, of course.

President Lula had stopped talking to the second tier right after the inauguration; his inner circle of ministers, aides and party stalwarts had formed an impenetrable ring around his office. But we were still at the beginning of Lula's first mandate, and the director-general didn't know exactly how things worked; he may have imagined that we PT militants had a direct line to Lula, and that all the major decisions were taken by assembly. That was the running joke about PT, that we didn't even change a light bulb without holding a national congress first. He probably thought I had a lot more power than I really did – and I did nothing to disabuse him of that impression. I had made myself clear. Either he did what I said, or he'd become every bit as vulnerable as the pawn he was trying to protect. His reluctance to take the necessary measures could be interpreted as collusion or, in the mildest hypothesis, as reluctance to align himself with the new government's self-styled 'ethical and transparent' methods, which promised to take a hard line on institutional cronyism.

The next morning, the *Official Gazette*, in which all government decisions are published into law, announced that the Superintendent of the Rio de Janeiro Highway Police had been removed from his post. Of course he wasn't kicked off the force altogether, which would have required a lengthy process involving a full investigation and, naturally, ample right to defence. But his wings were clipped.

From around midday, the ex-superintendent started calling me insistently. The aides who answered my cellphone were struck by the undisguised aggression of his tone:

highly unusual, as police officers usually respect hierarchy and codes of discipline, even under pressure. It would simply never occur to the rank and file to call up a National Secretary for Public Security, never. Not that I stood on that kind of ceremony, but this was definitely significant. The message he was sending me, incessantly, was very clear: he knew that I was behind his discharge, that it wasn't fair, and that he wasn't going to stand for it.

We put his impertinence down to a bout of panic, as we all realized the abyss the man was staring into. Given the gravity of the accusations against him, his removal was just the first step in an excruciating criminal and administrative investigation that would fall like a bomb in the ex-superintendent's life. His despair was understandable, especially when you consider that impunity had long been expected in Brazil. It was as if we were revoking a long-established right.

So I ignored the phone calls.

An hour later, we received an urgent message from the intelligence bureau at the Security Secretary's office in Rio. The crime hotline, a free service for anonymous tip-offs to the police, had obtained information that this same ex-superintendent was planning a hit against me. There was no ignoring this – even if it turned out to be just a ploy by enemies eager to see him slide still further into the mire. In a minefield, you can never really be sure where you're treading. My team and I were obliged to step up security, especially as I was scheduled to leave for Rio that same day.

That night, on Rua do Catete, a middle-class neighbour-hood in Rio, the decoy car in my security detail realized we

were being followed by four men in a white Passat. Our
guys were quick to overtake and close them down, but the
Passat's driver was swifter still: mounting the pavement, he
escaped down a one-way side street. Our number two car
wasn't authorized to give chase, as it could have been a diver-
sionary tactic to lure our rearguard away and leave us more
vulnerable. When we ran the Passat's plates, we found they
were fake.

The attack on my parents' building took place two or
three days later.

I started to receive more messages from the ex-superintendent, the man whose career I had ruined. He was basically
telling me that this wasn't over, I could wait and see. It
would all come to nothing: the messages mentioned a name,
one of the ex-superintendent's minions, and said that this
individual, a member of the same clique, would be his
replacement. The superintendency was Congressman
Roberto Jefferson's to bestow, and he would give it to
someone who would watch his back.

I took the matter to my superior, the Minister of Justice,
and told him everything, right from the beginning.

About a week after the gunfire in Laranjeiras, my pur-
suer almost lost an arm in an attempt on his life. He
survived by the skin of his teeth. Our intelligence people
went straight to the police department handling the case
and noted some curious interference on the part of the ex-
superintendent's brother, a member of the Civil Police,
who had registered the attack – obviously a botched hit –
as an attempted armed robbery. The pieces seemed to fall
into place: the ex-superintendent had probably been paid

in advance – and before his removal – for 'services' (rigged road blocks) or 'goods' (dodgy fuel) he was no longer in a position to deliver, and for which he was now a marked man.

I told the minister the whole story, and urged the utmost caution in appointing a new superintendent. I asked the Director-General of the Federal Police (the Brazilian equivalent of the FBI) to launch an immediate and rigorous investigation.* The situation was becoming increasingly complex and tense.

Some days later, in Brasília, I felt distinctly queasy as I read the copy of the federal *Official Gazette* brought to me by a distraught aide. The Minister of Justice had appointed precisely the man the ex-superintendent had said he would. I took the private staircase between my floor and the minister's in leaps and barged into his office, breathless and speechless; he was standing there, as if waiting for me. He spoke first, saying that he knew why I was there and could imagine how I felt. He said he, too, was upset and uncomfortable about the appointment, but that there had been nothing he could do to prevent it. José Dirceu had negotiated the superintendency with Congressman Roberto Jefferson and it was a done deal.

José Dirceu was Lula's Chief of Staff and his right-hand man. He'd helped found the PT, of which he was national

---

*In Brazil, there are two national police forces, both of which answer to the Justice Ministry and thus to the Federal Government: the Federal Police, responsible for investigating federal crimes, and the Federal Highway Police, responsible for patrolling and monitoring highways across the federation.

president, and had co-ordinated the victorious presidential campaign. A sort of Bolshevik Bismarck, he was to fall two years later under accusations of mounting and operating what was, at the time, the largest corruption scheme in Brazilian political history, involving cash payments for congressional support. The whistleblower was that same Roberto Jefferson, a Congressman for Rio de Janeiro and President of the Partido Trabalhista Brasileiro (PTB).* To back up his accusation, Jefferson confessed to his own involvement in the scheme, an admission that cost him his mandate. Both were found guilty and handed prison terms by the Federal Supreme Court in 2013. Dirceu was sentenced to seven years and eleven months

---

* Upon taking the presidency in 2003, Lula decided to form a congressional majority that incorporated a host of minor parties he knew would trade support for a share of government-appointed posts. In 2005, the media blew the lid on a congressional vote-buying scheme nicknamed the 'Mensalão' (monthly payout), which showed that these congressional bit players were avid for more than just advantageous job titles. They wanted cash too, in monthly stipends. Congressman Roberto Jefferson of the PTB – no relation to PT – was the whistleblower who made the scheme public. He basically sacrificed his political future and personal freedom in order to get back at the government for leaking a video that showed a Post Office director (the Brazilian Post Office is a State company) appointed by Jefferson receiving bribes in the Congressman's name. Facing serious corruption charges and hobbled politically, Jefferson decided to take his enemies down with him and denounced the whole vote-buying scheme. In the end, his downfall would be sweetened by a taste of vengeance.

and hit with a 676,000-reais fine (roughly US$300,000 at the time); Jefferson was given seven years and fourteen days and fined 746,200 reais. In July 2015, while serving the rest of his jail term under house arrest, Dirceu was arrested yet again, this time on charges of being the main operator behind an even larger corruption scheme involving kickbacks and bribes from construction companies awarded lucrative contracts by the State-run oil giant Petrobras. Lula's former strong man thus found himself back behind bars.

Jefferson and Dirceu's convictions, though, had nothing to do with the events I was investigating, for which there was no concrete evidence of any criminal wrongdoing on their part — whatever one might think of using key public security posts as currency in political bargaining.

The ex-superintendent was arrested by the Federal Police in 2004. The accusations against him were upheld. He had been nominated for the job by Congressman Jefferson, just as his successor was.

When the minister mentioned Dirceu and Jefferson, I was taken aback: I'd never before heard their names spoken in the same breath, as allies. We all know that politics requires a certain degree of flexibility — concessions have to be made and deals struck — but there are boundaries, and I saw that they were being crossed. This wasn't the first episode involving backroom dealing that had shaken my faith in the PT and its leadership, but it was the one that knocked me sideways. I found myself confronted by my own impotence. I had long been outspoken about my beliefs and values, and

the graft and double-dealing was a major political and personal embarrassment to me.

From October to December 2002, the transition period
between Fernando Henrique Cardoso's outgoing administration* and Lula's newly elected government, associations
representing sixteen Federal Highway Police regions,
believing – correctly as it turned out – that I was a likely
candidate for a key role in the incoming administration, had
asked me for a joint audience. At the time I was just a member
of the transition team, albeit the only one with a background

---

*Fernando Henrique Cardoso was elected President in 1994 on the
strength of an economic plan he had devised and implemented as
Finance Minister to outgoing President Itamar Franco (who had taken
over from deposed President Fernando Collor de Melo). Inflation,
which had been running to over 1,000 per cent per annum, causing a
tailspin of misery, widening the social gulf and rendering the nation all
but ungovernable, was cut to single digits with the introduction of a
stable new currency, the Brazilian real. The plan had extraordinary
effects across the board. In a single year, abject poverty was reduced to 17
per cent of the population. Stability and predictability stimulated long-
term planning, fostered investment and breathed new life into the
economy. Cardoso was re-elected in 1998 and launched the candidature
of his former Health Minister, José Serra, as his successor for 2002. Serra
lost to Lula in the presidential run-off. With two months to go in his
final mandate, as a gesture to show that Brazil had reached institutional
maturity and that political opponents could now treat each other as
adversaries rather than enemies, Cardoso offered Lula, the president-
elect, seventy posts in his federal administration, to be occupied by
people of Lula's choosing, so that they could start the transition ahead of
the 1 January 2003 inauguration. The aim was to ensure a smooth transition, and it worked.

in justice and security. Whatever the future held, and I had no way of knowing then, it was still my responsibility to convey their recommendations to the incoming authorities, whoever they turned out to be, and that was reason enough to grant their request.

The largest meeting room on our floor wasn't big enough for the crowd that arrived, and despite the extra chairs conscripted to form a second row around the large oval table, many still had to stand. The spokespeople of the various associations had advised me in advance that they were there to make a single request, which, I'd assumed, was about a pay rise. Beforehand I had rehearsed the lines I'd use to explain to them just how hard it would be for the president, at the very beginning of his mandate, to authorize a pay rise or benefits increment, no matter how deserved they would be. The economic situation was extremely delicate. Fears of socialist radicalism on Lula's part had scared capital investments away and destabilized the currency. The dollar had gone through the roof and the country faced a crisis of confidence among the international markets. After all, despite the nerve-soothing 'Letter to the Brazilian People' issued during the campaign period, PT had always positioned itself as a socialist party, the sworn enemy of capitalism, committed to not paying down the national foreign debt until a full audit had been conducted, and wholeheartedly in favour of State control of the markets. But, with all these justifications and more on the tip of my tongue, ready to urge my interlocutors to be patient and allow the new administration some grace, I was unprepared for the demand that came. 'We ask only this,' said the leader of the group, pausing for emphasis before going on: 'that the next government not do what all the others have done – and which is, frankly, killing us.'

I waited, not breaking the silence that fell upon the room, wanting to see where this grave tone was leading. 'All we ask,' continued the spokesman, 'is that the Lula government not use the Federal Highway Police as a bargaining chip; that it not hand over our superintendencies to state chiefs to be auctioned off to the highest bidder. That's how it's always been done. It's a humiliation to us, it truncates careers, hobbles the institution and makes our work impossible. How can we act autonomously when the head of the force in each state owes his job to a politician allied with the Federal Government? If you'd like to know who really runs the Federal Highway Police, you can start by forgetting it's a federal organ. It's not, because it's been carved up. The real power lies with the local honchos. You want to know who runs the FHP in Bahia? Antonio Carlos Magalhães. In Pará? Jader Barbalho. In Maranhão? José Sarney. These men are leading politicians and the heads of political clans with immense power in their home states and on the national scene. They have all attracted constant accusations of nepotism, cronyism, trafficking of influence and corruption. Regional political powers in Brazil have long acted as feudal lords. The FHP has become a bargaining chip in political negotiations.' The young man spoke with emotion.

I told them that I'd never forget our meeting that afternoon, because it was wholly unprecedented. I'd never been to an audience with what was effectively a union organization where the order of the day had not been limited to run-of-the-mill matters. Those police officers were there to ask for help in rooting out corruption and clearing the way for more effective policing. If the new government couldn't help, they wanted assurances that it wouldn't be a hindrance either. They asked for nothing else. They wanted professional respect and regard for their institution and for the public interest. There's still hope in Brazil that we can one day build a democratic republic worthy of the name — that was all I could say to them. And I meant it. I said I couldn't promise them better wages, but I was prepared to offer my personal guarantee of more respect and a harder line on corruption. Whatever role, if any, I ended up playing in the new government, they had my word that FHP jobs would be taken off the negotiating table.

The memory of that afternoon didn't sit well with the minister's blasé lament, side-stepping the issue without a second thought, as if it were a muddy puddle on the pavement. Tacitly, what he was saying was this: 'I've got a broader agenda to attend to. I can't waste time on such trifles.' He didn't say that, of course, but he let it be understood. He was an elegant, sophisticated man, and gave the incident the attention a mere incident deserved — none. Basically, his time was too valuable to be squandered on the micro. The glass walls of Oscar Niemeyer's beautiful building brought the Three Powers Esplanade into the room. His posture, his tone, his economy of words, everything about the minister's demeanour was crafted to convey the message that he was of a superior order, and that his mind was on the greater interests of the nation; he was a higher being, and his horizon was history. So what could I, a mere mortal, do but leave with my tail between my legs?

I left his office with my head ablaze. I felt a deep sense of shame and an urge to clear out my desk there and then. The problem, as I now realized, was that this depressing situation was only to be expected. The assurances I'd given the men from the Federal Highway Police were based more on my own wishful thinking than genuine conviction that I could do anything to change the culture. I think, at the end of the day, it was myself I'd been trying to convince.

2002 had truly been intense. Lula was a presidential candidate for the fourth time in a row and now had a real chance of winning. In Rio de Janeiro, I'd been offered the vice-governor's slot as running mate to Benedita da Silva, formerly vice-governor of the state and acting governor since April 2002, when Anthony William Matheus de Oliveira – Garotinho – the governor, decided to quit office and run for the presidency. In Brazil presidents, governors and mayors can run for re-election. When Garotinho stood down to devote himself to the presidential campaign, Benedita, his vice-governor, took over what remained of his mandate and was therefore eligible to run for re-election in October 2002 in his stead. After some hesitation, I'd agreed to be her running mate, but on two conditions: first, that Bené, as she was affectionately known, governed in a transparent fashion, in dialogue with social movements, and that she put together a plural Cabinet of respected names from civil society, people with proven technical credentials over and above any party affiliations. These weren't just my ideas; they were shared with the party faithful. And it wasn't just a pipe dream either. There'd been some very positive work done in this regard by PT mayors and governors. If she governed in that way for the nine months leading up to the elections, she had a real chance of winning the governorship. And even if she didn't win, she'd at least have left an inspiring legacy.

We were worried that Garotinho would leave us a time bomb as a parting gift: empty coffers, rolled debts, broken contracts, suspended services, cold payrolls, information shortfalls. Hence my second condition: that, as soon as she became governor, Bené was to submit the public accounts and financial records for independent audit. If she failed to do so, she'd be running the risk of inheriting Garotinho's chaos and leaving herself open to accusations of improbity. That might seem a tad over-zealous or even paranoid, but it wasn't. Unfortunately, outgoing administrations in Brazil have been known to practise this kind of sabotage with the sole purpose of destabilizing their successors, regardless of the cost to the city or state.

Over dinner that night, Bené agreed to both conditions and we toasted our partnership. She's an extraordinary individual. The first black woman from a shanty town – and a former maid – to occupy a major government post. To be her running mate in Rio de Janeiro in 2002 would be an enormous privilege and I was willing to give it my all. The first task she set me, and which indicated her disposition to come good on our agreement, was to start sounding out potential candidates for the Secretariat.

It didn't take long for the cracks to appear in my rose-tinted glasses. In late March 2002, on the eve of her governorship, after a whole day of discussions, Bené announced her proposed Cabinet over dinner at her house in the middle-class West Zone neighbourhood of Jacarepaguá. The names she read out were neither supra-partisan nor of proven credentials. With the odd exception, her list of department secretaries was made up of PT militants with ties to Congressmen and Deputies up for re-election and a handful of technocrats put forward by political patrons. Rather than the promise of a real governorship, however brief, capable of genuinely tackling the serious challenges facing Rio de Janeiro, the Cabinet Bené was offering – to her visible discomfort – was one big concession to her party's spread of electoral interests.

Once in the post of governor, she found herself facing a deplorable financial and administrative mess. The situation was far worse than we'd anticipated. There wasn't enough money even to cover the most immediate social welfare commitments, and the grassroots backlash came hard and fast. The best we could do was try to show with whom the real fault lay, and the only way to do that, as I had insisted, was through an independent audit, which had to be done urgently, or it would be too late to defuse the bomb. In the end the governor reneged on her promise to contract an independent audit, which meant she was acting against her own interests, good sense, her promise to me and the appeals of the party militants. Why?

I phoned her every day, and she didn't take or return my calls. When she did finally ring me back, a week later, she was terse: 'Luiz Eduardo, why don't you answer my calls or call me back? Where are you? Why don't you want to talk to me?' So I changed tack. Instead of phone calls, I started paying visits to the governor's residence in Laranjeiras Palace, where she couldn't fob me off. Our meetings were frustrating, difficult and disheartening. The governor responded to my questions with an emotional rant about how complex a time it was, and the virulence of the attacks against her, the injustices to which she was being subjected. As was to be expected, society and the media were not at all happy about the delayed disbursements, stalled construction projects, and all the other consequences of the empty coffers Garotinho had left us with, and she was the target for their ire. Without mentioning the audit directly, she said, between sobs, that what she needed now more than ever was support, solidarity and understanding, not more demands and pressure. I got the message and backed off. However, as the effect of her guilt trips waned with repetition, meeting after meeting, I gradually started to state my case more assertively, but not even then was I given a straight answer. Nevertheless, our relationship remained affectionate throughout the slow, painful descent toward a first-round electoral defeat, a bitter setback in some way neutralized by Lula's presidential win.

Bené's re-election bid had failed, but as payment for her electoral sacrifice she was awarded a ministerial post. As her running mate, I rolled in on the same bandwagon. My suspicions about why she had decided against the audit were confirmed in 2003 on a visit I paid to her as the new Social Development Minister at her office in Brasília. Bené finally admitted to me that she had not undertaken the audit because she had been ordered not to. It was part of a secret agreement Lula and Dirceu had struck with Garotinho before he'd stepped down as Governor of Rio. Bené would spare Garotinho's blushes and take responsibility for the financial mess he'd left in return for his backing of Lula in the expected presidential run-off against José Serra. Lula and Dirceu had basically sold Rio downriver in return for a better shot at the grand prize. Rosinha Garotinho, Anthony Garotinho's wife, was elected Governor of Rio: Rio itself could go to hell. Bené had never been PT's real candidate. She had taken one for the team. Our campaign had been dead in the water from the very beginning.

None of that, however, was anything compared to what I'd encountered at the front line of the gubernatorial and presidential campaigns in Rio. One morning, when I arrived at campaign headquarters, my secretary blurted:

'You know that pain in the ass who's called about a thousand times?'

I was stuck: pains in the ass weren't exactly a rarity on the campaign trail. She continued:

'That pest who calls every day. I've used the entire lexicon of excuses on him already.'

I suggested she tell him I was about to travel and that she didn't know when I'd be back.

'That's what I did.'

'Great, then,' I said. But she wasn't finished:

'That's the problem. He wants to know what flight you're going to be on so he can tag along and talk.'

I was stunned. It crossed my mind that maybe she was pulling my leg.

'He really said that?'

'His secretary did.'

Whoever he was, it seemed this guy really, really wanted to talk to me. He wasn't going to let up. Better to just give in now and spare myself further trouble. I'd never heard of him (and, for legal reasons, can't name him now), and I always tried to avoid meeting up with people I knew nothing about. If we were going to talk, it had to be in a public space. I was to speak at a seminar on violence at a well-known hotel in Rio's South Zone, so I arranged to see him in the lobby. It seemed a safe enough spot.

Late that afternoon, after the seminar, a middle-aged man approached me with a smile and said my name. We exchanged pleasantries and sat down at a small table in the hotel café. What followed were the tensest, most disturbing minutes I'd experienced in politics. He went straight to the point: 'The scheme in place to raise off-the-books campaign funds here in Rio is rookie stuff. It barely brings in 300,000 a month. You know, the numbers racket, slot machines, bingo halls, that's all peanuts, and could end up causing problems. It brings in a pittance but could cause a truckload of shit.' Then he laid out his proposal, which he said could generate millions per month for PT's concurrent national and state election campaigns, with a percentage for me and the governor 'off the top' – once he'd taken his cut, of course.* He assured me he knew what he was doing and that everything would be conducted professionally and in total security. All he'd need were a couple of strategic positions in the Rio government for his operators. Going through the government structure in detail, he pinpointed certain possible channels through which to siphon off funds from the budgets of State-run bodies and secretariats. He knew exactly where in the State apparatus the rivers ran deep and which tributaries to tap. He spoke like an experienced hydraulic engineer. Indeed, he was an expert in his field. Eloquent, quick and precise. A genuine corruptologist.

At the first opportunity, I told him I had no power to distribute positions and that I knew absolutely nothing about the scheme to which he'd referred at the start of our conversation. I stood up, wished him a pleasant afternoon, signalled to my secretary, who was waiting for me at the other end of the lobby, and left the hotel with my head in a spin.

There was no way of knowing if there was something deeper going on here, but I felt I would be remiss to keep this to myself. My first step was to share what I'd been told

---

*Brazilian political parties are obliged to declare campaign funds, donors, and expenses to the Electoral Court. To enhance their chances of success, campaigns tend to accept and solicit under-the-table donations from companies that may want or need to secure future favours or government contracts. As these funds are off the books, 'commissions' can be taken for personal benefit. In this particular case, the man in question was referring to US$150,000 per month channelled into the PT campaign from the illegal gambling racket.

with the governor, who reacted as she always did, lamenting that I kept bringing her problems instead of solutions. Bené said nothing about what I'd conveyed to her, just complained. Her nerves were frayed. The pressure was immense. Requests, demands, criticism – she could barely breathe. As for a private life, forget about it. The government was treading water: Bené had to rob Peter to pay Paul, just to keep things ticking over, at the very least disburse the 'citizens' cheque', the state's most popular social programme, and cover the civil service payroll. She'd suspended all investments and cut all public spending that wouldn't cause an immediate meltdown. But the ledger still wouldn't balance out. The situation was worse than critical, it was borderline bankruptcy.

I called a meeting with PT state Deputies and Congressmen at my home, those I felt were closest to me and truly committed to an ethical brand of politics. I told them about the proposal set forth by the graft engineer I'd met and expressed my concerns about the 'scheme' he said was already in place with the illegal gambling racket. I said I was afraid it might be true. The meeting ended without anyone saying anything at all useful. Some looked at me as if I'd just arrived from Mars, others seemed almost to sneer, while others still exchanged whispers to the effect that they wouldn't be at all surprised. The message was unanimous: on with the campaign; there's so much to do and so little time before election day – 6 October 2002, D-Day for the presidential and gubernatorial tickets. It just wasn't the time to get picky.

I had one last hand to play. Two members of the party's national board would be in Rio in the coming days. I scheduled a dinner at a restaurant in Flamengo and took my wife along. Despite the circumstances, the conversation was pleasant enough. I laid out the facts, names and all, and asked them to look into it. If the lobbyist's accusations turned out to be substantiated, I wanted them to put an immediate end to it. I said that, besides betraying our most fundamental principles, the very reason we were in politics at all, and the raison d'être of Lula's fourth presidential run, negotiating with racketeers made the most important social democratic project in the country's history hostage into a two-bit mafia. If it was true, it was the most wildly irresponsible misadventure I could imagine. *If* it was true. Their response to my plea was discreet but friendly, which gave me a glimmer of hope. If there was anything to it, they'd sort it out. That night I slept like a baby.

Two days later, in the morning, an old friend and comrade who'd become a leading light in the state government, on my recommendation as it happens, called to say he was on his way to see me. He didn't mention what it was about, just asked me to wait for him. His visit was brief. He had come to me with information, and it was up to me what I chose to do with it – he felt he owed me that much. He'd been at a meeting of Bené's inner circle, the select few who effectively called the shots. They'd decided to exclude me from the campaign – informally, it seemed, but gradually my name would disappear from the posters, flyers, banners. Most importantly, I was off TV and radio and would be dropped from campaign meetings. I thanked him, and we chatted for a while before he headed back into the eye of the storm.

I considered revoking my candidature, but that just wasn't viable. It wasn't the responsible thing to do. It would harm the campaign nationally, no matter what excuses I came up with, whatever personal reasons I might cite. The sudden resignation of the PT gubernatorial candidate's running mate would be high-calibre ammunition in the hands of the rival camps. I wouldn't have been able to live with the guilt of having in some way contributed to another Lula defeat. What was more, however authoritarian and arbitrary the party was turning out to be, there was still no hard evidence of a corruption scheme other than the indiscretions of an obvious scumbag in a hotel lobby. Maybe I was being sidelined for having had the temerity to cast aspersions on the national board. Maybe I was wrong to have pushed the issue. Maybe the best way to have played it would have been to skip the middlemen and go straight to the party president himself. That would have seeded less paranoia, but it was too late now. It was time for damage limitation. I'd have to swallow my indignation and deal with the new reality, acting as discreetly as possible.

The Benedita-Luiz Eduardo ticket lost in Rio. The Lula-José Alencar* ticket won the presidential election. The federal victory eclipsed the state defeat. I joined the celebrations. Though a part of me couldn't shake off the shadow that had been cast over the campaign, I still believed in the

---

*José Alencar was an important businessman in the Liberal Party and Lula's guarantor for the conservative segments of society and the elites, who always feared the PT's radicalism.

future of Brazil under the leadership of that extraordinary factory worker from the barren north-east. Lula's story was the sort you wanted to see come full-circle, the kid from the drylands of Pernambuco who'd arrived in São Paulo with his mother after a thirteen-day journey in the back of a truck. A shoe shiner at the age of twelve, lathe operator at fourteen. When he was nineteen he lost a finger to a metal press, and the shoddy treatment he received from his employers sparked his interest in the unions. It didn't take him long to become a leading light of the union movement and rising political star. During the dictatorship, Lula organized major strikes in the industrial-belt towns outside São Paulo and, in 1980, co-founded the PT, alongside leading left-wing intellectuals and union leaders. He ran for President five times in all, losing three elections in a row before toning down his radical leftist rhetoric to win the presidency in 2002. Teaming up with José Alencar had been a marketing masterstroke, as Alencar, a respected captain of industry, did much to assuage market fears and underwrite Lula's promise of a moderate, centre-left approach to government.

At a gathering of congressional colleagues in Brasília a few days after the election, a friend of mine from the south, the PT Congressman and human rights activist Marcos Rolim, asked the party president, José Dirceu, what role I would likely assume in the Lula government. Dirceu's response came as a surprise to Rolim, but not to me: 'If I have anything to do with it, none at all.' Faced with my friend's obvious perplexity, Dirceu explained: 'He boycotted our campaign in Rio.'

Despite resistance, I was invited to join the team that negotiated with the outgoing Cardoso administration to ensure a smooth transfer of power to the Lula government. Once the transition was complete, I was to assume the post of National Secretary for Public Security. However, in October 2003, after ten intense months, I was asked to resign. An apocryphal dossier forged inside the Justice Ministry, of which my secretariat was a part, hit the press, and it was full of serious accusations, including a charge of nepotism against me. This made the headlines for some reason, though the dossier was packed with far more abject stuff than that. For example, it was alleged that I had received kickbacks on the purchase of cars for state police forces using the national security fund, of which I was manager. I'd apparently bought the vehicles at padded prices. The problem with that charge was that the national security fund doesn't make purchases, it merely distributes funds to the different states, which decide what they buy and how much they pay. Another allegation was that I had disbursed a few million reais to 'a group of friends' to conduct some research and pocketed a percentage of the sum. This group of friends was ANPOCS, a respected national postgraduate research association in the field of the social sciences. The recipients of the funds were selected by an independent panel of academics, with no input from my department. This was the calibre of the accusations against me. They were so flimsy that when I did finally get access to them I made a point of publishing them on my personal website and taking them apart one by one, with documental evidence supporting direct, brief explanations. No public inquiry was launched and formal charges were never brought. Not a single judicial institution gave them any credence whatsoever. It was mud-slinging, pure and simple.

As I said, I had access to the accusations only after they had been made public, but it didn't take long to ascertain the source of the smear. When I went to the relevant powers for help in rebutting the false accusations, I found myself face to face with their author. I felt like Mia Farrow's character in Roman Polanski's *Rosemary's Baby*. Alone and terrified, she runs to the one person she can trust, the doctor, only to find that he has been the orchestrator of her torment all along. My 'doctor' was the new party president, José Genoíno. A guerrilla fighter during the dictatorship years in the 1970s, Genoíno was now a party whip and go-to man for realpolitik. In 2012 he was to be sentenced to six years and eleven months in prison for his part in the Mensalão corruption scandal. Later acquitted on one of the two charges against him, his jail term was shortened to four years and eight months. He served the remainder of his sentence under house arrest.

I knew I was my only line of defence. The accusations against me were ham-fisted and baseless. All I asked of him, however, was that if party militants turned out to be behind the dossier, they be punished accordingly. That afternoon Genoíno called a press conference at which he made the following declaration: 'Luiz Eduardo is behaving like a skunk, causing a stink to divert attention from his own wrongdoing.' I had resigned from my post a few days before this declaration, and I immediately wrote to the Rio state president of PT, Jorge Bittar, informing him of my disaffiliation from the party.

Two years after my resignation, major scandals began to emerge involving top-ranking party leaders. In 2005 the dam burst when a video was leaked to the press showing 2002 footage of a party representative negotiating a 300,000-reais (roughly US$150,000 at the time) under-the-table campaign contribution from a known racketeer. As it turned out, public funds from the state lottery were being misappropriated.

Back in 2003, an outcast from a government at the height of its popularity, I could find few interlocutors willing to hear my side of the story. At the time, anyone questioning the PT's ethical commitment and the immaculate probity of the Federal Government was given no credit whatsoever. Badly burnt by the turn of events, and only moments before I took leave of my team and function, I asked my secretary to call the organizer of the national conference of judges, Dr Andrea Pachá, cancelling my participation at an event to be held that weekend – 23–26 October – in Salvador, the state capital of Bahia. The message was simple: the invitation to deliver the inaugural address had been extended to the National Secretary for Public Security, a post I no longer occupied, so I would not be attending. I offered my thanks and apologies for the inconvenience. Andrea, however, insisted. She had invited me, not the National Secretary for Public Security. Her warm reassurance was as moving as it was convincing: 'You and your wife are most welcome. She, too, is our guest. The Bahia air will do you both good, as will the beauty of Salvador and the company of people who greatly admire your work.'

In mid-2003, during my brief stint as department Secretary, an old friend of mine from Rio contacted me to say that he had an important, delicate message to pass on, and that he would travel to Brasília in person to do so.

The message was from 'Lulu', Luciano Barbosa da Silva, the crime boss in charge of the Rocinha favela, the largest in the South Zone of Rio. Lulu didn't fit the drug lord stereotype: he wasn't violent, never attacked the police and didn't violate the rights of the favela's population. In fact, the aid he sometimes extended to the locals had earned him their respect and admiration. Lulu wanted my help to get out of the favela, out of the life of crime, so he could make a fresh start somewhere else. He had realized that the life of a drug lord was a dead-end street, but he didn't trust the police or justice system enough to turn himself in. He was pretty sure he wouldn't survive prison; indeed, there would be little hope of making it through his first week inside. Prison murders are easily disguised. There's no shortage of cover-ups, or of internal affairs investigators willing to cut the cops some slack. This type of murder, known as file-burning, is simply part of the routine in Rio's jails. Therein lies the paradox of police corruption. It works a treat for drug lords and other hoods because it gives them cover and freedom to act, even if they have to split the proceeds for the privilege. On the other hand, if deals fall apart, all hell can break loose. Convicts who were, only yesterday, police partners suddenly become potential snitches. Sitting ducks, they know there's a very good chance they'll get whacked.

Lulu wanted to escape from Rocinha, break with the Red Command, the umbrella crime faction to which he was affiliated, and go underground. His abdication would send shockwaves through Rio's crime world. Was there any way I could help him? As a person, I wanted to try to save his life. I felt the future would afford him a healthier, more peaceful fate far from crime and prison. It would be the best thing for him, for society, for everyone – or almost everyone, as I would understand later. But the institutional role I was sworn to fulfil obliged me to contribute to his arrest and imprisonment. How could a National Secretary for Public Security aid and abet a known criminal in his escape from justice? Of course I couldn't. All I could do was send Luciano Barbosa da Silva a message that said: the National Secretary for Public Security lets it be known that should he come into any information as to your whereabouts he will use that information to have you arrested; the individual Luis Eduardo Soares, on the other hand, wishes you the best of luck and a long life away from crime. It was frustrating and ambiguous, but sincere.

Six months after this episode, in late October 2003, it was my turn to face a life change. I packed up, cleaned out my desk, saved my work on an external hard drive and thanked my aides, whom I advised to stay in their posts until the new National Secretary for Public Security was appointed and do whatever they could to ensure a smooth transition. I feigned serenity and resignation, which couldn't have been further from my actual feelings. In Salvador, where I had been invited to address the conference, my wonderful hosts did their utmost to keep me from sinking into depression. Out of the government line-up and without access to the dossier that levelled accusations against me, of which I only knew what had so far come out in the press, I was contacted by a major weekly magazine. The reporter called me at around ten o'clock on a Friday night. He wanted to hear my defence. I told him I didn't even know what the accusations were, so how could I defend myself? The line kept breaking up, and I was almost out of battery. Leaving the restaurant, I tried frantically to find better reception. Meanwhile, the reporter was insistent: he was on the edge of his deadline, the report was about to go to print. He was giving me a chance to state my case – though I couldn't make out on what. He couldn't hear me any better than I could him. I was shouting at my end, he at his, both of us making a last-ditch attempt at dialogue. Then the call dropped. His number had been withheld, so all that came up on my screen was 'unknown caller'. I had no way of calling him back. I waited for a while out on the restaurant patio, gazing at the Salvador sea. I was, as the Brazilian saying goes, as lost as a goose in a snowstorm.

Devastated, my world crumbling around me, I didn't have the energy or the will to leave the room that Saturday morning to attend the lectures, interact, take a swim in the hotel pool or even go for a stroll along the beach – nothing could tempt me out. But when a Bahian friend of mine invited me to come with her to the Candomblé *terreiro* she attended, I jumped at the chance. As an anthropologist I've always had a keen interest in Afro-Brazilian religious traditions, of which Candomblé is one. As an individual, I have a deep respect for all trance-based rituals and beliefs, with their dances, music and catchy beats and vibrantly coloured settings adorned with statues made of ceramics, clay, wood and metal, in all shapes and sizes. Candomblé first developed in Bahia during the early 1800s. Based on Yoruba fundamentals, the religion's syncretic rituals are carried out in *terreiros*, or clearings. Candomblé priests are known as Mães de Santo (Saint Mothers) and, less frequently, Pais de Santo (Saint Fathers). A cousin of Voodoo, Candomblé has a colourful and often morally ambiguous pantheon that can be flattered and cajoled into granting all sorts of favours. A visit to a *terreiro* is always an experience, so I couldn't resist.

It was after five in the afternoon when we got there. Like this tradition's rituals, which often involve the channelling of spirits, the hilltop site was quite disconcerting, just the place for otherworldly visitations. Before the proceedings began I lined up with the others to receive the Saint Mother's blessing and protection. As I waited in the queue, with my wife at my side, I looked out over the woodland and its windy soul. Between broad palm leaves and twisted branches came flashes of sea and the sharp shadows of the city. The *terreiro* was a large house, open to all comers, where atabaques rumbled: drum leather, the slapping palms of the ogã, the pride of the African nations, the collars and bracelets of seeds and grains, the enamel jars, the thousands of tiny pots and the solar gold of the straw. The queue shuffled forward with serene anxiety, the busy traffic of saint children waiting for their turn.

Just then I felt someone tap me on the shoulder. He whispered something and smiled. He said my name. He wanted to know if it was really me. Yes, it's me, I said. We've never actually met, he said, though we've been in touch. Looking at the stranger's face, his identity dawned on me.

And so I greeted Lulu for the first and only time.

'Yeah, I kicked it all,' he said in a whisper. 'I left the life of crime behind me. I abandoned Rocinha, the drug business, the lot. Heard things aren't so good for you either. I hope they get better.'

I thanked him and said I hoped he managed to start afresh: it was much better to see a free man with a sparkle in his eyes than a convict behind bars, chained to his past. My wife heard every word, and leaned into the conversation.

'You'll be called back to Rio,' she whispered. 'You'll want to go back, they'll try to reel you in, but don't let them. Don't give up. Don't go back. Never. Never look back. Mark my words. For the sake of your happiness, your life; keep on going.'

I echoed Miriam's words, underlined the message. Don't forget what she's said, Lulu. She's right. Don't go back to Rio, ever, no matter what. He seemed to understand and agree. He was sure of his decision and conveyed that. I was happy for him. I felt an almost brotherly affection for someone as fucked as I was, as knee-deep in shit as I was, shaking his bones and gazing up at the sky as if trying to pretend he wasn't just this, a man.

On 14 April 2004, in Rio, Lulu was shot dead at close range by a police officer. He was surrounded at his house in Rocinha and made no attempt to resist arrest. He came out, hands up. He was marched through the favela in handcuffs, as the people watched from their windows and spilled out into the streets. They looked on in silence. The Bope squad, the special branch of the Military Police, frogmarched their trophy through his own turf. They made him sit on a low stone wall in an open square. Without warning, and for no apparent reason, the soldier sitting beside him raised his handgun and shot him in the head.

The gunshot echoed through the dusk. Hundreds of grieving favela residents packed the São João Batista cemetery to pay their last respects. They carried banners and chanted 'police assassins'. That night, the TV news claimed that Lulu's men had paid the protesters to turn out. Not a word was said about the fact that theirs was genuine grief for a peaceful gangster, a friend of their community, a provider in a place where the State never bothered to go. The official version of events was that the police had done their duty: an armed felon had resisted arrest and was killed in an exchange of gunfire. One more 'act of resistance'. In 2004 there were 983 such deaths in the state of Rio de Janeiro, a sum distinct from the tally of 6,438 homicides committed that same year in Rio alone.

The media never said, blogs never wrote, investigations never ascertained quite why Lulu had gone back to Rio. The Rio police had discovered that he planned to hide out at his mother's home in the backlands of some north-eastern state. They tracked him down en route, not long after our chance encounter in Salvador. But he wasn't arrested. He was kidnapped and blackmailed: if he wanted to live, he was told, he had to go back to Rio. A powerful group within the Civil Police in Rio needed his managerial abilities, his logistical expertise, his authority, his contacts with suppliers, his leadership and his knack for defusing inter-faction disputes, which destabilized police agreements with dealers and were generally bad for business. To the police, the drug lords are an assurance of peace and prosperity: without them the population – inflamed by the media – demand action, arrests and drugs and weapons seizures. Remove the dealers from the equation, and police heavy-handedness turns directly on the populace. End result: an increase in public insecurity and a sharp downturn in drug sales, because jittery users are too scared to go uphill into the favelas or circulate in the vicinity. Corrupt cops couldn't do without Lulu, especially not with summer around the corner, when drug sales and profits rise with the mercury. With Lulu in command, the favela was under control and business boomed. In the middle of Rio's most affluent heart, Rocinha had been the jewel in the drug trade's crown.

Given all this, Lulu never had a choice. Re-submerged in the cauldron of Rocinha, just as pretenders to his throne had steeled their nerve and whetted their appetite, Lulu found his old alliances in tatters. He had to repel successive invasions and ended up being dragged into a war between factions. Summer had passed, and his underwriters' coffers were all full. The police could do without him now, especially because things had changed: with the gang wars headline news, the police and the authorities were in a corner. They had to be seen to be doing something – to sacrifice a scapegoat. When we met on that hilltop in Salvador, Lulu had only a little under six months to live. He told anyone who would listen about what had happened to him, and sent me numerous messages foretelling his demise. He died exactly as he said he would, without any of us who had wished him a second chance being able to do a thing to save him.

What greater irony could there be for a city that prides itself on its beauty and virtues, for a nation that claims to be democratic, and for a justice system that considers itself deserving of the name?

Rio Revelry

I was delighted to hear from my Swedish friend. Delighted and surprised. She would be arriving the following week with the whole group. They were booked into a hotel, but they'd pay me a visit as soon as they were over the jet lag. They were eager for some Rio hospitality and to see how this tropical way of life of ours really worked, in practice, beyond the tourist guides and movie folklore.

When she'd said, some months earlier, as we exchanged goodbyes in Stockholm, that she'd be over to Rio de Janeiro to see me, I thought it was just a Swedish version of Rio's perfunctory niceties. In Rio, to the horror of Brazilians from other regions and the general confusion of foreigners, we have a habit of promising visits we haven't the slightest intention of ever making and of inviting people over safe in the certainty that no one will ever take us up on the offer. Promises and invitations of this kind are part of the carioca's ritual of farewells: 'drop by sometime'; 'don't forget to look us up next time you're in town,' 'pop in to see us, won't you?'. Or, pre-emptively, there's the 'let's meet up,' 'I'll be up for coffee sometime soon,' or 'I'll drop by your office and take you out to lunch,' 'I'll call you'. It's just hot air, nobody actually means anything by it.

If these promises were to be kept and invitations accepted, the people of Rio would have no time to do anything else but make and receive house visits. In Rio, formulaic phrases of this kind are just a way of showing affection and taking the sting out of farewells. For the carioca, 'adieu' is way too real and irreversible, so they opt for 'see you soon' instead, making the future more open-ended. In Rio, every goodbye is a bye for now.

The reader might interpret these clarifications as the guilty confession of a serial deal-breaker, but that's not it at all. The carioca feels no such guilt, because he's fundamentally unaware that he's an inveterate liar, manipulator and fraudster, altogether free and easy with his word. If we saw the practice as at all iniquitous, that would mean that Rio's celebrated vocation for congenial festivity was just a sham, a front, a ruse concealing an underlying stand-offishness. The heresy of it. Who would dare suggest that we cariocas were, deep down, a bunch of closet hermits, austere and circumspect, bashful Apollonian sheep dressed up as Dionysian wolves?

The story that follows was told to me by a couple of friends, husband and wife, whom we'll call Paulo and Sofia. Their account wasn't at all detailed, and one continually corrected and complemented the other's version of events, but the general gist was this.

Paulo and Sofia found themselves in a pickle with a nice young Norwegian tourist they met on Leblon beach one sunny Saturday. They got chatting, sat with the lad for a beer and exchanged business cards. At the end of the afternoon they said goodbye with the customary 'drop by sometime'. Later, as the couple were getting ready to leave to meet some friends for dinner, the doorbell rang. Sofia,

who was already dressed – they were running late – went to
answer the door while drying her wet hair with a towel. She
opened the door and was momentarily stunned and speechless to see an unlikely caller: the Norwegian. She got a grip
on herself, invited him in and told him to make himself
comfortable, that she'd be back in a minute. In the bathroom, on the verge of a nervous breakdown, she mimed the
news to her husband. Paulo either didn't understand or
didn't believe her, so she launched into an extravagant performance, whispering at full voice.

'He's here.'

'He who?'

'The guy.'

'What guy, Sofia? Calm down. Talk properly. What
guy?'

'The guy, the tourist from the beach.'

'The Norwegian fella?'

'In person.'

'The Norwegian guy is here? In our house?'

Sofia didn't need to say anything, she just furrowed her
brow, closed her eyes and let her arms drop open. Paulo
tried to convince himself that it was all just a joke, that his
wife was having him on.

'The Norwegian guy from the beach is here.'

In an awkward situation it's always good to have someone
to blame. It doesn't change anything, but it helps. Paulo was
the scapegoat, and Sofia let him have it:

'You invited him . . .'

She almost added: '. . . and he came.' But it seemed redundant. Paulo had understood that much perfectly well.

'What do you mean *I* invited him? Where did you get that idea?'

'You did say: "Drop by sometime" didn't you?'

'I said drop by, sure, what's the problem. I'm a polite guy.'

'Polite, is that what you call it?'

'What's that supposed to mean?'

Sofia turned to leave the bathroom, but Paulo pulled her back:

'Wait. Where are you going?'

'The guy is in the living room on his own. What will he think of us? That we're rude? That we don't know how to treat a guest? I'm going out there.'

'Wait. Let's think. What are we going to say? We can't turn up late for dinner.'

'Think of something. Who's the lie expert around here?'

'Are you going to bring that up again, Sofia? This is no time to start that fight again. For the love of God, I don't deserve this. Today of all days. How could this happen? I knew I caught him copping a look at your legs.'

'Cut it out, Paulo. Don't be ridiculous.'

'Ah! Now I get it. The gringo went nuts when he saw you in *that* bikini, they're not used to it. They see a pretty, half-naked woman and they lose it. Especially after a whole afternoon of sun and beer.'

'You gave me that bikini, remember? And who offered to buy him a drink? You. If anyone seduced the guy, it wasn't me.'

'So why did you lie belly-down on your towel and ask me to rub suntan lotion on your back and thighs just as the guy was coming back from a dip? You think I didn't get the timing?'

'Stop talking crap and come up with something quick. Something believable. In the meantime, I'll go and see to our guest.'

'Offer him a drink, a coffee, tell him I'm getting changed.'

The misery wore on, because there was a complicating factor. The carioca refuses to set a time for parties, visits or dinners to end and it's considered impolite for the hosts not to protest against their company's first attempts to leave. Any observation on the part of the guests that it might be getting late and perhaps they should go must be roundly repelled by the hosts as a way of demonstrating the high regard in which they hold the caller's presence.

As good cariocas, polite and nice people, Paulo and Sofia tried to find some painless way of cutting short the conversation and ushering the visitor out, but they politely resisted any attempt on the lad's part to leave. The hosts waited in vain for the Norwegian to pick up on the ambiguous rules of the game and insist on going, despite their effusive protests. The comedy of errors stretched on into the early hours, putting paid to their dinner date and ensuring some pre-dawn conflict and mutual accusations after the undesired guest's final withdrawal.

I remembered this story when I invited my Swedish friend and her group over for wine and cheese one night. It was a real invitation, not a sublimated goodbye. I laid out a fine spread. I bought wines as good as my income would permit and the best cheeses available at the local emporium. The bakery there makes some irresistible bread. I felt obliged to repay the Swedes for the kindness and moving generosity with which they had treated me in the various towns I visited, from Uppsala to Malmö. The dinners I attended at the houses of friends had been like something out of Bergman's marvellous films with Liv Ullmann and Max von Sydow – the dense, contained atmosphere and economy of words. At the table, there were silent lulls that extended beyond the Brazilian's anxiety threshold – especially that of a carioca. After the meal everyone would remain seated at the table. A song sheet was handed out, and we all looked over the words, following the order of the songs, and then the singing would start in chorus. The diners never seemed particularly enthusiastic about it. Nobody moved a muscle. In fact, the slow rhythm wasn't exactly conducive to movement. The singalong was like a natural continuation of the dinner, which avoided powerful flavours or exalted spirits at all costs. At least that was the impression I had – prejudiced, perhaps, as travellers' impressions often are. When we visit other countries we expect to find our own customs mirrored in theirs, and this can prevent us from experiencing the full richness that lies in difference. I confess that I could not help but feel bored by the monotony of these social conventions. Perhaps I was mentally reliving those Swedish films instead of opening myself up to the new.

Friday, five to nine at night. The guests would be arriving in five minutes. The Swedes are a punctual lot. I had five minutes to root through my pre-selected CDs for something to set the tone for our reunion. I was thinking of receiving my guests with some bossa nova, which had forged the musical sensibility of my generation – João Gilberto singing 'Chega de Saudade' or 'Samba do Avião', Tom Jobim playing 'Wave' or 'The Girl from Ipanema', João Donato doing 'Até quem sabe' or 'Capim'. But I hesitated, because my guests were a politicized bunch and might perhaps prefer Caetano Veloso and Gilberto Gil intoning 'Tropicália 2'. Then again, maybe a traditional samba was more appropriate, so I put on 'O Bêbado e o Equilibrista' (The Drunk and the Tightrope Walker), a sort of hymn to amnesty which Elis Regina sang beautifully. This song never fails to move Brazilians who, like me, experienced deep within themselves the struggle for democracy. My Swedish friends would be welcomed by the sound of João Bosco and Aldir Blanc in the voice of Elis Regina: 'The night falls like an overpass and a drunk in funeral suit reminds me of Chaplin . . .' Though she only knew our expected guests from my descriptions, I asked my wife for her opinion, and she approved of the choice.

The doorman rang up to say that thirteen guests had arrived. We double-checked the table, the order of the chairs, the sobriety of the flower arrangements in the middle of the living room, the classical elegance of the little objects of art on the library shelves. I turned down the volume of the music. The atmosphere seemed suitably receptive and serene. I opened the door and waited by the lift. I wanted them to feel welcome.

They leaped into my arms in a sort of frenzy. They screamed my name in chorus. There were some rounds of 'viva Rio'. Between shoulder clutches they told me that they had never been happier than during their week in Rio.

They extolled the heat, the warmth of the people. They paid no attention whatsoever to the music being played and went straight to change it. They'd bought some CDs from a street vendor on a shanty town visit which they were anxious to hear. I introduced my wife and she was warmly hailed, though they barely disguised their eagerness for the CDs, beer and party atmosphere – they'd brought crates of beer with them and hardly anyone touched the wines. They turned up the volume. A bolt of inebriating energy throbbed through the apartment as the place filled with the sounds of Rio funk. Men and women alike, young and old, took to dancing, moving their hips in horizontal and vertical thrusts without the slightest embarrassment. The women were dressed like the local girls, whose daring is backed up by physical assets my Swedish friends did not possess. And yet, what they lacked in natural aesthetics they made up for in choreography. After all, sensuality lies within the grasp of all. The blaring music, however, was an impediment to conversation. The chatter was something else; the frenetic rhythm fuelled exchanges that would normally flow elsewhere. My sitting room was too small for such an effusive celebration. Expanding one's mind requires space. The group fanned out into the two bedrooms, the hallway, the kitchen. They sang without words and danced till they dropped. Here and there, they paired off in couples which were soon unmade as they blended back into the group. Myself and my wife looked on in bewildered amazement. From the very beginning it was clear that we would have no control whatsoever over what went on in our house. We tried offering drinks, trotted out cheeseboards, but it was useless, our guests were in charge. The Bastille had fallen to the sound of the most furious funk; the Winter Palace had been overrun by masses exuding eroticism from every pore; the fridge had buckled under their assault and fallen into rebel hands. All we could do as hosts was resign ourselves to the spectacle, and pray for a little grace from the neighbours.

Six hours later, when we finally said goodbye, our Swedish friends were exhausted, drunk and effusively happy. They sang at the tops of their voices in the hallway. As they left, they said: 'Thank you Luiz, thanks ever so much for throwing us a real Rio house party. This was an unforgettable night. The "cidade maravilhosa" sure lives up to its name!'

Those hours with my Swedish friends showed me that no one throws a genuine Rio party quite like the tourists, because they have the motivation and the opportunity to aim for the most idealized image of what a genuine Rio party should be. We, the actual cariocas, dialogue with the images we have of ourselves, but we always keep a certain distance, because there is no ideal that can withstand the impurities of the everyday and the variations of real experience. However, we don't delude ourselves, we live by the cliché too – that same powerful, magnetic, transnational cliché of what it means to live in Rio de Janeiro.

I am convinced that one should never underestimate the power of clichés. Their success and longevity are by no means accidental. There is something revelatory in the caricature, not so much in the information it synthesizes as in the fact that it is rubber-stamped and recognized by society.

That authorization and recognition means that society believes in the portrait it renders of itself, which, in turn, implies the following: by believing in the truth of the image, we perpetuate and confirm it in action, so that, over the long term, the reality bends to the image. In other words, the content expressed in the cliché is not so much a representation of things as they are as a hypothetical model of things as they could be perceived. A hypothesis sent into circulation and positively received becomes a safe bet and prognosis. When society embraces a cliché, it becomes a self-fulfilling prophecy.

This line of reasoning helps me understand the episode I will now relate, which is, in a sense, an inversion of the previous one: the obsession with sex and sexuality again, only this time seen negatively. After all, a cliché turned on its head is still the same cliché: Rio, the 'marvellous city', oozing sensuality and listlessness, pursuing its unending cult to Bacchus, except now seen from the perspective of an eroticized chastity steeped in a glamorous and kitschy popular aesthetic. That's how I've come to understand the events that follow, and which I witnessed first-hand.

In the first half of 2007, singers took turns on the stage of the biggest concert hall in the Baixada Fluminense, with the audience accompanying each evangelical hit at the top of their lungs. The twenty-square-metre stage sat inside an arc over ten metres high. With the exception of the three floors of boxes and galleries, all the tables and chairs had been removed from the auditorium, leaving a wide, open floor for the faithful to pack into. The songs sounded redundant, and the 'flock' were screaming like fans at a pop concert.

After about an hour of gospel performances by special guests, the pair of hosts who'd been running the show up to that point suddenly disappeared and all the lights went out. The darkness lasted just long enough for the pastor to appear in a pool of spotlight. It was done with such theatrical aplomb that it looked as if the light was emanating from this man, of medium build, standing alone in the middle of the stage, teetering slightly from a problem in the left leg that had resulted in a permanent limp. Despite his asymmetrical boxer's face and the wear and tear of a life of ups and downs, a rags-to-riches story spanning various incarnations, from prison inmate to TV evangelist, he looked pretty much his forty-five years. The spotlight blended with the aura of his odd charisma. He had come on stage to pontificate, strut and gesticulate, belt out rhetoric with his booming baritone, but most of all the master of ceremonies was there in the dual capacity of preacher and father. Famous, feared and respected throughout Rio's slums and suburbs, he was there to celebrate the nuptials of his own daughter.

The audience went wild. Three thousand people sang the praises of the Lord. The pastor worked the crowd like a ringmaster or the host of a variety show. When the response seemed lacklustre, he paced back and forth and drummed up more noise: 'What was that? I can't hear you!' So the crowd shouted 'Glory be to God.' He'd shuffle closer to the edge: 'Glory be to who?' The decibels rose to his will. He was there to celebrate the wedding of the year. The more enthusiastic members of the crowd would say 'of the decade'. Being there was an honour, a privilege. The bride and groom were stars of religious showbiz. Their gospel songs were a huge success, and not just among the members of the pente-costal denomination founded and led by the father of the bride.

He addressed the crowd, especially the authorities in attendance, whom he hailed and welcomed for their show of solidarity and affection, then launched into prayer and some reflection on the union of two souls in holy matri-mony, a bond forged by divine blessing and sealed with fidelity. He then announced the evening's main act: the wedding. He called the families and sponsors of the bride and groom onto the stage. The crowd opened like the sea before Moses, clearing a path with almost athletic syn-chrony. The long corridor was bathed in light as one of the bride's greatest hits started to play through the sound sys-tem. The pastor received them all on stage and, after a pause for dramatic effect, called upon the groom, who appeared into view in an impeccable white suit, flanked by his father and ushered in by a retinue of maids of honour and children and teens in angelic gowns. They made their way toward the stage, walking slowly and waving discreetly.

With the groom and his entourage safely accommodated on stage, the spotlight was flung to the far end of the hall, to the beginning of the aisle formed by the crowd, where the bride and her father (having slipped off stage unnoticed) began the wedding march behind a celestial cortège, sending the crowd into hysterics. The bride, dressed in the typical white gown of her church, and her father, in a light beige suit, beamed and waved at the adoring flock. Back in command of proceedings on the now busy stage, the pastor proclaimed: 'The bride, ladies and gentlemen, and the groom.' And he hugged them both affectionately, coaxing a tear from the bride's eye. She produced a handkerchief as she waved and gave thanks, blowing kisses left, right and centre. The bride and groom, on either side of the pastor, microphones in hand, sang a duet to each other, after which they took their places among their respective sponsors, as family and friends rose from their seats down the back of the stage.

The pastor began his sermon calmly and moderately, in a confessional tone, as if speaking over the dinner table in the privacy of his home. Gradually, however, his oratory took on vigour and speed as he warmed to his subject, and pretty soon he was in his stride, brimming and frothing. Of his words, I can remember the following:

'They have never touched each other. Never seen each other naked. She is pure. Immaculate. This beautiful young lady has never known sex. She weds here today with no knowledge whatsoever of the temptations of the flesh. She has never even imagined the filth of sex, the depravation. She reviled the sin without tasting its tang. I am her witness. As her father and her pastor, as the officiator of her wedding, I declare before God and all gathered here today, my dearest brothers, my dearest sisters, that she, in her twenty-fifth year, has not once gazed upon her own body in the shower. And if she ever did, it was accidental, an innocent glance. I can assure you that had she ever so looked upon herself, it would have filled her with remorse. This girl here does justice to the white she wears. Her mind is unblemished, it knows none of the vulgarity, the torpidity of humanity, it has never been burnt by the flames of sex that engulf the world in disgrace. Sex is the root of all evil. The bride, my daughter, I am proud to say, I bring to her groom a virgin, assured that the libidinous devil has never licked her soul with the forks of his blazing tongue. I have been by her side, always watchful. Satan has never tortured this girl's spirit with the searing prongs of his trident or the shaft of his scorching horns. I did not let him. I have been her shield and today, praise the Lord, I deliver her unto her groom unstained by sin.'

The evocation of his daughter's solitary nudity, the insistent references to lust and lasciviousness, the carnal passions and delayed physical contact inflamed the erotic imagination and enthralled his audience, who now shared the carnal expectancy of the happy couple. The toxic images were invoked and dispelled, dispelled and invoked, and the atmosphere filled the sacred space with an almost promiscuous awareness of sex.

The pastor asked the groom to read from the Bible and then had his daughter do the same, though her voice trembled. He went through the matrimonial motions, handed them their wedding rings, prayed with them and blessed them. They were now man and wife, but that was not the end of the ceremony. It was time for the pastor's public confession. As if inebriated by the mystical rite, he embarked on a series of effusive tributes to his own wife, the bride's mother, and begged her forgiveness. 'When I look now on this ageing woman, worn by years of suffering, I feel ashamed, and yet it also fills me with thoughts of praise for the Lord. For many years I was possessed by the devil and wallowed in a mire of sex, drugs and alcohol. My nights were spent in debauchery and orgies. Then I would arrive home and beat this woman.' He enumerated his infidelities, and the crowd met each sordid disclosure not with silence and perplexity but with gushing Biblical exhortations. As at an auction, each item displayed, each sin described in graphic detail, always related in some way to sex, coaxed a roar of 'Christ won the day,' 'Glory to God' and 'Good will triumph'. The deeper the descent into hell, the more effusive the words of praise, the more intense the mystic catharsis. This community in ecstasy loved chastity with a fervour so visceral it aroused an ambiguous sensuality. It was a cult to Bacchus turned inside out, a paradoxically erotic exorcism of sexuality, evoking the power of lust in what is perhaps the most Dionysian of halls in Rio de Janeiro.

In 2013 the pastor in question was convicted of rape and sentenced to fifteen years in prison. In 2014 he was released on bail by decision of the Supreme Federal Court. He is appealing his conviction.

You Are Strictly Forbidden to Die*

Day breaks hot in the Baixada Fluminense, the second-largest region in metropolitan Rio de Janeiro, part of what some call Greater Rio. The sunrays sparkle on the metal of the cars, buses, motorbikes, vans, the knot of heavy city jams throwing up dust and noise. The groaning traffic adds its own heat to the solar swelter and colour overload. Such is the glare that Sérgio, who recounted his adventure to me, is impelled to retreat behind the shades he brought back from Europe, even inside the cab. He's talking to Mariana on his cellphone:

'You know me. That's just the way I am. I prefer it this way. Alone. Just one more face in the crowd. That way I'll feel more or less —'

The cab pulls over and Sérgio stops mid-phrase to pay the driver. He steps out of the cab, cellphone in hand, and looks

---

*The story told in this chapter has been pieced together from interviews, direct observation and first-hand accounts gathered over the last twenty years. Each episode concerns real situations and alludes to real people, though the sequence of events is not exact, the connections have been redrawn and the names changed. Though not verbatim quotes, the general tone and content of dialogue and statements have been maintained. We felt that this was the best way to produce a narrative that was as true as possible to the circumstances in which crime and politics intertwine in Rio de Janeiro, including the greater metropolitan region, from which the city is indissociable.

up at the colossal public hospital building in front of him, a little spooked, but also dazzled by what he's experiencing. He goes back to the phone.

'— what people feel when they get here. I've arrived. I'll call you later.'

He surveys the chaos of patients, next of kin, ambulances, staff and pedlars hawking water and sandwiches at the entrance. He crosses the 'concourse of miracles' and goes inside the building, where he negotiates his way around queues and an archipelago of small gatherings en route to the reception desk. The hall resonates with angry voices, railing against abandonment and humiliation, hurling imprecations at no one in particular. He passes small groups engaged in hushed, private conference, while others pace anxiously in near-circles. An elderly lady swoons and almost faints on the spot. Pregnant women and mothers carrying febrile infants shuffle by in numbers. Someone complains of the pain. Nurses and other staff rush in all directions, some pushing patients on trolleys.

Sérgio finally gets the attention of an attendant at reception. Her heavy make-up clashes with the environment, striking a dissonant chord that just adds to the general confusion. He says to her:

'I have an appointment with Dr —'

At that moment, like a caravan in the desert, a squat, fat man in his sixties wearing a white coat struts into the lobby with a retinue of four wardrobe-sized security guards, heavily armed and wearing bullet-proof vests. Sérgio watches the director's wagon roll by and turns back to the attendant:

'Is he going on safari?'

The girl gives him a puzzled look. He explains:

'Hunting.'

The penny drops:

'Sort of, except he's the game. What do you want?'

'I have an audience with —'

'No audiences here, only appointments, exams, surgery or meetings.'

'A meeting.'

She goes on:

'Scheduled? With who?'

'Dr Franco Emiliano.'

'Are you the hunter?'

The girl picks up the phone and announces the visitor, then turns back to Sérgio:

'ID.'

She takes his ID card, punches in the numbers and hands him a badge:

'Someone will be down to escort you. You can wait over there.'

Without further ado, she barks:

'Next!'

After ten minutes' waiting, Sérgio decides to take a look out on the concourse, where he walks straight into a dramatic scene. At the entrance to the São Tomé funeral home, located down the back of the building, a woman pulls her husband by the arm. His name is Nelson, but everyone in the favela calls him by the diminutive Nelsinho. He's dazed and reeling, cursing as loud as his lungs will let him,

'Vampires, fucking bastard vampires.' His wife tries to calm him down:

'Stop it, stop it. Come away from there. Isn't losing one child enough? You want more? You want to be next? Leave me a widow, is that what you want?'

The couple's teenage nephew, Deco, tries to contain his uncle. An elderly woman comes to console the traumatized mother and leads her into the concourse. A little fresh air and a walk will do her good. Nelson breaks away from his nephew and makes a beeline for the sombre funeral home. Deco, shouting and sobbing, tries to stop his uncle, but there's blood in Nelson's eyes and his nerves are about to snap. He bawls at a funeral home attendant:

'Vampire, monster. Go on, suck the blood out of him, suck him dry. Take him wherever you want. I've lost everything. I've lost my son. Bloodsucking son of a bitch.'

The funeral attendant excuses himself to some people with whom he's been discussing funeral costs and coffin types. He approaches Nelson with professionally decorous contempt, the spiel already reeling off his tongue:

'I am sorry for your loss, like I said. But there's nothing I can do. The law is the law. Right or wrong, that's not my problem. It's city law: if it dies here, it gets buried here. If you want to take the body for burial outside city limits, it'll cost you 400 reais. Read it. It's right there on the wall. It's the law.'

Deco holds his uncle, who's now sobbing silently.

At the other end of the concourse a notary approaches the mother and her elderly consoler, who are wandering arm in arm.

'Excuse me. I know this isn't a proper time, but if I can just have a moment of your attention. You see, I think I can be of assistance. I've been told that you are the next of kin of the . . . the young man . . . it's such a tragedy. May God keep him, God rest his soul . . . the youth who so tragically lost his life in a car accident on Dutra in the early hours of this morning. The youth who was driving a blue Fiesta, licence plate SEG 2537.'

The women stare at him in shock, then start to cry. The notary is not deterred:

'I know what it means to lose a son. I, too, lost my child. God bless his soul. So I know that some extra money can be a great help at a time like this, a huge help, yes indeed. Terribly bad form to speak of money under the present circumstances, I know. Practically blasphemous. But it does help, which is why I ask if you were aware that you have a right to claim back your "DPVAT" mandatory car insurance. The sum of 2,000 reais. If you'll just sign this authorization form, I can take care of all the paperwork, hassle-free. All I need is your signature.'

A Military Police car rolls slowly by, occupied by a driver, one soldier and a sergeant, to whom the various figures working that patch turn with deference. In file, numbers game touts, street pedlars, clandestine cabbies, funeral home directors and flower stall women approach the sergeant's window for a bout of ring-kissing and palm-greasing. The notary hails the Military Police officer from a distance:

'Sergeant, a sad day, very sad.'

He rests a hand on the grieving mother's shoulder as he passes the paperwork to her companion, who takes the form but doesn't read it. He leaves the two women and heads over to the police car, where he discreetly makes a 'thumbs-down':

'Slow, very slow.'

On the other side of the concourse, the uncle's fury has rubbed off on Deco and the kid decides to set the funeral attendant straight:

'Not your problem? It is your problem. Everyone knows this piece-of-shit funeral home belongs to councillors Tonico do Posto and Beto Churrasco. Everyone knows they hold the lease on the municipal cemetery. Some fucking law this is. Who passed this law? The council, that's who. So if it's your law, it's your problem. Go fuck yourself.'

The lad goes for the attendant and the roles are suddenly reversed: now it's Nelson who's holding Deco back. In the ruckus they end up falling over a wreath.

The shouting and mayhem at the funeral home catch the women's attention and that of the sergeant, who signals to his driver to stop. The manoeuvre is swift. The Military Police officer gets out of the car, heavy, sweating and slovenly, and heads for the funeral home. Inside, the attendant is waving and calling to him from the fray:

'Sergeant, where were you, man? You can't leave like that, look at this shit! Look at the shit!'

He spreads his arms in front of two women, mother and daughter by the look of it, who work at the funeral home. Chairs, coffins, wreaths and bouquets are knocked everywhere as uncle and nephew crash to the floor. It's no longer clear who's trying to contain whom, or who is more furious and indignant. When the sergeant comes in, semi-automatic in hand but not raised, the uncle and his nephew stand up and separate. The soldier recognizes Nelson.

'Is that Nelsinho? Had to be. You can't stay outta trouble, can ya?'

'I'm gonna report you lot, I'm gonna finish with you once and for all.'

On the other side of the concourse, the mother snatches the papers from her companion's hand and shoves them back at the notary:

'My son was killed by the militia. They put thirty bullets in him. Thirty.'

Sérgio reckons it's best not to intervene, so he returns to the lobby. After a few more minutes' wait he decides to take a look around, scout the terrain, get the lie of the land. Wearing all the airs of someone who's supposed to be there, he goes into wards and corridors, noting every detail of what he sees, and it's perplexing, sapping and enraging. He pulls his cellphone out of his pocket and starts filming the sorry scene: patients abandoned on trolleys in the corridors, heaps of dirty towels in the corners, filthy puddles on the floor and scant lighting. He's suddenly grabbed by a security guard, who shoves him through a half-open door. Sérgio just about manages to stay on his feet. He tries to steady himself and take in his surroundings, a service stairwell. The security guard grabs him by the shoulders and growls at him like a wild dog about to tear a rabbit apart. He stamps on Sérgio's cellphone and twists him into an armlock. With his free hand, he radios through to someone:

'Got another journalist here, copy?'

Now assisted by a colleague, the security guard frog-marches Sérgio into the director's office, one wall of which is covered with security monitors showing CCTV from different parts of the hospital, another with framed medical diplomas and show-jumping rosettes. Inside, Sérgio recognizes two of the three security guards standing to attention around the director's desk. They were part of the caravan, safari or pretorian guard he'd seen strut through the lobby. The third is the guy who just captured him, with all the grace and gentleness of his noble profession.

Rattled and dishevelled, his shirt torn, Sérgio is deposited in a chair facing the director, who examines him from his comfy armchair with a clinical stare. Nearby are two other chairs, another armchair and a desk busy with papers, two walkie-talkies, a bullet-proof jacket, three medical textbooks propped up by bronze horse bookends, a photo of the director as a younger man receiving a trophy as he sits proudly astride an elegant thoroughbred, a statue of Saint George slaying the dragon and a bust of Hippocrates. The director finally breaks the silence:

'You requested a meeting with me . . . Sérgio, that's your name, isn't it? . . . and I accepted because you told my secretary over the phone that were you were a doctor, not a journalist.'

'I am a doctor.'

'So what's with all the filming?'

'What's with roughing up journalists?'

'Damn it, are you a doctor or a journalist?'

Sérgio fires back, as if he's rehearsed his whole life just to say those words:

'I'm a hospital director.'

'Which hospital?'

'This hospital.'

'What are you on about?'

'Have you forgotten there's a new mayor? Things are going to change in health, starting with this hospital.'

'I wasn't informed.'

'I'm informing you now.'

The director waves the security guards out of the room and waits for them to leave, then raises his tone:

'What way is this to treat an authority of my calibre, with a history of public service as long and distinguished as mine?'

'What way is this to treat a journalist?'

'Christ, are you a journalist or aren't you? Is this some sort of set-up? Are you filming this conversation?'

'I came here with the best of intentions. I came to talk to you as a sign of respect. I came here as a regular citizen to get to know the reality of this hospital. I wanted to discuss your egress before it was officially announced so that we could arrange for a smooth, co-operative transition that would be good for all concerned. Especially for the hospital and the population. But what did I find? A director who swans around with armed goons on the hospital premises. An office that looks like a bunker. Oh, and I nearly take a beating from a hired thug. What is this, the Wild West?'

'Sérgio, where are you coming from? Mars?'

'Germany.'

'Mars.'

'Where I was doing a doctorate.'

'And then you just parachute right into the thick of Rio de Janeiro. The theory's rather different here, lad.'

'It always is, but I have years under my belt as a medical practitioner in Rio. I spent fifteen years working at private hospitals here, but I came back because I wanted to get involved in public health. The mayor is young, bold, idealistic, and he's known me for some time. I was a colleague, in fact, an apprentice, of his father's, who was a doctor, a great doctor.'

'You speak of the new mayor as if he were a friend. You can forget that for a start.'

As he speaks, the director stands up, takes off his white coat, puts on the bullet-proof vest and pulls his suit jacket off the back of the chair behind his desk, then reaches into a drawer for a gun, which he sticks into a holster on the back of his belt.

'Are you going somewhere? Weren't we going to talk?'

Sérgio stands up.

'The guy who sat in this chair before me was killed. The guy before him cashed in his chips and left the country. The new mayor might be idealistic, bold, whatever, but a friend —'

He opens the heavy bunker door and looks back at Sérgio, before leaving him alone in the empty room:

'He's no friend.'

Alone in that cold bunker, Sérgio recalls the conversation, two months earlier, with the mayor-elect. A little older than Luiz Claudio, and nowhere near as fit, Sérgio struggles to keep up with the politician on his morning run.

They are trailed by security guards, jogging along behind them at a respectful distance. They're all wearing campaign T-shirts with the slogan 'Nothing should ever seem unchangeable'. Sérgio is having a hard time of it, but his interlocutor not only ups the pace, but seems to have no difficulty speaking:

'Not counting the capital, metropolitan Rio has a population of four million people, and 70 per cent of them, living wherever they can raise a shack, have no access to basic sewage disposal. The towns are growing with no urban master plan, no respect for the environment, no development strategy and a civil service that doesn't work — that is, for anything other than nepotism and jobs for the boys. Education's been abandoned. Health, sold to scrap. That's where you come in.'

Luiz Claudio slows down and stops. Sérgio does the same, and bends over with a stitch, sweating buckets. Luiz dries his face and head, and goes on:

'Look, Sérgio, you know that our hospital is a tremendous challenge. It's municipal, but it caters for the whole Baixada population, plus the city. It won't be easy. I need you. I want you to be the new director. I'm giving you carte blanche. However . . .'

He smiles, turns to face Sérgio, puts his hands on his shoulders and says, in a half-jocular tone:

'There are three commitments you'll have to undertake. Number one, improve the services; two, root out corruption; and three, don't die.'

Sérgio looks at his friend with whatever seriousness his breathlessness will allow. Luiz insists:

'The last one is the most important. I mean it, bro. You are strictly forbidden to die.'

They smile and walk on, arms round each other's shoulders.

Sérgio snaps back from his brief reverie. He looks around the office as if unable to believe, or understand, what he's heard and seen, and still sees around him. He turns and heads for the bunker door.

An imposing black pickup, a luxury import, crosses the arid landscape of Rio's West Zone. Few vehicles travel that semi-desert road. In the passenger seat a short, fat, middle-aged man wearing blingy gold chains and rings sweats profusely despite the Swiss air conditioning. He's Camargo 'Bonebreaker', aka Sergeant Camargo of the Rio de Janeiro Military Police, the militia chief. The skinny guy of indeterminate age driving the car in a colourful shirt and cursing at every pothole or ruck is Private Meneses. In the back is Congressman Ivo Cury Lízio, the new partner in the Firm – that's what they call it, the Firm – a chirpy fellow in his thirties. The darkened, bullet-proof windows make it clear that something of the metallic city sun has been lost in translation on the tint of the militia's mobile HQ.

The pickup slows suddenly. The driver leans to the right, craning his neck for a better view:

'Isn't that that son-of-a-bitch Nelsinho?'

The fat passenger answers with a question:

'The guy on the bike?'

A moment of indecision.

Having passed the cyclist, the vehicle speeds ahead, pulls a brusque u-turn and comes back the same way. The fat sergeant jumps out of the car with the unlikely agility of an athlete, right arm tight to his side, and crosses the street, appearing in front of the cyclist like a ghost conjured out of the asphalt. The rider brakes and takes his feet off the pedals. He says something inaudible, but something certainly, because his lips are moving. The right door of the car is wide open, and the private climbs out of the driver's side and approaches the cyclist and the chief. The Congressman is now the only occupant of the car.

The fat sergeant raises the arm glued robot-like to his flank and fires at point-blank range. The driver, carrying an automatic rifle, stands over the lifeless cyclist and gives the coup de grâce.

They climb back into the car and the Congressman twists in his seat to stare at the dead body and what's left of its head. He just about manages to open the door before puking his guts out. The sergeant is tart:

'Fuck it, man. We just had lunch.'

The politician spits, pulls out a handkerchief to wipe his chin with and slumps back into the car, slamming the door. Not a word.

The truck u-turns again and returns to its original route, driving over the dead man's body on the way.

Feeling the bump beneath the car, the unexpected intimacy with the corpse is too much for the Congressman and he returns to the outside world his protein-heavy campaign lunch. The fat sergeant is inconsolable:

'Jesus Christ. Fucking hell. The car was spick and span, man. Just came back from inspection yesterday.'

Some people come running down the road's edge, looking startled. They see the black truck and scatter. A rusty
old Gol 1000 slows down as it approaches the corpse but,
seeing that the armed perpetrators are still at the scene,
speeds up and disappears. Nothing can trouble the three
horsemen of the Apocalypse. They're on their way to
electoral victory and success. The victim is just roadkill, a
hiccup dealt with by skilled shooters, an inconvenience to
be expunged from the Congressman's memory by force
of will.

Late that afternoon, Manuela is in shock as she looks down
at the disfigured corpse lying at the side of the road. She was
the first to find him, and she returns to cover him up. A
crowd has now gathered around the body, blocking the road
and holding up the scant traffic. She walks away to make a
phone call:

'Cardoso, send a team out here. I came alone. Send a
photographer at least. Send Barros, and make it quick.
They've murdered a community leader. Yeah, seems he
fingered some militiamen. Let me give you the address.
What? What do you mean "Who cares about another crime
in the West Zone"? So what if it was the militia? What
difference does that make, Cardoso? I know we're not a
tabloid. I know exactly what a serious broadsheet is,
Cardoso. Very well.'

She hangs up, her eyes filled with tears.

The next morning she goes into the young editor-in-chief's
office with a newspaper under her arm.

'Coffee, Manuela?'

She sits down, in silence.

'What are you scowling about?'

'Is this what your serious broadsheet does?'

She slaps the folded newspaper on the desk and taps a small note that reads: 'Murder becomes routine in the West Zone.' She continues:

'This is bullshit, Cardoso. This is fifth-rate.'

'I know you blew a day's work trekking all the way out to that world's end, Manuela, and the paper appreciates your effort, but —'

'Don't shit me, Cardoso. You don't know the difference between a cold truck heist and the murder of a grassroots leader any more.'

'Manuela, our readers —'

'What about our readers, Cardoso? Our reader doesn't want to know unless the corpse is in his own garden? Because it's not Ipanema that's stinking of gunpowder and grey matter? Because the dead guy's poor and black and from the slums?'

'If we cover every turn in the war between militias and drug lords, the paper will become one long obituary, a police report.'

'This wasn't gang warfare, this wasn't a turf war. The victim's no criminal. He was a community leader. While your readers are enjoying a sea view, a tsunami is brewing out in the West Zone and in the Baixada, out in no man's land. A tsunami that's going to hit City Hall, the cops, the justice system and sweep the pretty world of your readers right off the map.'

'Manuela, let's do this. I'm going to give you an opportunity. You deserve it. How about your own column in the culture supplement, with your photo on the side.'

'Maybe some day this story will be told and we'll all have to shoulder our share of the responsibility.'

Manuela gets up and leaves.

A week later, Sérgio is in the antechamber to his office surrounded by doctors, nurses and other staffers, eager to welcome their new director. The group disperses and a young woman comes up to Sérgio and hands him an envelope:

'My resignation letter.'

'Why?'

'Change of director, change of secretary. Isn't that how it works?'

'No. This time it's not just the director that's changing, but the method, routine, mindset. Don't worry, your place is here if you want it.'

He angles to read the name on her ID badge, but she spares him the trouble.

'Mariângela.'

'It's a pleasure, Mariângela. So what's on the agenda for today?'

He heads for the door with 'Director's Office' on it, but the secretary beckons to him before he grasps the knob.

'Dr Sérgio, there are some people waiting to see you.'

'In my office? Inside?'

The secretary nods, but Sérgio is stunned at the intrusion.

'What are they doing in there?'

He doesn't wait for an answer. He opens the door and sees two men sitting comfortably in his office, one maybe twice the age of the other. They stand up and introduce themselves:

'Ramires. It's a pleasure.'

'Ramires Junior. How are you, sir?'

Sérgio tries to keep a lid on his indignation:

'I don't recall scheduling this appointment.'

The father takes the initiative:

'Apologies, Director. We'd scheduled with your predecessor, Dr Franco Emiliano. But now . . .'

'What's this about?'

'Oh, just to introduce ourselves. I know you are only settling in and haven't had time to get up to speed yet. We won the tender for the new ambulances.'

Between irony and perplexity, Sérgio repeats these last words:

'New ambulances.'

The son explains:

'Ten ambulances and two mobile ICUs.'

'Your company is . . .'

'Economic Solutions Inc.'

Sérgio ponders:

'Solutions . . . it doesn't ring any bells.'

'Based in Cuiabá.'

'Cuiabá, Mato Grosso. And you travelled sixteen hundred kilometres to take part in a tender in Rio.'

'Congressman Ivo Cury Lízio was the author of the congressional amendment.'

The lights come on in Sérgio's mind and he repeats the words as if by way of confirmation.

'The funds are from a congressional amendment.'

'You know how it works, of course? Each Congressman has the right to earmark a few million for a social project of his choice. Most of them choose something of public interest in their constituencies, but a lot of them are at a complete loss. We help them. We get in early, at the start of the year, and we present an important initiative with high voter impact. We handle all the red tape, negotiations with the Health Ministry, everything. When the local authority makes a call for bids, we've already ironed it all out at ministerial and municipal level. It's a win-win situation, especially for the population. It's a very nimble and secure system, I can assure you.'

Ramires Junior adds:

'We've been bidders in over three hundred tenders, Brazil-wide.'

The father is more precise:

'Three hundred and fourteen. Ivo takes care of the municipality's affairs in Brasília. He represents the mayor.

The son adds emphasis:

'He works with the mayor. They're very much in tune.'

Sérgio interjects with an important but overlooked detail:

'There's a new mayor now.'

'Yes, but the city is still here, isn't it? And it can't get by without political connections at a federal level.'

Ramires Junior rounds off the edges:

'Partnerships.'

The father gets back to the point:

'See, the thing is Congressman Ivo Cury Lízio has already been paid.'

Sérgio squirms:

'The Congressman has been paid.'

'Quite, but we haven't, because there was an election in the middle of things. But we delivered the ambulances and advanced Ivo his cut to help out with the campaign costs for his councillors.'

Sérgio elaborates on the point:

'Who will be sitting in opposition to the new mayor.'

Ramires Junior bats this away:

'Now Doctor, we all know there is no such thing as opposition. People always settle into place.'

Sérgio insists:

'The political reality is different now.'

'But municipal health can't wait.'

Ramires stands up, ready to shake the director's hand.

Ramires Junior, a true patriot:

'An election can't be allowed to stand in the way of health, can it, Doctor?'

Father and son prepare to leave.

'Here's my card. For all the city's health needs, we're here. We get things done quickly and smoothly. Thank you, Doctor.'

They say goodbye and Sérgio watches as they show themselves out.

One hot Sunday two weeks later, Aureliano throws a barbecue for some friends at his country mansion in the exclusive Pedra de Guaratiba area of Greater Rio. Though sixty-six years old, he's still got his athletic build and handsome Italian movie star good looks. He's wearing white slacks and a muscle shirt that shows off his three tattoos. Adding a finishing touch to the style, that of a sort of Hare Krishna monk, is a pair of Indian leather sandals. The country house, famous among entrepreneurs who shoot their way into business, politicians, bent cops, militiamen and pop stars, has a helipad on the terrace, a wave pool, sophisticated stables, an airstrip with a private jet on standby, a tennis court, football pitch, fully equipped gym and shooting range.

The host circulates among the different groups scattered about the grounds. In the garden, men and women are chatting and eating around a sun-shaded table. As he turns his body, Aureliano shows off his tattoos: a classic atomic mushroom cloud, a dove and the words Las Vegas encircling an imposing casino.

'Power, the power not to use power, and the simulation of power, because play . . . what is play? It's simulated warfare.'

Silvinha, a large-breasted, meaty-thighed woman, asks the obvious:

'Las Vegas?'

'Las Vegas, the temple of play. The great theatre of war that isn't war.'

She whispers something into Aureliano's ear, and he responds aloud:

'You gotta be kidding me, sweetheart! I don't believe it. How long have you and Colonel Saraiva been married?'

She flashes two fingers as she chews on a canapé, finding it all so very humorous. The host is horrified:

'Hey Saraiva, get over here, Saraivinha.'

The colonel is ten years Aureliano's junior, but looks much older, tottering around behind a rotund gut. He approaches, glass in hand, to hear the host's admonition:

'Have you no shame, man? Your little lady here's been spilling some beans . . . And you aren't coming out of it looking too good . . . Is it true you never took her to Las Vegas?'

Silvinha's husband tries to mount a defence:

'Las Vegas is a big hole you throw your money into.'

'Worried about money, Saraivinha? You? Give me a break.'

Aureliano turns to the colonel's wife:

'Your name?'

'Silvinha.'

'Silvinha, do you know how much this weasel brought in last year?'

He shuffles over to a nearby group chatting and eating on the lawn and gathers up Aírton, Ivo Cury, Inspector Sarmento and Congressman Roni Anderson, and reels them into the conversation.

'Hey, get this. Come here. You too. You know this S.O.B . . . Colonel Saraiva. Fuck it, man, I'm talking to you.'

Saraiva turns back, perks up:

'Yeah, boss.'

'This weasel here never took his wife to Las Vegas.'

The men protest in unison:

'How low can you go, Saraivinha?'

'Cruelty, pure and simple.'

'Don't they have a support group or NGO for women abused like this?'

Ivo Cury is emphatic:

'For me, if it's a party, it's Las Vegas: Christmas, New Year, Easter. Pops loved the place.'

The host corrects him:

'That's a lie, your father loved Punta del Este, God rest his soul. He used to borrow my jet, with a couple of broads . . . But we're getting off-point. We're talking about Saraiva here, listen Silvinha, this guy wouldn't spend Christmas; he's never gonna take you to Las Vegas. Listen, sweetheart: you know what he made last year, in security alone?'

He goes over to the colonel, nose to nose, and eyeballs him ironically, tweaking his voice for comic effect:

'The security he pays bent Military Police a pittance to provide . . .'

His voice returns to normal. He focuses his attention on Silvinha:

'We're talking just on the concert halls on Dutra, the saunas in Morro Agudo, the casino over in Caxias, the bingo hall in Meriti, the numbers game stalls in Mesquita, Belfort Roxo, São Gonçalo and Santa Cruz?'

He whispers into Silvinha's ear. She's the only one who hears him, but she repeats what he says aloud:

'A million? Millions? Ten?'

She shrieks, and the pitch makes the dogs bark.

Saraiva's in a funk. He goes over to his wife and tries to take the glass out of her hand, but she resists:

'How could you, Saraivinha? And all this time I've been scrimping at the mall.'

Saraiva's getting grumpy and wants to put an end to the banter:

'Enough. Enough.'

Aírton whispers to Roni and Sarmento:

'To say nothing of the slot machines, contraband and select unmentionables.'

Sarmento adds:

'Saraiva took a beating in Morro Agudo. Ivo Cury got away scot-free, though. He'd already pocketed his cut on the ambulance deal, before it all went belly-up.'

Roni asks Sarmento:

'Wasn't Saraivinha going to lose control over the lowlands, what with the changes in the Military Police?'

'The colonels had a sit-down. Drew up a Treaty of Tordesillas.'*

Roni chimes in:

'With Aureliano's blessing, I'm sure.'

Aírton stirs the pot:

'They learned from the chief inspectors. But you know who's getting fucked over a barrel? Carlinhos Tanajura. And Macedo and Ramos too.'

Roni:

'I saw Macedo recently. He was out with some broad who looked like a Carnival float.'

Sarmento and Aírton speak at the same time:

'The transport guys.'

'And the garbage collection guys, and the clinics on the public health system. That Sérgio Borba has cut the money line.'

---

* Of 1494, which established the division of the globe between Spain and Portugal for purposes of colonization.

Roni, a veteran politician, has a wider, more precise reading of the situation:

'The problem's Luiz Claudio: new broom with pretty bristles.'

Sarmento, an inspector with the Federal Highway Police, spits it out:

'Someone's gotta do something.'

Roni, quick off the mark:

'Yeah, I'm gonna get a beer.'

He moves away from the group, grabs a beer off the tray of a passing waiter and heads over to the pool, full of kids, young mums and nannies in whites.

On the other side of the pool, near the football pitch where a five-a-side kickaround is in full swing, there's a pair of toilets and a kiosk serving drinks, French fries and sandwiches. Pop-infused country music blares out of the open boot of a hatchback nearby. Ivo Cury, with his unmistakable egg-yolk dye job, approaches a group huddled around the grill. Among them is Sergeant 'Bonebreaker' Camargo, dripping with his usual gold, and his sidekick Meneses, inseparable from his coloured shirt. Meneses is holding a spit of grilled meat.

'Grab a plate, Congressman. Have a slice.'

Ivo grimaces and bares his teeth:

'It's still bleeding.'

Another group is gathered around a large tent attended by waiters, with a freezer, a generator and trayloads of pastries and tapas. Aureliano and Otacílio are standing nearby, deep in conversation. When he sees Roni approaching the tent, the host beckons him over.

'They treating you OK, Roni?'

To Otacílio:

'Do you know Congressman Roni Anderson?'

'Who doesn't?'

'Otacílio Alves, it's a pleasure.'

Roni shakes his hand and nods appreciatively. Aureliano continues:

'It's good you came over, Roni. I was just saying to our friend here that I don't discriminate along party lines. I support Roni's party the same way I do all the others that work with us. Ideology doesn't interest me.'

Roni nods:

'There is no ideology any more. That's so last-century. This whole Left and Right thing, that's just barn dancing, that's all.'

Otacílio is amiability personified:

'Which no one does any more.'

They laugh, and Aureliano gets back on subject:

'I don't care about parties, Otacílio. If the PSDOB* want to come on board, I'm good with that . . . I treat my friends well. But enemies? I got no time for enemies.'

Roni follows the thread:

'Joining forces is good for us, and for Brazil. João Daniel came to me with something interesting . . .'

Otacílio jumps in:

'The election.'

'Something about us putting forward a running mate . . .'

Aureliano turns to Roni in surprise:

---

*Partido Social do Brasil (Brazilian Socialist Party), created in Rio in 1985 by dissidents from former Governor Leonel Brizola's PDT.

'Pedro Raimundo's running mate? He's a future president, he is.'

'Tempting, tempting.'

Otacílio cuts to the chase:

'Together, our two parties would be unstoppable. We carry the weight of leftist tradition. Pedro Raimundo's idea is to present a milder face, one more palatable to the middle class. Your party could really support us in that. It would be wind in this new guy's sails.'

Roni pulls the rug:

'There's just one problem, though: your party sends flowers and blows kisses while stabbing us in the back.'

'I know what you're referring to, but you can be sure of one thing: it's not the party that's doing that. Quite the contrary. It's a personal thing of Luiz Claudio's. That'll change.'

Aureliano stamps his authority on the conversation:

'Otacílio, tell João Daniel and Pedro Raimundo that we are the dynamic hub of metropolitan Rio. We forged unity in the Baixada with iron and fire. Look at this tent. Almost every mayor from the region is here. There are judges, chief justices, captains of industry, celebrities, footballers. That's our strength. We elect together, and we govern together.'

Roni puts the boot in:

'We can't just stand idly by while some flyboy destroys what we built with sweat and tears.'

'And blood, Roni. My family spilled a lot of blood on this land.'

A fortnight after being sworn in, Sérgio agrees to meet the ex-director, Franco Emiliano, in the hospital store room.

Emiliano peeks out through the ventilation flap and leans up against a crate. Sérgio stands before him, arms crossed.

'Look, Sérgio, what you're doing is very risky. Others who tried the same thing before you came a cropper. I'm warning you because I've been in your shoes. I know what it's like. A new mayor, fire in the belly, idealistic, and you think you can do it all. That you'll be allowed to do it all. But when the backlash comes, and it does, it's your neck on the line. Not the mayor's. You're collecting enemies. You're declaring war on too many fronts at the same time: the cemetery and funeral racket; mandatory insurance, the DPVAT, there are a lot of fingers in that pot, those of lawyers and notaries; the accredited clinics; the hospital suppliers; and now this debacle with the ambulance tender. You broke a deal that had already been struck. Ramires was caught on the hop, he feels betrayed. He won the tender. Congressman Ivo had already been paid. It's a lot of money. You're playing with fire.'

Sérgio lunges at Emiliano and grabs him by the scruff of the neck:

'Listen, you son of a bitch. I came down here because I still gave you the benefit of the doubt, as a fellow doctor. But you're just a thief. A two-bit lousy little thief. An old son of a bitch running errands, passing on other people's threats. So run back to your bosses with a message from me: they can go fuck themselves. And tell them that the mayor sends a message too.'

Sérgio's palm slaps Emiliano's face so hard he almost reels out of the door.

About a fortnight after the episode in the store room, Inspector Lucas and Manuela are sitting in an unmarked police car with the windows up and the air conditioning on. Theirs is just one of the many cars parked in the shade of a tree-lined square surrounded by middle-class apartment buildings and small commerce.

They finally hear the metallic rasp of male voices coming in over the wiretap:

'Hey, Teixeira, finally, hey? You been screening my calls, eh?'

'What's up, Netinho, spit it out, coz I'm sort of in the middle of something here.'

'You're the one who better have something to say, Teixeira, because the boss is done waiting.'

'Tell him it's going ahead, I'm just waiting for the right time.'

'When will that be?'

'He'll find out. First I've got to talk to the boss, in person. You think I'm gonna whack an authority without checking with him first? If you wanna do it yourself, be my guest.'

'The son of a bitch is meddling in everything. He's causing the boss some damage.'

'I know that and he knows it too. But things don't work that way. The guy's a chess player. Politics is one big headfuck.'

'Headfuck, now you're talking. Like that. OK, one more day, got it? One more day.'

Lucas grabs his gourd and fills it with hot water from a thermos flask. He sips his *chimarrão** through the metal straw.

---

* *Chimarrão* is a green tea commonly drunk by Gauchos, people from southern Brazil, Uruguay and northern Argentina. Some more ardent drinkers carry a gourd full of dried, ground mate leaves and a thermos flask of hot water with them wherever they go.

He offers some to Manuela, but she can't understand the appeal.

'How can you drink that stuff in this heat?'

'It settles the nerves.'

Manuela is won over:

'Give it here.'

He pours in more water and hands the gourd to Manuela. She sucks on the straw and thinks out loud:

'An authority who's disrupting the boss's business dealings. The boss has got to be Aureliano, the old numbers game racketeer, and granddad of the militias. Yeah, Lucas, the old king of the Baixada is still calling the shots.'

'This is all wrong, Manuela. You shouldn't be here, doing this, it's illegal.'

'Ah! Cut it out, you're like a broken record. What a bummer. It's all illegal, Lucas. Everything.'

'No, it's not.'

He turns and looks out the window, as if staring at something:

'Morro Agudo.'

Lucas turns to Manuela and continues:

'The wiretap is legal.'

He shuffles in his seat as he turns the key in the ignition:

'But the judge didn't authorize any eavesdropping journalist.'

He pulls out into the road. Manuela responds:

'You owed me. Who gave you the goods on the Nelsinho murder? Or you think the witnesses would be willing to tell a cop what they told me? Everyone in the West Zone knows that ratting out the militia is a death sentence. And you owe me for other stuff too, Inspector Lucas, remember? And anyway, I'm your only guarantee. Who else is going to vouch for you if the sky comes falling down?'

'The sky doesn't fall, not like that.'

'Chief Inspector Selton?'

'Only one place I know where the sky's falling down.'

He speeds into traffic and starts to weave.

'If the world caves in on Lucas it's because it caved in on Selton first.'

'The old world. Creaking.'

'Don't count on Selton. Even if he says you can.'

'Manuela, I'm the weakest link in all this. I'm where the chain breaks.'

Lucas continues to drive like a maniac.

'No. Not this time. The difference between you two is salary only. What does an inspector earn? Half of what a chief inspector makes?'

'I wish.'

'You and Selton are in this together. So who's the bigger threat to the dons? The chief inspector, that's who. Not you. Anyway, where are we going?'

The car accelerates. The vicinity of the main square in Morro Agudo, in metropolitan Rio, is one big tailback, so Lucas pulls over and they continue on foot. Manuela still doesn't know what the rush is about. They find themselves in the middle of a protest in front of City Hall, which is besieged by uncollected rubbish. The angry crowd, poor in the main, are chanting against the mayor and waving banners and placards that read 'Out with Luiz Claudio' and 'We want our jobs back'.

They squirm and push their way through the demonstrators. Manuela pulls out her cellphone and starts to film. Lucas just watches. The protesters chant: 'You bit the hand that takes out the rubbish'. From the back of a sound truck, a squat, bald councillor shouts:

'The people gave you their hand and their vote, Mr Mayor, and what did they get in return? Lay-offs. If you want to economize, why not take a pay cut? The mask has fallen: the handsome nice-guy has shown himself to be just another neoliberal who has condemned thousands of workers and their families to misery.'

A middle-aged councillor, with short hair and lips pumped with filler, takes the microphone:

'In the name of the councillors of Morro Agudo, and as president of the chamber, I can assure you of this: we are not going to just sit back and watch the people suffer. We will fight. We will push for the mayor's impeachment. Down with Luiz Claudio, traitor of the people, neoliberal!'

The two politicians paint their faces black and the crowd follows suit, chanting something about neoliberals and the devil. People circulate in the crowd, handing out face paint. The next speaker on the platform is a younger man, in his thirties, with bleached-blond hair. He receives a grand introduction:

'With us today is someone who never abandoned the people. Our representative in Brasília, Congressman Ivo Cury Lízio, to whom I am honoured to pass the mic.'

'The painted faces of Morro Agudo are here to say that the mayor is a barefaced liar. First was rubbish collection. The mayor broke the contract with the rubbish collection company and the city became a rubbish heap. He thinks it's cool to break contracts. He thinks it's revolutionary. Then came public transport chaos. The companies have pared back their fleets because the mayor doesn't want to pay what the municipality owes. And now you have been kicked out into the streets like unwanted dogs. Well I say it's time we kicked Luiz Claudio out into the street. Get, Mr Mayor. Shoo, Mr Mayor!'

The crowd repeats the slogan: 'Get, Mr Mayor. Shoo, Mr Mayor!'

From up in his office, Mayor Luiz Claudio watches the demonstration through the slats of his blinds, apparently unfazed. The room is full of aides and secretaries, waiting in silence for instructions.

'We know what's going on. Some call it politics, but I call it blackmail. Two thousand people fired because they were appointed to positions of trust by elected councillors and never put in a day's work. They're stooges. There's only one way to turn this around, and that's to play the game. Write this down, Narinha: in tomorrow's edition of the *Official Gazette* we're going to announce the readmission of nominees from 55 per cent of the council members. Let's divide these bastards in order to conquer. I've been on the other side, I know how it's done. One way or another, it's still progress: a 45 per cent cut in stooge pay.'

Down in the square, in the shadow of City Hall, Lucas pulls Manuela to a relatively calm spot and whispers to her:

'The target is right there.'

He points discreetly at the window of the mayor's office, on the left-hand side of the top floor.

'The "handsome nice-guy".'

'The "neoliberal"?'

Manuela takes a photo of the mayor's window as Lucas scans the crowd. She says:

'It makes sense.'

'This is where the sky is falling, here in Morro Agudo. There's no other part of Aureliano's kingdom where the old order is crumbling quite as fast.'

'Well, when the sky falls, it has to fall on someone. What are you going to do?'

Lucas is already on the radio, calling his boss. He cups his hand around the mouthpiece and moves away to talk.

'Chief Inspector Selton?'

Up in Luiz Claudio's office Narinha, the mayor's longest-standing aide, calls her boss into a corner and points at a cellphone:

'Mr Mayor, its Chief Inspector Selton Cruz.'

'Federal?'

'No. State Civil Police. It's urgent.'

'Did his secretary make the call?'

'No, he called himself.'

'Narinha, find out who this guy is. Use the radio.'

'What do I tell the chief inspector? That you'll call him back?'

The mayor beckons for the phone and takes the call with infectious bonhomie.

'Chief Inspector Selton, it's a pleasure to talk to you.'

Early the next morning, Luiz Claudio leaves his apartment building with a security guard providing cover. They're both wearing gym clothes. They are met by Inspector Lucas, who's standing in front of two unmarked police cars with only the drivers inside. Standing around Lucas are five security guards dressed in black. As Lucas told me later, the mayor's first reaction upon seeing them was to laugh:

'Man, what's this? Have you lost it altogether? When we spoke yesterday, I figured it'd be something more discreet.'

He greets the detail, shaking each guard's hand in turn. Lucas protests:

'No point in taking risks, Mr Mayor.'

'Lucas, it's over the top. It's just not my style. How's it going to look, me jogging with the whole elite squad behind me?'

Taking the mayor to one side and speaking in a low voice, Lucas says:

'The colleague of mine who was on the wiretap last night tells me that the attack is going to be today. Two arrests are being made as we speak. If they spill —'

Luiz Claudio feels the impact. He looks around him, looks up, as if counting the number of floors in the building. He's rattled.

'Attack? What sort of attack?'

'An attempt on your life, but we don't know how.'

'A bomb, at the office?'

'We've got some good people over there sweeping the place.'

'What about here, at home?'

'We're putting you under round-the-clock protection.'

'Clara and the kids have left town, as you recommended.'

'The people behind the hit have probably chosen now as a good time because there'll be thousands of possible suspects.'

'The people I dismissed.'

'Or their families, the councillors who appointed them, the list goes on. If you wanted to throw the cops a truckload of red herrings, this would be the time to do it.'

'So they'd just be red herrings? Is that what you're saying? The run's off today. I'm going to get dressed.'

In the mayor's car, the driver and a security guard sit up front and Luiz Claudio and Lucas in the back. The traffic is heavy-going, especially for a convoy of four. A motorbike zooms toward them at speed. Lucas is trying to stay calm, but his paranoid eyes are shifting about, expecting an attack at any moment.

'If they shoot up the car, we're done for, Lucas. It's not bullet-proof.'

'I know. Look, we've got a good team on this. Everyone's got their eyes peeled.'

A run-down ambulance overtakes several cars, but it's unceremoniously cut off by the last car in the security convoy, which takes a bit of a hit, triggering a cacophony of screeching brakes and honking. The ensuing blockage allows the lead cars to put some distance between them and the possible threat. When the ambulance does get back on track, it careers away down another route, leaving its intentions an unanswerable question.

The mayor tries to follow the ambulance situation through the dark windows of the official car. He breaks the silence:

'We could have put lives at risk here.'

'Or we might have saved the life of someone at risk.'

'That ambulance is a disgrace. It's falling apart. It's a deathtrap.'

'Municipal?'

'Afraid so. It belongs to our hospital. The shame of it.'

'You just took office, sir. There hasn't been time yet. The people understand that.'

'Maybe, until they find out we've just sent back ten brand-new ambulances and two mobile ICUs . . .'

'Sent back?'

'Prices were padded for kickbacks. Lucas, did you know that health is the biggest hive of corruption?'

'This process of sending stuff back, have you —?'

Lucas stops mid-question and leans forward, watching like a hawk. The mayor continues:

'Dr Sérgio blew the lid off a real cesspit. A national scandal.'

'How many people were involved?'

'Hard to say, but we're talking three hundred and something municipalities nationwide, plus Congressmen, people at the Health Ministry.'

'What about here, in the city?'

'The former hospital director, for one.'

'Is anyone in the group associated with Aureliano Bernardes?'

'Don't know. Couldn't say.'

Lucas pulls a little notebook out of his pocket and avidly flicks through the pages. Luiz Claudio remembers one name:

'The funding came from a congressional amendment proposed by Ivo Cury.'

'I don't know him . . . No, wait. Yes I do. He was at the demonstration in front of City Hall.'

'His father was a chief inspector who led extermination squads back in the 1980s. Before that he was a member of the dictatorship's counter-intelligence unit in the 1970s. He was also the founder of the most powerful militia in the Baixada and West Zone of the capital.'

'Christ, what a CV.'

'Curriculum mortis. What was the surname, Lucas?'

'What was the son's surname?'

'Ivo Cury Lízio.'

'Chief Inspector Lízio.'

'Romano Lízio.'

'That's it, Mr Mayor. Chief Inspector Romano Lízio. He was Aureliano's head of security.'

'Who do you think funds Ivo's campaigns?'

'Sérgio is . . . you mentioned a name . . . Sérgio?'

'The hospital director.'

'Who takes care of his security?'

'Are you kidding?'

'Like yours? Worse?'

Luiz Claudio, looking every bit as anxious – practically desperate – as Lucas, moves for his phone. Lucas completes his reasoning:

'I may have made a mistake. Mr Mayor, call —'

Luiz Claudio is already on the phone, waiting to hear Sérgio's voice on the other end. The mayor thinks out loud:

'No answer. Sérgio, pick up.'

'At this time of day, where'd . . .'

At that very moment Sérgio is driving down a quiet two-lane, one-way road. His windows are closed, the air conditioning is on and classical music is blaring out of the stereo. He's driving in the left lane, and there's a motorbike with two men in black leathers and black helmets tailing him. Sérgio pays no heed. The road bends left up ahead.

Before they reach the bend, the man riding pillion pulls out a walkie-talkie and radios someone.

High up a lamp post, a man dressed in electrical company overalls copies on the radio and fiddles with some connections on a circuit board.

A hundred metres ahead, a green traffic light turns straight to red and stays that way. At the curb on the right lane, thirty metres before the traffic light, two more men, also dressed in black leathers and helmets, are waiting on another motorbike.

Sérgio, relaxed in his own mobile world, takes the bend. His cellphone starts flashing, but the music drowns out the ringtone. Sérgio rolls up at the red light. The bike that had been trailing him accelerates, runs the light and disappears. Sérgio is rapt in the music, and stares blankly at the red LEDs. The bike parked at the roadside comes up behind Sérgio's car, in the right-hand lane. The man riding pillion has a gun in his hand. Out of nowhere, a run-down old ambulance from the municipal hospital comes rattling up behind them, sirens wailing. The bikers look back and hesitate. The ambulance accelerates, filling up the right-hand lane and bearing down on the motorbike sliding up to Sérgio's passenger-seat window. The ambulance shows no sign of slowing.

Sérgio checks the rearview mirror and sees the ambulance approaching like a meteor and instinctively edges left to make room. The motorbike wobbles as the driver veers right to get out of the way – not out of solidarity, but to save his own skin. All this happens in a fraction of a second, the very fraction in which the gunman pulls the trigger.

The glass shatters and Sérgio feels a burning pain in his right arm, near the shoulder, as if scorched by a blowtorch. Instinctively he opens the door and throws himself out onto the ground, as more bullets drill into the car. It's only then it really hits him what's happening. The biker has no choice but to speed off, and is followed almost immediately by the wailing ambulance, which screams by, fully intending to run the red light. But it doesn't. It screeches to a halt in the middle of the crossroads, the driver having realized he's just driven through a shooting. People start running from all directions toward the man lying injured on the hard shoulder.

That night, in his hospital room, Sérgio comes to, hooked to a drip and all bandaged up. Standing around his bed are a doctor, a nurse, his wife Mariana, Lucas and the mayor.

Mariana caresses his forehead.

'It's OK, love. You'll be OK.'

Luiz Claudio takes his friend by the hand:

'It's all right, bro. Your wonderful team took great care of you, isn't that right Doctor? Dr Paulo Roberto is here with us. The gunman just hit you in the arm, thank God. This is Detective Lucas, my guardian angel. I'm going to lend him to you. You needn't worry about security. Lucas and his guys won't leave your side.'

In the hospital lobby, Lucas walks over to Manuela, who's waiting for him:

'Sérgio is out of danger.'

'Thank God.'

'Teixeira and Netinho were taken in.'

'Wow, Lucas, good news at last.'

'Wait. There's more. Don't celebrate just yet. The super-intendent decided they should be sent to a holding cell at the Military Police barracks, because they're Military Police.'

'That's crazy. They'll break out.'

'Why do you think they were sent there?'

'Why didn't you do something?'

'Chief Inspector Selton went berserk, called up God and all his friends, but nothing doing. The police are the devil's turf.'

Manuela is sleeping soundly in her comfortable home in Rio's South Zone. Her cellphone rings and takes a while to wake her. The fog finally lifts and she answers:

'It's five-thirty in the morning, Lucas. What's up? You're kidding. They didn't even spend twenty-four hours behind bars. I'll put it on the newspaper website. Thanks, OK? Are you still at the hospital?'

Six a.m. and Lucas practically hasn't slept. Summoned by his superior, he heads to the police station in downtown Rio. He enters discreetly and makes for the chief inspector's office. Standing in front of an armoured door that would look more natural in a bank vault, he presses his thumb to the fingerprint reader, swipes his card and punches in the access code. The door opens majestically onto a high-tech oasis you would never imagine was ensconced in an otherwise worm-eaten building.

Chief Inspector Selton is sitting with his back to the door, in the middle of the round room. Beside him, two detectives man the eight-monitor station that controls the geo-referencing system. The chief inspector is observing a large central monitor. Without looking back at Lucas, he entones in his booming tenor voice:

'Look at this. My informant at the Military Police prison planted a micro GPS in Teixeira's clothing.'

With a laser pen, the chief inspector traces his route on the large electronic map up on the screen. Lucas asks:

'Have you followed his full trajectory since escape, sir?'

'Judging by the increase in velocity, we know the exact moment he entered a vehicle after breaking out of the barracks.'

'Were we able to pull photos of the area from the Traffic Department?'

'Have a seat, Lucas.'

Selton, still glued to the monitor, slaps the seat of a chair by his side.

'Sit, or you may have a nasty fall.'

Lucas does as he's told, while trying to guess what's coming:

'Was it a police car?'

'Not just any police car. Paulino, bring up the photo.'

The large screen fills up with the image of a Federal Highway Police vehicle.

Lucas mumbles:

'Fuck.'

'There's more. Otávio, show the satellite footage of the site where they are now.'

Selton aims his laser pen at the electronic map before it starts to zoom in on a suburban region near Avenida Brasil. Gradually, the image focuses enough to reveal a walled-in warehouse with tanker trucks coming and going at an incredible rate. As the zoom moves in, Selton narrates what he sees:

'Avenida Brasil, right there. Campo Grande on the other side . . . are you getting your bearings?'

The site is a bizarre mixture of an abandoned factory and heavy machinery depot, with a whole fleet of tankers and trucks. It's a hive of activity. The chief inspector asks:

'Do you know what this is? It's a fuel adulteration plant.'

'Is the place registered to anyone. A front?'

The chief inspector changes his glasses and reads from a printout.

'The Evangelical Church of Eternal Rebirth. Registered to Etelvino Lins and Aírton Neves. Etelvino Lins is the father-in-law of one Inspector Sarmento, Superintendent of the Rio de Janeiro division of the Federal Highway Police. We know nothing about this Aírton Neves.'

'So let's raid the police and bag the lot of them.'

'Easy, Lucas. This is just the tip of the iceberg. The monster's got to be a whole lot bigger. This is just the tail. We'll hit them when the time is right.'

Early the following night, at his office, Mayor Luiz Claudio says to Sérgio, recently released from his bandages:

'That's not it, for the love of God.'

'I know, I'm just kidding. But I think it's too soon. We've just got started.'

'It's all here, in your report: three hundred and forty-seven new protocols formulated and implanted. Training of personnel for the application of new methods and procedures in each area of the hospital – fully complete. It's a revolution, Sérgio.'

'First steps.'

'You've outgrown Morro Agudo. The party needs you to govern Brazil. It's not just me who's saying it. Remember?'

'A little praise from João Daniel. That's all.'

'You don't know João.'

'Of course I do. I greatly admire him. The guy led the resistance during the dictatorship. He went through hell and high water with the utmost dignity. Between you and me, he's bigger than Pedro Raimundo.'

'He thinks so too, that's the problem.'

'Pedro is the charisma. João Daniel, the organization, the brains and the strategy.'

'But it's Pedro who speaks to the soul of the people.'

'They complement each other.'

'If only, Dr Sérgio. That's just pretty packaging, a front for the faithful. In truth, they hate each other. Pedro will throw João on the fire the first chance he gets. Want to bet? But first he has to win the election. And to do that, he needs João. And you.'

'Are you saying I've just joined a pit of vipers?'

'Don't play stupid, Sérgio. You don't have a stupid bone in your body. Your discharge will be in the *Official Gazette* tomorrow, then you'll be free to devote all your energies to the campaign. Welcome to the dog-eat-dog world of politics.'

Sérgio hugs Luiz Claudio and turns to leave. The mayor calls to him just as he reaches the door.

'You be careful, now. Remember our plan: goal number three, don't die.'

'Look who's talking. Lucas told me you dispensed with the security detail he put together for you.'

'What, that mini-army? No thanks. No need to worry, though. The last thing our enemies want to do now is draw more police and press attention to Morro Agudo. Despite it all, brother, despite it all, we keep on going. What was that line from Brecht you said the other day?'

'It's from the end of *The Good Person of Szechwan*: "As you have seen, there is no solution. But there has to be."'

Luiz Claudio raises his coffee cup. A toast to the future.

It's About Too Many Things to Fit In

On the afternoon of 20 June 2013, I interviewed Dulce Pandolfi for the second time for the chapter on her life, perhaps the most fitting illustration of what Rio de Janeiro had been like under the dictatorship, and to what extent human dignity had been dragged through the mud in our tropical paradise.

The Rio branch of the Getúlio Vargas Foundation overlooks Botafogo beach. The Centre for Contemporary Historical Research and Documentation (CPDOC), where Dulce works, occupies the fourteenth floor. As I was waiting in the foyer, before the interview, I realized that Oscar Niemeyer, the architect who designed the building, had put one over on us yet again. The genius permitted himself certain liberties, one of which was this: to frustrate any expectations the occupants may have entertained that they'd be privy to one of the most dazzling natural landscapes in the world. Nothing stands between the building and that famous inlet at the foot of the Sugarloaf massif, not a single thing to spoil the view. But the great architect, like some mischievous or perhaps malicious conjurer, saw fit to shunt all the building's windows to its flanks, effectively ignoring the view and forcing its exuberance to take refuge in the imaginations of those working within a stone's throw of the sand. Architects like to play God, and they enjoy reinventing the landscape.

Dulce arrived a little late and apologized for keeping me waiting. I reminded her that if any apologies were due they were mine, for taking up so much of her time and making her rummage back through such traumatic memories. Like all good Brazilians with a window of opportunity – and cariocas are particularly guilty of this – we stopped off at the coffee shop before heading for the recording room. When we sat down before the microphones, the racket from an adjacent building site was registering as a dull thud through the studio's soundproofing. Beside the original Getúlio Vargas Foundation, where we were, an ultra-pretentious addendum was under rapid construction. Another Niemeyer design. The noise from the Foundation's flashy new building resonated at some subtle layer of mind, drawing out the connection between these two icons of Brazilian history: the architect and the dictator. I thought of Getúlio Vargas, the man who had ruled Brazil with an iron fist, who wrought major changes to the nation's economy and politics and who governed for nineteen whole years, from 1930 to 1945 and again from 1950 to 1954. These two modernizing heroes were associated with great transformations that left an indelible mark on twentieth-century Brazilian society: urbanization, industrialization and the inclusion of the urban workforce in the social compact through labour laws and social struggles. The link between the two said even more: Niemeyer had always been a champion of the Communist Party, with ties to Moscow, and it was this very party that allied with Vargas in 1945, despite the violent political repression he'd subjected it to. What bound them was intense nationalism and belief in State-induced economic development.

Vargas returned to power in 1950, this time by ballot, and he presided over the country in a relatively democratic manner until 1954. On 24 August that year he killed himself with a bullet in the chest in order to stave off an impending coup d'état. His suicide was his final political victory, an extreme gesture that would postpone the coup for another ten years. Niemeyer died on 5 December 2012, only ten days before his 105th birthday. Their lives were poles apart on many levels, but intimately linked by the modernist dream. While one cut his life short, the other became a walking symbol of longevity, a quality he extended to his work. Vargas laid the foundations of Brazilian industry. Niemeyer lent form to that historical process, moulding the monumental products of progress in his inimitable style. The next democratically elected president after Vargas was Juscelino Kubitschek who, inspired by his legacy, transferred the capital to the Midwest, raising Brasília out of the semi-arid wastes. The new city was to embody a modern Brazil, as if it were the picture and portent of its future. Kubitschek's partners in this mammoth endeavour were Lúcio Costa and Oscar Niemeyer. The Planalto, Alvorado, Justice and Foreign Office palaces, like Brasília Cathedral, the House of Representatives and the Senate, were concrete symbols of this new Brazil, the fruit of its people's ingenuity.

In parallel, Rio de Janeiro, though stripped of its capital status in 1960, continued to figure as the ultimate symbol of the nation. If Brasília was reason, competence and the triumph of construction over nature, Rio *was* nature. This symbolic equation was and remains so strong that even the attributes of the denizens of these two cities reflect their respective aptitudes. In Rio there's a natural talent for dance, a flair for music and the gift of the gab – the latter diverging into a morally ambivalent if not outright shady roguery on one side, and a warm and wholly virtuous sociability on the other. Looking at the world through this dichotomous and simplistic lens it becomes hard to see, for example, the solid presence of science in Rio. Few may realize that Rio is home to more research and academic institutes than anywhere else in the country. Chief among them is the Institute for Pure and Applied Mathematics (IMPA), whose alumni include the 2014 Fields Medal winner, Artur Ávila. Rio tends to be associated with Carnival, beautiful women, stunning landscapes and a Dionysian and festive vocation, but that's not the whole picture. These are clichés born of a certain machismo, prejudice, myth-making and image-peddling to bring the tourists in and boost popular morale, chipped away at day after day by constant violence and abiding inequality. But then, doesn't every cliché possess its grain of truth?

In the studio, sounds from wildly different sources mingled over the microphones. On one hand was Dulce's voice, that of an individual once crushed by the authoritarian omnipotence of the State. On the other was the music of 'progress' – the metronomic clanging of piles on stone, the scream of matter in mid-transformation. We were rummaging through the past while outside, on an adjacent plot, the future was beginning to sprout. In my mind's eye I saw the green and yellow flag, flapping on the effigies of Vargas and Niemeyer, overlap with the rags of barbarity, with rolled-up shirtsleeves spattered with blood. The words on the

Brazilian flag read 'Order and Progress'. Dulce's story shows the price paid for the order that allowed the progress to be made and which hand-picked its beneficiaries. During the dictatorship, the beneficiaries were few. Never had the nation been so unequal.

Dulce spoke for roughly two and a half hours. The last few minutes were the hardest. She had reached 9.30 on that fateful evening of 13 August 1970, when twenty armed men stormed her apartment and hauled her off, cuffed and hooded, to the army's torture rooms in the bowels of the Rio barracks. Where at only twenty-one years of age she had been introduced to the infamous purple room, desperately trying to figure out a strategy while the henchmen prepared the day's supplications. I couldn't bear to hear about them, and she didn't want to remember them. I asked if we could stop there and she asked to stop there, as her eyes welled with tears. I felt ashamed, not only for being unable to contain myself but for having put her through that.

I handed her a cup of water and she drank it. The silence was filled with practical matters, as I put away my notepad and asked how we'd arrange to have the recordings sent. I thanked her again, and promised to call to schedule the next meeting. As it happens, it was 5 p.m., the time the demonstration was due to start on Presidente Vargas Avenue. Vargas. Coincidence?

'Won't you come with me, Dulce?' 'I'd love to,' she said, but her trauma had its after-effects: agoraphobia was one. She felt uncomfortable and breathless in a crowd.

Our goodbyes were brief. I had to get out of there because I couldn't shake off her description of prison. We'd stopped at the Doi-Codi torture chamber, the purple room, the first electric shocks. It was harrowing enough.

She walked me to the lift and went back to work. She still had some business to attend to. I made for the nearest subway station, in Flamengo. I walked in a daze, paying no heed to place, traffic, pedestrians. How was I to reconcile the hatred I felt with my pacifist principles? Beside me two couples were exchanging placards and laughing at the slogans on them, excitedly scurrying as if late for a party. I ducked into a café and ordered a coffee so I'd be able to use the toilet. I closed myself inside the cubicle and gave in to the pent-up emotion. At that moment I felt I would never be able to write Dulce's story. I went back to the counter, where I drank my cold coffee. I ordered a bottle of water and watched the movement outside. I decided to stay put until I was sure I was composed enough to continue on my walk to the station. Some students filed by on their way to the demo, their shirts scrawled with words. They were shouting, and other shouts came in response: an exchange of slogans against the police and the politicians. Some of their refrains sounded aggressive: rhymed zingers embroiling the mayor and the governor in a couplet of invective. The atmosphere and vocabulary was Derby Day through and through, Cup Final frisson. Outside, a group of guys and girls replete with gothic tattoos and piercings, dressed in black T-shirts and black knee-length trousers, walked by in silence, exuding a hieratic pride that had a certain beauty to it. I studied the two girls bringing up the rear. They must have been fifteen or less. I pulled my notepad from my bag – I organize my mind better when I write – opened the pages and tried to find the tone to suit what I wanted to say:

'The loveliest woman of her generation turns sixty-five on 14 December 2013. Her name is Dulce Pandolfi. She's a lecturer and researcher at CPDOC, a department of the Getúlio Vargas Foundation, one of the leading academic institutions in Rio de Janeiro. She came down from Recife at the age of twenty-one to join the revolution. Her story has always been taboo: too harrowing to tell, as there'd be no gauging the emotions it might spark. To pry into it would be an invasion of privacy. That's why I've been putting off this interview since I first met her in 1973. I never dared ask her for the details of what happened to her. A general sketch was enough. However, she decided to collaborate with the Truth Commission set up by the Rio Bar Association and wrote out a deposition that was brave and moving, if scant on detail. "I knew I wouldn't be able to say it," she told me, "that's why I decided to write it down." Her discreet account, with neither description nor adjectives, was devastating all the same. The door was open for that interview I'd been putting off for forty years. Twelve whole hours of conversation spread across four meetings. I must admit that these encounters took more out of me than the hundreds of interviews I'd conducted throughout my professional life. I know the best interviewer is the one who disappears from view, lets the interviewee occupy the space, but here, in this case, some background on the relationship established during that dialogue is warranted, for reasons I will explain over the course of the chapter.'

Writing at the marble-top table of that little café, I realized that my emotional response had to be a part of that story. The conclusion had the odd and calming effect of providing something in Dulce's biography that could dock into my personal disquiet, my narrative perspective and the history of Rio de Janeiro, in its public and private facets. The sombre, violent Rio of the catacombs contrasted so starkly with the solar enchantment and idealized hedonism. I was now convinced that, in order to breach the boundaries between these two dimensions, the book would have to incorporate a confessional voice, which meant, naturally, and whenever possible, a first-person narrative.

I paid the bill and went back onto the street.

It was nearly six in the evening. I headed for the subway, figuring that the demonstration would have begun by now, even if it's hard to tell when such things begin or end. This was to be the third demonstration in Rio that June, and it was leaderless, largely organized over the social networks. The original touch-paper had been a proposed twenty-cent increase in public transport fares, but after the first march was dispersed by riot police using rubber bullets, pepper spray and tear gas, the backlash against police violence came to the fore. Other agendas joined in, demanding an end to old-school politics and to the multi-billion-dollar splurges on mega-events, namely the World Cup and Olympics. There were an untold number of other denunciations and demands, varying from protester to protester, and that was what made it all really new. Every individual there felt free to take to the streets to issue his or her own slogan or battle cry.

After the first two demonstrations, journalists, politicians and social scientists took to blogs, sites and TV to punt their ideas on the events. On 17 June, a Monday, Rio surpassed São Paulo by drawing 100,000 people downtown to Rio Branco Avenue. São Paulo had staged demos that had gradually swollen in size. After the first protest, which gathered some 10,000 people, the media had urged the government to come down hard and restore order. Two days later, 30,000 protesters suffered all manner of brutality at the hands of São Paulo riot police and, ironically, the worst hit were journalists. The number of serious casualties, the savagery of the police and the mayhem of the situation led those same media to change their tune, start criticizing the government and look upon the protesters with more sympathetic eyes. The 17 June demonstration in Rio ended in chaos. Faced with the lack of precedent, interpretations of it were as diverse as they were conflicting: for some the movement was right-wing, it was fascist; for others it was left-wing, it was anarchist; still others saw it as entirely depoliticized, against everyone and everything, led by infiltrators serving this or that interest, against the Federal Government, against the conventional media, and so on.

I published a piece in *O Globo* newspaper in which I called for the analysts and punters to surrender to their ignorance. It was better humbly and patiently to accept one's perplexity before that formidable, disturbing, exhilarating and wholly unprecedented state of affairs than to try to fit round pegs into square holes that served no other end than to show what the demonstrations were not: they were not organized, they had no chain of command or fixed agenda, they had no ties to any political party or union, and they were not targeting any clear goals set by general consensus. So what was the point in listing what these protests were not and did not have? They were happening and, as events, had certain identifiable properties, characteristics, a modus operandi. It was time to set the discourse on its head and actually describe what was going on with an open spirit, observing rather than judging with an arsenal of old concepts. I ended my article exhorting readers to go and join the demonstrations to see for themselves, first-hand.

Pro-government columnists with ties to the PT (Workers' Party), in power since 2003, couldn't get their heads around it: why are the masses taking to the streets now, if inequality has decreased in Brazil over the last decade, like never before? Why this tidal wave of unrest now? The conservatives had to be behind it, they concluded. But to me it was obvious: misery doesn't spur anyone to fight for his or her rights. Indigence generates only depression and apathy. Where hunger and unemployment reign, information about rights doesn't even filter through. Demonstrations only tend to happen when quality of life improves and people realize that it could be better still or that they stand to lose the ground they've gained. Better access to education also teaches people that everyone is equal before the law, that we are all citizens and that if there is a lack of equity in access to rights and justice it is because something is wrong and needs to be fixed. What's more, it shows that the solution requires their participation. So much has been said about citizenship in Brazil since the promulgation of the new Constitution in 1988 that people actually started to believe in it, especially when the pretty terms trotted out in government propaganda and in the classroom started to correspond, at least in part, to everyday experience. The active citizenry the sociologists love to bang on about was gradually seeping into society's vernacular, its practice, even in the slums and shanty towns.

Flamengo subway station was packed, as it always is at rush hour. I decided I'd get off at Uruguaiana, near Vargas Avenue, the meeting point. More and more people boarded at subsequent stations, and it soon became clear that the vast majority were on their way to the same destination. We flocked off the train at Uruguaiana, and as we poured toward the narrow flight of steps leading up to the exit the group compacted, cramming us all in like sardines. There was no way of avoiding physical contact. At times I even felt my feet lift off the ground. Resistance was futile. I decided to relax and get carried along by that human wave, limiting my movements to avoiding walls and handrails. Some people called for calm, shouting 'Easy, take it easy,' while others chimed in with derisory chants against the governor. One group of friends started some inside banter. One guy exclaimed in an intentionally loud voice that he reckoned his friend, stuck in the ruck further up the steps, was enjoying the proximity with all those athletic young men. A retort came from down the back, with someone shouting that it was time Brazil quit with the homophobia: 'Enough of the dumb-ass gay jokes.' Other voices were raised in support, until one joker provoked general laughter, bleating: 'Cure me, cure me. Can't anybody cure me?' It was a reference to a Bill presented by the evangelical right-wing bloc at

Congress which, if passed into law, would have authorized psychologists to offer the so-called 'gay cure' among their regular services. It was a blatantly homophobic supposition that associated homosexuality with mental illness. The Bill was rejected, but it caused a real stir all the same. When we were practically spat out of the subway on the crest of a collective impulse, the provocations gave way to slogans and chants: 'Come down into the streets, come on down into the streets.'

On Uruguaiana Street I took a deep breath and stuck my arm through the second strap of my satchel. I couldn't see further than a few dozen metres. The online rallying call had obviously worked, but then Uruguaiana is a relatively narrow road. Vargas Avenue, at ninety-odd metres across and just over three kilometres long (between Candalária Church and City Hall), was another matter entirely, and would probably swallow the tidal wave of people like a drop in the ocean. As I saw it, as soon as we turned onto Vargas, that crowd would break up into a harmless archipelago of dwindling islands. Or so I thought.

I proceeded with difficulty toward the avenue. I met some colleagues and students from the Federal University along the way, but I soon realized that the cast was varied and spanned the whole social spectrum. It was a first impression that would be borne out over the hours to come. The crowd was mostly young, as you'd expect, but there were men and women of all ages and backgrounds. In short, this didn't look like your typical white middle-class tantrum. When I got onto Vargas Avenue I climbed up on a concrete bench, stood on tiptoe and raised my arm as high as I could to take a picture of the sprawl. The throng was impressive, and had a powerful effect: the emotions exorcized at the café flooded back with a vengeance.

The flow carried me toward the north end of the avenue, where City Hall is. It was getting dark fast, and the copper sky, studded with the glow of street lamps, was being sliced by glancing shafts of spotlight from the helicopters. All sound was swept up in the cacophony of chants, except when one particular refrain caught on and was intoned in unison. Hundreds of youths took obvious enjoyment from waving their placards and flipping the bird at the chopper overhead, which was bombarded with anti-media chants. Someone passing by in a faster-moving group yelled over: 'It's a police chopper, not the media.' The information spread. The gestures continued, but the abuse changed. The two groups were approaching from the right. Further on, to the left, I saw a cluster of people dressed in the colours of the national flag. They were singing a saccharine anthem that irritated the more politicized throng: 'I . . . am Brazilian, with great pride, and all my love, oh, oh, oh'. Booing sounded from all directions and the nationalists soon clammed up. I tried to follow a group that was marching and chanting beneath a banner that read 'Evangelicals for free fare'. They were held in formation by a rope cordon. It was hard to stick to any course because the crowd kept heaving, sometimes in different directions at once. There was no point in even trying to sidewind.

A snack vendor who had probably figured he'd make a killing peddling to hungry, thirsty protesters was being bounced around in the throng, clutching his cooler for dear life and trying to find a way out. He wasn't going to earn a cent in there and he knew it, and was beginning to attract some invective too, which, as far as I could make out, went more or less like this:

'Join us, you're one of us; don't pretend you're just here to sell stuff. Don't come here looking to make a bit of money where we burn profit at the stake. Stop posing as a spectator, we're here to set fire to capitalism.'

'He's just a worker,' says another, trying to defuse the situation.

'Even more reason for him to take this seriously.'

'The guy's just doing his job.'

'This parasite's taking the piss. Revolution isn't a picnic. This is no Sunday at the beach, no game of football. Either you join us or beat it.'

'For fuck's sake, let the man work.'

Pushing and shoving starts, and the crowd bears down. The snack vendor withdraws with his tail between his legs.

The slogans on T-shirts and placards make for an endless array: 'Fare Free'; 'No to Fare Hike'; 'Love is not an illness'; 'You can cure prejudice, but not love'; 'Homophobia is a crime'; 'Come out of the closet and onto the street'; 'Love is worthwhile whatever the form'; 'Police for those who need them'; 'Demilitarization Now'; 'Disband the Military Police'; 'Scrap the MP'; 'Join the Marijuana March'; 'Legalize'; 'Prohibition of drugs = criminalization of poverty'; 'Viva Slut Walk'; 'My Body My Rules'; 'Zero Intolerance'; 'End the violence: Afro-Brazilian religions deserve respect'; 'It's not about the 20 cents. It's about too many things to fit on this placard'; 'No to relocations'; 'Rio does not belong to the developers, it belongs to us'; 'Out with the governor'; 'We have football. Korea has education. Let's swap?'; 'I want Fifa-standard healthcare'; 'Fifa go home'; 'Fuck Fifa'. A tall man dressed up as an Orthodox Jew was waving a sign that read: 'It is about the 20 cents'.

Along Vargas Avenue there are quite a few commercial office buildings and state institutions. When the front of the column was already approaching City Hall, at the far end of the street a few thousand protesters were still at Candalária Church. You could see this online in the coverage posted by live-streamers down on the asphalt and in the traditional media. The cellphone was a tool that broadened the protesters' reach, or at least it did until the signal crashed. At the height of the tension, and for about an hour after that, nobody on the avenue was able to send messages or access the internet. Coincidence? Traffic overload? Political intervention? I did what I could to pick up the pace en route to City Hall, but it was hard going. The sheer density of the crowd kept all movement to a medium tempo. As we passed below buildings where workers were still busy, the crowd chanted 'Come down into the street, come down,' and the lights in the office windows started flickering on and off in a show of solidarity. Mutually encouraged, the chorus in the street below and the flickering lights in the buildings above grew in equal intensity.

On the right side of Vargas Avenue for those looking north, a ripple of panic shot through the crowd, indicating that something was wrong. Strident shouting and the sound of crunching metal broke through the wall of noise rising from the thousands-strong crowd. I climbed up the steps of a footbridge to see what was going on. Lots of others had the same idea at the same time. Nothing down there was individual or solitary in any real sense. Squashed up against the grid along with hordes of others, I could see some black-clad figures attacking shop-front shutters with sticks, iron bars and the like. I don't know if they were actually trying to cause material damage or if it was just a crude way of adding to the general cacophony, and I couldn't make out the names of the companies or institutions they were attacking, which may or may not have been targeted. The undulations in the crowd sent people spilling in all directions. Gradually, and then more rapidly, like a house of cards that implodes layer after layer in ever-quicker succession, the crowd closer to the door-smashing started yelling 'No violence, no violence, no violence,' and the cry rippled outward, eventually reaching my neighbours on the footbridge, who cupped their hands around their mouths and shouted themselves hoarse. The 'black-blocs', as these rioters are known, had rolled out aspects of their repertoire at earlier demonstrations, but this was their grand debut at one of the largest street protests in the country's political history. I know, because I've been at every single one since 1968.

From up on the footbridge, just over one and a half kilometres from Candalária, I gazed across Vargas Avenue, entirely taken over by the crowd. There can't have been fewer than a million people there. I couldn't get Dulce's account out of my mind. The multitude, seen from above, was like a gleaming, undulating lawn. Were the torturers who had not succumbed to age and guilt now having dinner? Were they glued to their TVs, gobsmacked, watching an empowered citizenry flex its muscles? A million people, who could ever have imagined that? The long procession flickered with cellphone flashes. Guilt? They don't feel guilt, I thought to myself. I sincerely doubt any of Dulce's tormenters lose a wink of sleep or ever wake from nightmares of the dragon's chair in the middle of the purple room. The kids there on the avenue hadn't a clue what the restoration of democracy meant to my generation. And they're right, I said to myself; they're right to want more, to demand more, to refuse to settle.

Images of 1984 sprang to mind. April 10, a Tuesday. By early afternoon, 800,000 people had already amassed. By the time the last speaker had finished, the crowd had swelled to 1,100,000, all shouting, over and over, 'Direct elections now.' It was a different context back then, but the surge of collective vitality was the same. The political leaders who opposed the dictatorship, many of them only newly returned from exile thanks to the amnesty, called a rally and addressed the crowd from a huge stage erected in front of Candalária Church. They were all there for one and the same reason: to demand direct elections. Or so we were led to believe. A direct vote was hardly in some of their interests, but that's another matter. Back then, electing a president by direct vote was synonymous with freedom, the end of censorship, the imminence of a constitutional assembly. When I walked onto Vargas Avenue in April 1984, night had not yet fallen. The experience of June 2013 was just as moving. The sea of bodies seemed to go on for ever, and it assimilated differences of opinion, ideological nuances, modulations of sensibility, individual beliefs, different ages, different origins.

On 10 April 1984 I was exhausted. I'd had as much as I could take of the authoritarian regime. The dictatorship had desiccated two-thirds of my life. From 1964 to 1984, all we had had was twenty years of fear and censorship. All my energies had gone into the underground resistance, my youth had consumed itself in the shadow of imprisonment, in news of comrades broken by torture, murdered or disappeared. In the martyrdom of countless Dulces. I wanted to see all the political parties legalized. I was drained, but that world of people I met out there on Vargas Avenue blew away the tiredness of my thirty years, and any possible superfluity that might separate me from whomever was at my side, craning their necks with me to catch a glimpse of the speakers. It was a good sound.

When night fell and the political stars lit up the stage, and the most popular singers and artists came up to join them, we all sang the national anthem together, with Fafá de Belém at the microphone, and the multitude singing a cappella – 1,100,000 voices. Brizola and Ulysses Guimarães were there. The future presidents Tancredo Neves, Itamar Franco, Fernando Henrique and Lula were there too. Half a century of history went into the largest street rally the country had ever seen. The famous 'direct elections' march in Rio de Janeiro has never been equalled and, until 20 June 2013, nothing had even come close. The Dante de Oliveira amendment, which proposed direct elections, was rejected by Congress on 25 April 1984. It needed 320 votes to pass. It obtained 298. Even so, the pressure paved the way for

successive democratic advances that culminated in the in-
direct election of Tancredo Neves, the administration of
the vice-president who replaced him after his death, José
Sarney, and the convening of a Constituent Assembly and
promulgation of the new Constitution in 1988.

The footbridge started to shake. My daydream dissipated.
The grid began to buckle when those on their way down
met the crowd trying to push their way up. The result was
an angry coagulation, a pile of bodies crushed into a stale-
mate. Sensing the onset of panic – and I felt it growing
myself, seeing the potential dangers of the situation – the
people trying to climb down the steps started shouting 'Go
back, go back down', and followed the shouting with the
rather more convincing argument of sheer weight with
gravity on its side. We won. We scrummed our way out of
trouble.

I tried to quicken my step and came across all sorts along
the way: whole families, solitary roamers like myself, live-
streamers interviewing protesters and posting it all in
near-realtime, bell-ringing Hare Krishnas in flapping robes,
theatre troupes from the Fluminense lowlands dressed up as
political mafia and waving placards in support of the fare-free
movement, and hundreds, tens of hundreds if not thousands
of people with Anonymous masks hanging round their
necks, or pushed up onto their foreheads, or still covering
their faces.

The Carnival spirit reared its head here and there, but
withdrew before the stampede, recoiled at the drum roll
and fled when the bombs started going off. In fact, the

explosions and stampedes were growing closer and more frequent. The atmosphere was becoming denser, heavier, bloated by a vague but growing fear. Here and there the refrain returned in bouts: 'No violence, no violence,' and it rippled and gained momentum. The chorus was accompanied by a reaction adopted by everyone within a 300-metre radius: we would all just sit down. It was a way of containing the erratic flurries that were beginning to seed disorder, causing the first signs of panic. If we didn't resist, the herd was likely to break loose in all directions, causing chaos. After each sit-down, pockets of people would start standing up, and then dozens and hundreds, until we were all clambering to our feet, taking our lead from those around us. Ranks closed, the mass would proceed. It was only natural that the crowd would pack tighter after each interruption, as those down the back pushed into the barrier of bodies grinding to a halt before them. I tried to wriggle my way into some space, somewhere I could take a breather, manage to turn around and hold up my cellphone to take a picture. It was the only way I could get any idea of what was going on around me, 360 degrees. Another was to go online and look for live streaming transmissions from elsewhere in the crowd, or live images from electronic media channels. Internet was our roving eye until access was cut or, as I said before, user traffic crashed the servers. Let me insist on this: we never actually learned what caused that sudden, vast, collective solitude, but that was precisely what it felt like when I lost the internet and my phone went dead, and I realized the same had happened to everyone else around me.

I made the most of a brief clearing between two blocks of protesters and surged forward. I was less than 500 metres away from City Hall when the explosions started again. The riot police were dispersing the crowd with rubber bullets, smoke bombs, pepper spray and tear gas. There was nowhere to run. Flanking us and heading us off, the police were ready to repel any attempt at approach. Those in the front line were forced to turn and run, and that meant barging back into the crowd. Run is probably not the right verb, as it was more of an attempt at running. It was impossible to make any real headway through the wall of bodies, no matter how hard they tried. There was no co-ordination, no synchronicity that could have allowed those further back, and not directly affected by the police assault, somehow to assimilate those fleeing in panic. The scattering was pointless, sending people charging in all directions, gasping for air, their eyes red and swollen, some of them stumbling under rubber bullets, others pulling shirts up over their heads while inhaling vinegar – the more battle-hardened demonstrators carry a riot kit, full of effective remedies and protections against police weaponry. The result was a clash between those advancing and those trying to flee, and it sent shockwaves of panic spreading in centrifugal spasms. I suppose for someone watching from one of the helicopters it must have resembled gradually expanding concentric circles.

The cries of 'Don't run, don't run, don't run,' came first from a few, then from many, and finally from thousands. For those who bore the brunt of the stampede, it was a moment of despair. Though I tried to stay calm and clear-minded, as far as that was possible under the circumstances, and sought to weigh all the options with a modicum of common sense, I simply couldn't see any reasonable alternative other than to wait and hope for the best. Pray, even. Pray that the police would realize they were on the verge of causing a massacre; that the hundreds, maybe thousands up front would find some solution less counter-productive than panic and flight; pray that the masses further back would realize they had to stop and turn around, retreat to the Candalária in an orderly but sprightly fashion. We also had to hope that those blocking the streets parallel to Vargas Avenue had the good sense to pull out, allowing the main crowd to spring a few leaks. With so many variables, the overriding sensation was of total impotence. The worst part was seeing the elderly and pre-teens among us, many of them practically children. This wasn't a homogeneous group. Nobody in their right mind would expect a million people to disperse in a manner that was orderly or fast enough to avert disaster.

The lights on that part of the avenue kept flickering on and off. I sensed that an unstoppable avalanche was on its way. When the lights came back on, they lacked the same force as before, but it was enough to kindle some hope that we'd get out of there in one piece. Suddenly, the crowd before me tightened into compact nuclei, opening corridors like respiratory ducts in the vast organism we had formed. These openings were filled by people in flight, as if they were tunnels in a labyrinth. The ingenious solution adopted spontaneously by our huge collective body, governed by some invisible intelligence, helped but couldn't quite resolve the situation. Some of these clusters fell apart like so many staves in the wind. Others grasped and grabbed, pushed and shoved, fell over and got back up, swept on by the tide, propped up by solidarity, but totally disoriented. The dozens, hundreds, thousands of people separated from their groups came in my direction, ferreting for escape routes and heralding a flood.

At times like these, the instinct toward self-preservation kicks in and puts the right words in your mouth: 'Don't run, don't run.' Thousands of voices, tens of thousands speaking in unison spread this nugget of sound sense and injected a life-saving dose of reason into the herd we'd become: 'Don't run, don't run.' When I looked back, I saw that the rearguard had already turned and was retreating. If we were quick, everything would be OK. This new positive glimmer was contagious, winning over those who, like myself, had seen no way out only moments earlier. 'It's going to work,' some said as they walked. 'Easy people, keep it going, nice and easy. It's gonna be OK.' We spoke of calm, but moved as swiftly as possible. Mental flashes infused with indignation brought to mind the police brutality in shanty towns, the hundreds of extra-judicial executions that go on each year in Rio, without us taking to the streets because of them. But there we were now, and we were there for them too, to put an end to the ongoing massacre of underprivileged black youths.

I don't know how long the crisis point lasted, but it seemed like an eternity. I stopped thinking about the book, the history of Rio, about the government, the morally bankrupt parties, or even the political meaning of this milestone event. My consciousness was swirling toward the

plughole of survival. Noble values went up in smoke –
democracy, justice, human rights, participation. Suddenly
a new, less idealized street soul emerged: the rude soul of
things, stuck fast to the surface of the facts, the material
soul that fuses with our bodies. All that mattered was the
sweat, my throbbing feet, the panic, the gnawing thirst, the
pain running up and down my back, the hearing dampened
by the explosions and the bawling and screaming, my eyes
stinging from the cloud of pepper spray that came billowing in its target's wake, like some swelling, prodigious
ghost.

There we were: a rabble, a horde, a mob, a gang. The
black-blocs are my brothers, I wanted to say to whomever
would listen. The terror had instilled in me a new way of
regarding the experience I was beginning to emerge from.
The march was retracing its steps. Thousands were flowing
back toward the starting point at Candelária, or were slip-
ping away down side roads. Throughways began to open
across the vast avenue, leaving archipelagos where before
there had been riveted plates.

It was a long and arduous walk back, although the thin-
ning crowd made things easier. I decided to head for
Candelária, then take a right onto Passos, or Rio Branco,
further down. I thought I'd probably be able to find some
transport back to the South Zone on Rio Branco where it
meets the Flamengo landfill, by the shore. Walking from
there would mean I'd have covered ten kilometres since the
start of the protest. By that stage I'd have gladly taken whatever ride came along first – a bus, a subway, a cab. It wasn't
midnight yet, so I thought I might still be able to catch a

train, unless they'd closed the subway early for security reasons.

They had. The expression came to me quite naturally, and that made me reflect on what it meant. I hadn't said to myself that the service might have been closed, I'd said that *they* might have closed it. In other words, I'd attributed the suspended subway service to a hidden and powerful entity, some group with the authority to take such a decision. OK, it made sense under the circumstances, but that was not the case when the word 'they' was normally used – as it commonly is, especially in Rio – as a way of washing one's hands of responsibility and shifting the blame onto some murky cast of powerful others. And it's something we do daily, when faced with the most diverse situations. It's common to hear a cab driver, a neighbour, a colleague say, 'Look, it's been like that for ages and they don't do a thing about it. They couldn't care less. They don't want to know.' The problem in question could be a pothole, a spent street light, a badly run school, a dilapidated building, beggars in the street, a broken traffic light, a closed-down health centre, rising inflation, growing unemployment, precarious security, etc. It doesn't matter what the complaint is, whether it's major, minor, provincial, municipal, structural, federal. What strikes me as telling is the vague, shadowy, generic nature of the supposed culprit. Those to whom the blame is assigned are known only by the pronoun 'they'.

It wasn't the first time I'd wrestled with this turn of phrase, habit of mind and language, which sounded very much to me to indicate a remiss, evasive, individualistic behaviour that was averse to all responsibility. I'd sometimes provoke my interlocutors by asking: 'They who?' Nobody ever answered. I'd insist: the politicians? The powers that be? The authorities? The government? The elite? The rich? The ambiguous, stuttered response was always some variation on 'Yeah, that's it, them, they're them.' In other words, they're *others*. The 'others' are not like those who say 'they'. The others are remote, diluted in some diaphanous, untouchable, almost immaterial collectivity. If it's the others who do and undo as they please, then I am condemned to powerlessness. In principle, nothing outside the strictly private sphere concerns me. Seen from this perspective, public space is far from shared, far from belonging to one and all. Public space becomes a no man's land. That's why – my imaginary interlocutor will say – I don't see any harm in throwing litter on the street, because I don't feel co-responsible for what is going on around me. So there is really nothing to be done other than to look after oneself and one's own, and damn the rest. It is also perfectly justifiable for those wronged by the predatory 'they' to act exclusively in their own interests, regardless of rules or law.

So what is left to those who evoke the 'they' if they think and feel in this way? Besides a sense of powerlessness, and disdain for all things public, there is also the feeling of being a victim, and that eats away at self-esteem. What's left, then, is resentment. And an inaptitude to participate in society. What's left is a chronic inability to experience the 'we'. If 'they' are indefinite and vague, then there's no 'us' substantial enough to recognize.

Traditionally, demonstrations were organized around specific demands summed up on large banners raised at the head of the march. The slogan on the banner would then be fleshed out, in all its demands and positions, in speeches and announcements by the protesters' spokespeople. A lot went into that banner; it was the succinct result of a great number of proposals filtered through assemblies and meetings. These successive filters corresponded more or less to the tiers of leadership, and they ended when the core was reached. In other words, behind every slogan, every carefully worded banner, was a certain type of organization, a power structure that ran through the social movements, political parties and trade unions. To whom were these slogans and perorations directed? To the State and its occupants, to governments and to the legislature. The movement's general interlocutor, the addressee of its big block letters, was the State, and its message was received either through the media or directly.

To my right was Santana Fields, 155,200 square metres of wooded parkland encircled by railings. My musings on the pronoun 'we' and the darker underside of Rio culture were the direct result of what I saw there. The railings were plastered with overlapping posters and signs, stuck on and threaded between the bars, forming a magnificent open-air mural. As they left Vargas Avenue, the protesters had deposited their placards there like totems, offerings or lit candles on some profane altar. The park's perimeter runs for one and a half kilometres, so how many placards were there? My first impulse was to photograph that mosaic of words, as if it were an installation, a collective work in which the scrawls connected thousands of anonymous authors in a single unspooling text, enveloping that whole park. I contemplated that paper chain and drew comparisons with the Occupy sit-ins happening all over the world. What I saw in that toppled, horizontal Babel was a sort of fledgling occupation. With neither the nomadism of the march nor the sedentariness of the sit-ins, it was a symbolic demarcation of territory, perhaps stemming from a collective desire to retake the city, make it public again, save it from the voracity of business.

I wanted to photograph it, but I didn't have the strength left to do so, and perhaps it wouldn't have made any sense to try. It was a concatenation whose beauty resided precisely in its ephemerality, as with any happening. There were thousands upon thousands of placards, but what really mattered was the chain reaction triggered by the gesture of the first individual who decided to hang his or her placard there. Each sign deposited on the Santana railings was an act of co-operation with a seed action, which it replicated. The sheer volume of co-operative gestures demonstrated the enormous power of collaboration between individuals. No rules, no coercion were needed. No grammar organized the creation. No individual or entity dared claim legitimate authority over the mural, or purport to speak for the myriad desires it expressed, which could never have been conveyed by a single traditional banner. Right there was the 'we' that gets lost in the resentful, atrophying mythology of the 'they'.

Suddenly it all became clear, and so simple. On the one hand, the large, overarching banner of the traditional demonstration communicates succinct messages, refined through successive filters, and addressed to the Stare – the political and rational equivalent of that phantasmagoric other subsumed under the generic 'they'. Interestingly, those who took part in the 20 June demonstrations left behind a mural of customized placards addressed only to those willing to come close enough to read them. Their interlocutor was not the State or some greater other, but the other standing right next to them, a protester just like them, marching the same road. The personalized placard was an invitation to converse, to share, to forge a bond, to play the I off the you. A collectivity was in the process of forming, stimulating critical lucidity and the unconscious mind alike, rational discourse and its symbols, the political and existential vocabulary expressed in speech, writing, the body and collective choreographies. Perhaps the younger generation realized, without knowing it, that the construction of Brazilian society was a work in progress. Not everything depends on the State. Not all blame lies with the State, not everything is its fault or to its credit. An attitude that values co-responsibility saves the individual from impotence, resentment and victimhood. Individualism infused with liberating and creative possibilities and collectivity are not mutually exclusive. The propagation of a generous individuality could be the chance we need to reinvent collectivity in a more democratic and just light.

I opened the recorder app on my cellphone and said the following: anyone who tries to capture the demonstration of 20 June 2013 in a nutshell risks wasting what was perhaps most essential to it: its dispersiveness.

I was tired. I confess the exhaustion was more mental and emotional than physical. I decided it was time to forget about the book and about politics and go home. I'd taken

sufficient notes for the chapter I intended to write and had
made my contribution to the march by joining it. I could
relax now, switch off, maybe have a beer while waiting for
the crowd to thin out. After all, the demonstration had been
a success, even if its critics would question exactly how I
defined that. 'What did it aim to achieve?', they'll ask, 'And
did it achieve it?' I had no interest in measuring the march's
success in those terms, I'd reply, opportunely. It was time to
rest. Mission accomplished.

Far from it.

I decided to head for Passos Avenue. My cellphone signal
was back. Around me I saw lots of people walking alone, in
pairs or in groups, some in silence, others chatting excitedly,
unharried and unworried. I learned of episodes of police
violence against demonstrators as they left Vargas Avenue.
The activists had not attacked the police, nor had they van-
dalized any property, they were simply dispersing. They
fled the offensive in the direction of São Francisco Square
and hid at the Federal University. Some fellow lecturers
there later confirmed the details. The police seemed to be
lacking any chain of command or clear strategy. This flight
to the university would give rise to a group whose role
proved important over the course of the coming months.
The excessive use of force by the police led to interaction
between groups, creating new initiatives for the public
sphere. I learned that some bank branches had been damaged
by vandals in balaclavas. It was impossible to know whether
they were black-blocs, undercover police agents or delin-
quents hired by politicians to further their own nefarious
aims. There were all sorts of hypotheses.

I felt safe on Passos Avenue. The atmosphere was peaceful until the police cars turned up, gun barrels protruding through the lowered windows. The cops regarded the pedestrians with less than professional sneers. They were there to toy with us. All of a sudden smoke bombs loaded with tear gas exploded like real grenades. All hell broke loose around me as people scattered. I covered my face with my satchel and shirt and made a run for it myself. I got the impression that the noise and the chaos had precisely the effect the police had been looking for, creating the kind of tumult they could now respond to. Retrospectively, however crazy it sounds, they were causing turmoil in order to justify the kind of action by which that turmoil had been created in the first place. They were playing cat and mouse with us. In the blink of an eye calm turned to hate. Some of those among us, who had showed no inclination whatsoever toward vandalism before, took to kicking in shop fronts, shouting and yelling. They couldn't take their anger out on their sadistic aggressors so the metal shutters would have to do. Our revulsion stung like the pepper spray that gnawed at our eyes, lungs and throat.

I decided to cross left, avoiding São Francisco Square, and ran with a group of strangers over to Rio Branco and on to Cinelândia. There was barely time to stop for breath. I needed water and a toilet, but the bars and restaurants were shutting up shop. There was quite a crowd at Cinelândia, but no disorder, just protesters sharing their experiences, exchanging photos of police brutality and narrating events that would have sounded like exaggerations to me if I hadn't just witnessed something similar first-hand. I sat down for a bit on the steps of the City Council building, alongside some others. We spoke to strangers because we were united by the situation, especially by our repudiation of the police behaviour. Random detentions had been rare, but they were starting to become more frequent. Again police cars pulled up, spreading panic. They slowed down on Rio Branco Avenue, returned down the wrong side of the road, stopped on the corner outside the Municipal Theatre and hurled smoke bombs and tear gas grenades into the huddle of people. Shots rang out. It was as if the cops thought rubber bullets were playthings to be used liberally and without necessity. Despair and disorder followed. The police force was bringing on exactly what it is supposed to combat. The guardians of public safety were taking delight in provoking chaos and even more delight in quashing it by force.

We fled to Lapa, the bohemian centre of town. There were no police cars and some restaurants were still open, with people eating and drinking at tables out on the pavement. I went into the first restaurant, a modest but comfortable place, where I could find a vacant table. I had to drink something and rest before planning my route home – I had yet to see a single form of transport anywhere along the way, not even private cars.

I went online and saw some truly impressive scenes. The police violence had run to a far broader spectrum than the acts I had witnessed. There were some much more serious incidents. It's hard to overstate the role of the live-streamers, especially the so-called Ninja Media group, who had transmitted the whole demonstration live online from the thick of the action, but their participation would become even more important in the aftermath, as they followed the police to record their brutal hounding of the dispersing crowd. In addition to the militant reporters – social network activists armed only with cellphones – countless other individuals made vital contributions in recording and sharing scenes from the streets. Many acts of police brutality dispensed with explanations. These visual denunciations went viral, forcing the department to issue official statements which the images quickly debunked. Criticism of the conduct of the police was virtually a running commentary on the acts of brutality themselves, reaction following upon action within seconds.

I hadn't been in the restaurant for very long when the explosions started again, some distance away. But they grew closer and louder, and pretty soon it was bedlam outside and a cloud of tear gas was billowing against the window, blocking the view. Frightened people, shirts pulled up over their noses and mouths, heads down, came rushing into the restaurant. Some of them needed medical attention, and were promptly assisted by customers who seemed to know what they were doing. I waited for the smoke to clear, then paid the bill and left. The roads were still empty and the footpaths packed. But there was no tumult other than that caused by the police. I listened to people's accounts and asked some questions. It was the same story over and over: the cops were enjoying themselves hounding the public and terrorizing them with their grenades.

A police car rolled up and people scattered. I hid behind a tree so I could see what was going on in relative safety. About fifteen metres from where I stood I saw the police laughing and chatting before flinging two or three smoke bombs into two restaurants that were going about their legitimate business. The pavement tables were all empty by this stage, but the interiors were packed, especially one of them. The bombs are so loud they cause panic, even though their smoke is harmless. Mayhem broke out, and the tree couldn't protect me from the drifting gas so I had to run too, eyes closed, satchel and shirt covering my face as I tried to hold my breath. I didn't actually see the shooting, I only heard the gunshot. A guy took a rubber bullet in the shoulder just before the police car screeched away. He'd been dissing them and waving his arms around to signal that he was filming the whole thing.

I walked through Glória looking for some transport. On Catete Street, dozens of us marched in single file along the narrow pavements. There was no vandalism; in fact, we barely spoke as we made our exhausted way toward Machado Square, where we hoped to find a bus or cab. We heard more explosions further ahead, but we didn't retreat; we couldn't have, as a police car was tailing us at a distance. All of a sudden the car came screaming toward us and we bore the brunt of another by now routine smoke bomb and tear gas attack. Our only option was to spill down the side streets, but they were dangerous as we could easily get corralled. A haze of smoke hung over Machado Square, and we saw dozens of people pouring bottles of water over their heads to counteract the gas. Nobody knew what to do. All we wanted was to get home, but the police wouldn't let us. They kept circling, attacking, causing us to disperse and regroup. Supreme irony. According to the police commissioner interviewed on

TV the following day, Military Police interventions were made only to avoid depredations and break up crowds that posed a danger to property or to the physical integrity of the population.

I walked on, alone now, through Laranjeiras toward Cosme Velho. I'd covered twenty kilometres by that stage. Staying together put us at greater risk, as it was groups the police were looking for. That said, walking around alone was even riskier, as there was no telling what the police would do to the captured straggler. By lucky chance I saw a cab driving along a parallel street and managed to wave it down. The cabby took pity on this dishevelled protester, who reeked of tear gas and the milky stench of smoke bombs.

TV the following day. Militia's Police interventions were made to avoid depredations and ... crack up crowds that posed a danger to property and ... ... the integrity of the population.

... spilled out along now, through a banquet, forming a semi-vehicle towered foamy bloomers by taut wings ...

'Don't be Lazy'

Tony – Antonio Lemos Bisneto* – from Rio de Janeiro, was arrested in London on charges of conspiracy to import two tonnes of cocaine. After the longest criminal trial in modern British history – fourteen months in all – he was condemned to twenty-four years in jail. Having served a third of his time in Britain, he was allowed to do the rest back home in Brazil, where the sentence was commuted in accordance with more lenient national legislation.

Considered a dangerous criminal, Tony served eight years in a control unit at Britain's largest 'supermax' security prison, four of these in solitary confinement in what amounted to an impenetrable vault wrapped in an impregnable bunker. A jail within a prison. Maximum security is perhaps a euphemistic description of the regime to which Tony was consigned. At forty-minute intervals, day and night, a warden looked in through the hatch in the door to check on him and report briefly on his state and actions in a special journal. Typical entries would run something like: '9.00 a.m: the prisoner is sitting on the edge of the bed, with his face in his hands, staring at the wall'; '9.40 a.m: the prisoner is still sitting on the bed, staring at the wall'; '10.20 a.m: the prisoner is restless; pacing around in circles'.

* All names have been changed.

Deprived of his freedom, privacy, human contact and access to areas other than cramped, concrete enclosures, Tony found himself on the verge of madness. His weekly sun-time was taken in a narrow well with a retractable ceiling operated by a technician. His letters were read by the authorities, and so had to be translated first, which meant correspondence took months. He was moved about only when absolutely necessary, and a whole convoy had to be mustered for any excursion: two sedans and two SUVs escorted the armoured transporter in which he sat cuffed and shackled, with a helicopter providing aerial cover. In the rare event of inter-urban transit, the helicopter was replaced with a small plane, flying in circles overhead.

The Hedonist Dream and Nightmare of Drugs

Tony's involvement with drugs was gradual and started during his time as an economics student at a Rio university in the mid-1970s. After graduating, he embarked on a very successful career in the capital markets. With a mixture of luck and talent, and at a time that was particularly propitious to financial speculation in Brazil, Tony managed to amass a small fortune. His first, whirlwind marriage ended in divorce after six months, when he learned that his wife was cheating on him with his best friend. He'd lost his bride and best man in one fell swoop, but that wasn't all: he'd also lost his will and his way, the ground beneath his feet. He slumped into depression, tears and despair, and though he had his mother, Mila, to fall back on, maternal support alone was never going to be enough. Perhaps in an attempt to shirk maternal guilt, or occult some earlier root cause (which amounts to the same thing), to this day Mila blames her son's later problems on this romantic let-down. Tony took a month off and went travelling in Europe. He embarked in a suit and tie, but came back a tattooed, long-haired hippy in shorts. He'd really taken to the Age of Aquarius – now in its death throes – and realized that there was a lot more between heaven and earth than air travel, money, career and urban comforts. There were boats too, and seas to sail. There was sun, and pleasures to be had. A mapful of nautical adventures awaited him, so he bought himself a yacht and sailed the oceans on a couple of four-year expeditions. It was at one of his ports of call that he met Angelique, who became his second wife and was to be the mother of his two children, Ana and Michel, the loves of his life. To a roll of hedonistic pleasures that included sun-drenched sex, marijuana and hashish, he slowly, and sparingly at first, added cocaine and morphine.

Ten years later, back in Rio with a new wife and two kids, Tony suited up again for a second career as a movie producer. He cashed in the yacht and left his sailing days behind him. But not the drugs, one of which – morphine – took over his life and almost evicted him from it. It also drove him back into his past, where he picked up the thread of some dangerous connections.

One sunny afternoon at Rio's Gloria Marina, as he spent his lunch hour gazing at the constellation of yachts, imagining a future restored to the happiness that drugs had stolen from him, Tony heard someone call out his name. It was a voice he recognized. Gordon Wright, an old friend, fellow seafarer and party animal, was hailing him from the deck of a boat.

Wright, who spent his life sailing between the Caribbean, England and South Africa, called him aboard to show him the reason for his Rio visit: suitcases, travel bags and chests. He told him to open any one of them and take a peek. Dollars. Lots of dollars. Ten million of them, to be precise. Tony was stunned. All he could do was stare. Even in his halcyon days on the stock market he had never seen so much cash. His friend's mission was astoundingly simple: all he had to do was hand the bags over to whoever came calling and could tell him the exact amount of money contained in one of them. Wright planned to head to Cape Town as soon as the drop was made. In the meantime, there was something he wanted Tony to do for him, a favour for which he would pay in dollars: he needed a kilo of blow. Just a little souvenir for some South African mates.

Two days later, Tony turned up with the order. Gordon Wright was seasoned enough to sense that something was amiss. He excused himself for a moment and went to weigh the package. His suspicions were confirmed: Tony's delivery came up 250 grams short. Back on deck, he looked Tony straight in the eye but didn't say a word. He didn't have to. He knew his old Brazilian buddy would never pull something that rank unless there was a pretty cataclysmic reason. Tony squirmed. He'd never felt so ashamed in his life. He could not have imagined he'd sink that low, a petty thief and cheat, selling his soul for a measly quarter-kilo of coke. Gordon asked him if the problem was cocaine. Tony confessed: it was morphine. The sailor pulled a wad of

dollars out of his pouch and stuffed it into Tony's pocket.
'Your call,' he said. 'You can buy a plane ticket and come
spend some time with me in Cape Town, and let me help
you get clean, or you can riddle yourself with morphine.
Jab yourself to death. You choose.'

Tony chose both: he bought morphine and a plane ticket.
At the airport in South Africa, already missing his kids, he
dumped his stash in a toilet bowl and headed to Gordon's
place, where he went cold turkey. A month and a half later,
after sweating the venom, chewing his fingers off, damning
the world to hell, biting his lips till they bled and hurling
himself against every available wall – in short, having spewed
his soul, he emerged fourteen kilos lighter and white as a
sheet, but clean. He was morphine-free. Gordon Wright was
so proud of Tony's courage and the titanic effort he had
made to beat the habit that he offered to take him back to
Rio on his boat, where he would put him in touch with
someone very special – someone through whom he could
make more money than he had ever imagined. A few weeks
later, back in Rio, Tony was introduced to Albino, 'The
Ghost', and thus began his involvement in the international
drug-smuggling business.

Albino: A Network between London and the Amazon Rainforest

Albino came and went like a ghost. He was a master in the
art of disappearing. He wasn't just a stickler for security, he
was obsessed with it, and never emerged in person until he

was fully sure his associate hadn't been followed – which usually entailed a rigmarole of phone calls from a series of pay-phones, often miles apart. But a meeting with Albino was worth the hassle, patience and diligence, because it was a pleasure – and a very rewarding one at that. Among Tony's very tight circle, The Ghost was considered warm and kind, concerned for his associates' families and asking after each member by name. Better still, the friendly chit-chat was always a prelude to a tantalizing offer. Tony never did figure out The Ghost's nationality. Nobody knew anything of substance about the man – where he was from, where he went, how many drug routes he controlled, who his contacts were among the producers (plantations, kitchens, wholesale supply lines), moneymen and political stringpullers. He spoke English and Spanish like a native, so he could have been Mexican-American. On rare occasions, The Ghost made house calls. He'd turn up with flowers for the wife, wine for dinner and gifts for the kids. He was talkative and sweet, and then he'd disappear for years on end. The most striking thing about Albino was that he was, indeed, albino, which made his chameleonic vocation all the more puzzling. How could someone so apparently distinctive disappear in plain sight, without the slightest trace?

His routine was one of constant travel, and though certain destinations had to be revisited, the same route was rarely used twice. For example, he frequently had to go into the Colombian backlands to negotiate with the cartels. From what Tony was able to glean from Albino, these powwows were brief, and basically came down to a few dozen words, half a tonne of pure cocaine and £150 million.

Getting there was a near-oneiric peregrination that took him by plane out of Bogotá to Pasto, and from there to the foothills of the Galera volcano, where the cartel bosses were waiting for him.

The airport was a few dozen kilometres below the town, but still way above the cruising altitude of commercial flights crossing the Andes, weaving their way among the magnificent natural peaks. When the flight attendant announced that it was time to fasten seat belts and prepare for landing, the plane tilted 45 degrees upward and rose with engines at full throttle, then levelled out and came in slowly, checking the wind. The landing strip is basically that, a strip, running along a sliver of plateau perched on sheer bluffs overlooking an abyss. Albino's job was to get the cargo to its destination, distribute it to the dealers in return for payment, and get the money back to his Colombian suppliers, who controlled production and took care of the first leg of transportation, from the jungle to the coast. The cocaine was usually dropped into the ocean in twenty-kilo cigarette crates, which Albino's people fished out of the water.

Each departing flight cost the drug lords $US150,000. That was the toll charged by the military in control of the airstrips. The fee bought a single day's grace per week, so a lot rode on luck, as weather conditions in the jungle often made it impossible to land or take off. The cartels' planes were small and could only do 1,300-kilometre round trips, and as the airstrips were 160 kilometres inland they had to dump their load 500 kilometres out to sea at the very most. The drops were made on rough open ocean and the target was a stretch of water between Albino's group's boat and a raft drifting at a distance of roughly twenty metres. The planes would come in low and drop their payload in batches of three 500-gallon crates, which the crew of two aboard the raft would have to retrieve despite the chop and squall. Even if the drop was well placed, fishing the crates out was a task that required strength, courage and skill, but if the pilots missed their mark, scouring ocean waves for the bobbing boxes became a near-Herculean labour. After nine or ten drops, an average of twenty-five crates would be recovered, with a couple lost to the swell. Once they were stocked aboard ship, the boat would stop for provisions at a Caribbean island before sailing to its final destination, which was occasionally Miami, but, more often than not, some southern English port.

Anyone flying above the sailing boat as it made its way from the Caribbean to Britain would see a pair of bikini-clad women lying face-down on beach towels on either side of a man in swimming trunks, propped up on his elbows and taking in the view. The highly persuasive scene, which could be staged at a moment's warning, was cover for the real industry going on in the hull below, where the crew were busily hiding half a tonne of Colombian cocaine. As there was always a chance that the sailing boat would be intercepted on the high seas, the waterline was repainted to make it look as if the heavily laden hull was riding light and airy on the water. Seen from a distance, the boat would appear to cut lithely through the waves with nothing on board but the crew.

As it entered British waters, the sailing boat made anchor and waited for a smaller craft to arrive from the nearest port, with two couples aboard. The cargo was then 'coopered' to the smaller boat. A boatload of local day trippers would hardly be searched by the coastguard, but a large sailing boat certainly would, and it would come up clean, with the paperwork in order and no sign of anything untoward. To avoid arousing suspicion, as soon as the crates were transferred the crew would dump all the sophisticated navigational equipment; consigning expensive technology to the sea bed was a small price to pay for the immense returns. A group would be waiting to offload the cargo from the smaller boat and take it by van to nearby garages, where the crates were stored pending distribution.

The street price in Europe and the USA was (and remains) far higher than the costs involved in production, transportation, storage and distribution, because the drug the end consumer snorts is only 15 to 30 per cent pure. In other words, every gram exported by the suppliers is multiplied three to sixfold on the local retail market. It is this profit margin that keeps the globalizsed drug economy purring even in times of crisis. An investment of £150 million sterling can turn in yields of between £450 and £900 million. The gross profit on half a tonne of pure cocaine is in the region of £200 million. Not bad – Tony used to say – for any business, despite occasional drug busts and seizures, which Albino's operation could easily absorb without affecting overall profitability. The cartel would distribute Albino's payment among its members to hedge against possible losses.

With the cogs of exportation well oiled, medium-term profits are guaranteed. And that means there's always a steady stream of replacements to meet turnover demands in the various operations, from money-laundering and transportation of funds and cargo to distribution and sales. Tony was considered a competent operator who could be trusted to move drugs and drug dollars. He carved out a reputation among the inner circle and earned the trust of Albino and the other king-pins, whom he never actually met. Despite his speciality, Tony was always willing to help out in other areas, too, and that was exactly what he was doing during the final chapter of his involvement in the transnational underworld of drug-trafficking — or should that be in the marine world of the transnational transit of coke and yachts.

A Faustian Pact with The Ghost

On his last meeting with Albino, in Rio in 1998, after the customary zigzag and sequence of phone calls from payphones in Leblon, a fancy neighbourhood in the South Zone, Tony was given four jobs and a mission code: 'Don't be lazy'. Good code keys had to be easy to remember and contain ten letters, with no repeats. Each letter corresponds to a number, from one to zero, left to right. The code was their way of concealing passwords and bank accounts, phone numbers, addresses, flights, dates and times. Another tactic was to use simple equipment to clone telephones and select the numbers at random, which made the calls hard to trace.

Upon completion of the four tasks, Tony would be paid the sum of £1 million. It was enough to retire on, so he could devote his energies to his kids, as he'd long dreamed.

He wanted to spend more time with them, be there for them – in short, be the father he felt he hadn't been so far, though the kids idolized him.

His first task was to train DaCosta, a rookie whom Albino had recruited in Rio's swanky Barra da Tijuca neighbourhood, and take him with him on the journey to England.

Training DaCosta would take time because, in the crime world, experience is the only real tutor. Even so, there was a thing or two he could teach him. For example: how do you walk $US100,000 in cash through tight international airport security? When posed the question, DaCosta gave the answer most mortals would: 'Avoid attracting attention; stay calm and act natural.' Wrong. Tony taught his apprentice that if everyone reasoned that way, surely the cops did too. In other words, wouldn't the police be on the lookout for those who simply sailed on by, like they'd nothing to hide? Nothing made you look more innocent than a little awkwardness, such as dropping your jacket, tripping over your wheelie bag, spilling your documents onto the floor or leaving loose change in your pockets so the metal detector would go off, and then apologizing effusively as you fished out the coins. Tony taught him all this and showed him how to pull it off. He also trained him to use the code, clone a phone, take convoluted routes so as to shake off a tail, and spot good places for private conversations – Horse Guards Parade was a safe bet, as it gave 360-degree visual control. Paranoia was the rule. Be suspicious even without apparent reason because, in this business, danger was rarely apparent. Everything was a possible trap. The slightest slip could be fatal.

The second task was to take care of the customary banking transactions, distributing the proceeds from the first phase of the deals and shifting the rest to tax havens and back to Brazil. The third task was to re-establish contact with a segment of the network that had been cut loose since the sudden arrest of one of Albino's men in July that year, ratted on by some suburban London drug pedlar as part of a plea bargain.

It was important that Tony rebuilt the bridge, as the merchandise from Colombia was stockpiling and had to be distributed. The fourth and final task, albeit a pivotal one, was to call in a debt owed by a retail distributor in London who was refusing to pay Albino's emissary on the grounds that the collector was being followed. Tony was authorized to threaten to call in the 'Indians' if he didn't stump out.

The Savage Dance of the 'Indians'

Those who did business with Albino knew that death was the price of betrayal. In Europe and the United States the dirty work was conducted by the 'Indians', a multinational pool of professional hitmen. For security reasons, any given Indian was hired once and once only and was instructed to enter the country, eliminate the target and leave that same day, without talking to anyone. To expedite the process, the Indian would arrive at a pre-arranged address where he would find maps, a weapon, a photo of the victim and specifications for the time and location of the hit. The identities of the hitmen were never known and Albino only ever

uttered the words 'call the Indians' as a last resort. In Latin
America the system was adapted to suit the local reality,
which required far less stealth and expense.

A few months before Tony's last mission, Albino summoned up an 'Indian' to take out the rat in London who had
landed his man in jail and caused the temporary knot in his
supply line – which Tony was called in to fix.

Once in London, Tony settled DaCosta into a hotel and
arranged to meet the debtor. After a labyrinthine runaround
designed to throw off any potential tail, he arrived at the
restaurant and warned the associate that the Indians would
be called unless he paid what was owed. The debtor repeated
what he'd said the last time: he couldn't even talk about the
debt – which he acknowledged and was willing to pay –
because Tony, like the last guy, was being followed. In fact,
he was risking his neck even talking to him.

Having made no headway on that part of his mission,
Tony turned to task number two: taking care of the financial transactions. This went smoothly and earned him his
fortune in advance, delivered to him in a suitcase by an old
associate. On that same day there was some good news and
some bad news. The bad news was that a major traffic accident had gridlocked London, causing mayhem; the good
news was that this meant he wouldn't have to take so many
different roads, side streets, cabs and Tube trains to cover his
tracks. The chaos alone would be cover enough. He decided
to hide the suitcase first, which was no major problem for
someone with his experience, then pulled DaCosta out of
hiding at the hotel and spent the next few days trying to re-
establish the broken link in the supply chain. He used this as

fieldwork training for his apprentice, showing him that the safest way between two points is a zigzag line that takes leg-work and multiple Tube journeys out to the most unexpected places.

With most of his mission accomplished, Tony took DaCosta to the airport. The underling was tense, and was only able to breathe freely once the airplane doors were secured for take-off. False relief. The plane was ordered to open up again and he was arrested with $US35,000 on his person. He denied knowing Tony, even when shown airport CCTV footage of them together at the airport. During his trial, his declarations were so absurd that they got him off the hook – to the cops, he was just a chump being played. A couple of hours after DaCosta's arrest, sometime around daybreak, Tony was sleeping fitfully through a dream of a real-life episode – a scary encounter with some whales during an Atlantic crossing. The sound of the huge cetacean banging against the hull of his yacht overlapped with the thumping on his hotel-room door. The pummelling continued. It was the police: open up. Not long after that, Brazilian Federal Police raided his apartment in Rio. Presented with a search warrant, Angelique and Ana were informed of Tony's arrest in London in connection with the smuggling of two tonnes of cocaine, roughly a quarter of which had been seized in some London estate. Ana hurried little Michel out of the apartment. From the street below, she called her fiancé Rogério, a cop. Between sobs, she managed to tell him that it was over, that her father's arrest for drug-running would only endanger the career he had worked so hard to build. Deep down, however, she harboured suspicions that maybe Rogério was behind it all. It would take years to dispel those doubts, but, by then, it would be too late for them.

That very day, 24 February 1999, with the exception of Albino himself, the whole gang was taken down.

The Crown versus Antonio Lemos Bisneto

During the trial, Tony saw and heard his secret conversations in Hyde Park, which had been recorded loud and clear using sophisticated technology he didn't even know existed and had no defence against. He saw his convoluted peregrinations reduced to slapstick comedy on a screen. He watched dozens upon dozens of hours of footage, heard his own voice in hundreds of tapped phone calls, saw himself in countless photos and discovered that there'd been no fewer than twenty-eight agents watching his every move, day and night, in seven-man crews working six-hour shifts. As it turned out, the debtor had not been lying when he said that Tony was being tailed. He'd been followed the whole time, with the exception of the rainy Tuesday afternoon when a car crash brought the city to a halt. Of that brief but decisive period there was no record or account. It became clear to Tony that the police knew nothing about the operations in Colombia and the Caribbean, much less about the ghost at the helm, Albino.

From the dock, Tony played a walk-on part in the archaic power play of crime and punishment, there merely as supporting actor to the weighty leading part, that of the judge. In his impresssive wig, the Right Honourable Chief Justice Arthur Brown did not look the buffoon Tony had expected; on the contrary, the wig conferred an ancestral yet timeless aura of authority. Tony was struck by the judge's intellect, keen perception, speed of thought and vast knowledge, so unimpeachable as to leave no grounds whatsoever for resentment on Tony's part. The judge seemed to have inexhaustible reserves of compassion, which must have caused him some distress, seeing as his function was to uphold and enforce the law with cold reserve. Tony felt this strange, paradoxical and latent emotional bond with the judge and admiration for the obviously paternal figure he cut, however hard he may have striven to conceal it.

More than a year after the beginning of his trial, Tony set foot in that temple of British justice for the last time, and with no hard feelings; exhausted, on tenterhooks, heart about to burst, but with absolutely no rancour. Each protagonist was in his rightful place, and acting accordingly. He totally understood that in hounding him, probing him, pinning him against the wall, the barrister was just doing his job. His huntsman's tenacity was purely professional. It was all a game. He understood that. His lawyers spanned a three-tier hierarchy, with the courtroom the sole preserve of the barrister, the eldest of the three.

Tony was offered all manner of plea bargains. He wouldn't have to inform on anyone, just provide the addresses of properties bought with drug money. That alone would chop numerous years off his sentence – how

many was up to the judge to decide. But he remained loyal
to his fellow adventurers; perhaps because he considered
himself an honest guy – true to his own peculiar brand of
ethics – but more likely because he weighed the years he
would have to serve against other factors known only to
himself. After all, flipping had its price in his line of
business.

There were many harrowing moments, and hearing his
sentence read was the worst of them. The Right Honourable
Arthur Brown set aside the ironic tone and blasé formal dic-
tion with which he usually tried to disguise his tendency to
side emotionally with the weak and the vulnerable. He
turned to Tony, mustered the full gravitas of his authority
and said: 'That you have committed serious crimes has been
proven beyond reasonable doubt. However, as I do not want
this to be the final chapter in your life, I shall opt for leni-
ency, and pass a lighter sentence than I really should. Instead
of the determinate sentence of twenty-seven years . . . I
hereby sentence you to . . . twenty-four years in prison.' It
wasn't a cruel joke. Arthur Brown really did sympathize
with Tony. And he knew the value of a year – having lived
some seventy-odd of his own.

Only one other experience rivalled the sentencing for
sheer intensity. After a little over a month in the dock –
which he affectionately called 'the gallows' – subjected to
meticulous (he preferred to say 'sadistic') grilling by the
prosecutors, having his version of events picked apart by
cross-examinations, witness testimony and audiovisual evidence, Tony imploded. On the outside he remained firm,
seated, together, but on the inside he was dissolving. His

mind short-circuited and he began to watch the court proceedings from above, in the air, seeing himself move, speak, answer, sip water, surveying the whole choreography of frenetic stenographers, prowling barristers, waiting cops and expert witnesses, the rapt, attentive jurors. He watched the whole ritual play out from above, in the top corner of the courtroom, floating free of his own body. It was painful, terrifying, mortifying. How do you ask for an adjournment on the grounds of an out-of-body experience? How do you ask for an adjournment so that the defendant can re-embody? There was no escaping the absurdity of it. So he turned to the judge and did precisely that. The judge summoned a court psychiatrist and, to the prosecutor's chagrin, adjourned the case for two weeks.

If, at this point, the reader feels a chuckle coming on, let me just say that floating free of one's body is no laughing matter and, contrary to what one might think, it's not at all pleasant. The experience eventually waned, but the sensation, according to Tony, was downright devastating.

While Tony was in jail in England, various difficulties meant that visits by his family – despite their strong bonds – were limited to just two or three. The first, two years into his sentence, stuck in his memory for its special intensity. Ana, his daughter (then twenty-one), Michel, his son (then eleven) and Mila, his mother, flew across the same ocean he'd sailed so many times with different crews. Monitored closely by CCTV, it took them hours to get through the successive security points, amid mounting anxiety. When they did finally come face to face Tony's kids saw their father weep for the first time.

Visit to the Bunker

Michel jumped straight into Tony's lap and fell asleep, lulled by his father's familiar scent. Years later he would explain his unwavering admiration for his dad, despite it all: 'He never picked up a gun; he detested violence. He sold drugs because people bought them. Is the product he sold bad for people? Yes, it's dangerous . . . but so are alcohol and cigarettes. But try explaining that to the Crown or my grandmother!' For Michel, his father was the victim of the hypocrisy of a failed system.

Michel was his own man long before he became an athlete, to his mother's dismay. And not just any athlete. Michel would be a Brazilian pioneer of the French sport of parkour, a radical urban choreography that turns every straight line into a baroque flourish, transformed by aesthetic pleasure and a love of danger. Curiously, these are traits he inherited from his father, who made a habit of straying from straight lines in pursuit of risk – tortuous meanderings he shared with the 'Indians', Albino and the police obliged to follow in their footsteps.

The parkourist scales overpasses in bounds, leaps between buildings, teeters on the highest ledges of cathedrals and, most of all, systematically avoids the obvious, the simple, the practical, the everyday. The parkourist is a devotee of excess, of the discontinuous, the useless, subverting the very principles that govern our cities. In his world, the shortest distance between two points is almost never a straight line. Tony, Albino, the 'Indians' and their lookouts lacked the parkourist's art and skill but shared his aversion to the beaten path, and applied the same logic in making connections, identifying, understanding and achieving their goals, and milking them of their consequences.

For Tony his adventurous, fearless, talented son, with his own ideas and, admittedly, a touch of cynicism, is 'a well of affection and an inexhaustible source of pride'. Michel was to move to France, to live with his French mother, and take up French citizenship. The lad also saw his sister as something of a second mother, and for good reason. During the years he suffered from early depression, Michel convinced Ana to come live with him and her stepmother in Paris – a move that earned her a French passport as well.

No sooner had Michel snuggled into his father's arms than Mila, railing against the draconian restrictions of the British prison system, which wouldn't even allow her to embrace her son, ripped into Tony for betraying her family's honoured history and for 'tarnishing' (she'd picked the verb carefully from her prized vocabulary) the good name her father had earned through a lifetime of hard, honest work.

However, it was Ana who set the tone for the visit, appealing to her grandmother's milder side – or for a little good sense at least – and using the time to address practical concerns for their future, because they still had a future, she insisted: freedom lay at the end of these travails. As far as she was concerned, Tony's fate should follow a lucid plan, and she was intent on carrying it through, 'come what may', she'd insist energetically, with her uniquely but paradoxically exuberant pragmatism. No matter what it took, she would get him home, and that she did. Six years later, after sacrificing much of her youth, Ana's relentless wrangling

with lawyers and politicians paid off, and Tony was transferred to prison in Brazil, where more lenient legislation
commuted his sentence and saw him released back into society twenty-four months later, many years ahead of schedule.
This faster track to freedom was the main reason why Tony
opted to swap the asepsis of the British panopticon for the
miserable insalubrity of Brazil's sweltering prisons.

Back to Rio

In all, Tony spent over four years in a supermax control unit
and three years in lower-security prisons in England. He
arrived back in Brazil on 19 May 2006, where he would
serve the rest of his sentence, which was adapted to national
legislation. There are three imprisonment regimes in Brazil
and the law allows prisoners to graduate progressively
toward more lenient forms of detention, from closed to
semi-closed and finally open prison, or parole. The first
glimpse of his homeland was the grey sprawl of Cumbica
airport in the São Paulo satellite town of Guarulhos. When
he finally touched down at Santos Dumont in Rio de
Janeiro, he couldn't contain his emotion and had to dry his
eyes with cuffed hands.

However prepared he thought he would be for the culture shock, his time in Brazil's penitentiaries scared the
life out of him. It was like leaping between totally different worlds. The aseptic, maddening isolation of the
British vault was replaced by the terror of Brazil's torrid
dungeons.

When it came to considering the option of transferring to Brazil, Rio specifically, he had mulled over many factors, but not the actual material conditions of incarceration. The desire to get back home spoke louder than anything else. His mother had warned him about the heat, and Tony laughed it off. His mother's letters described the temperatures in Rio's cells as torturous. In Rio, she'd said, prisoners roasted in their own juices. The stench was rank. The environment was medieval and disease – TB particularly – was rife. Brazilian jails were disgusting on every level, from the food to the flea- and tick-infested mattresses. Surely he knew that. Tony scoffed at the thought of the micro-fauna and rodents; he didn't mind being a Noah's ark as long as it got him home. His mother's list of objections was a small price to pay for release from Her Majesty's sterilized cube. Tropical heat would be a welcome change, evoking turbines, steam, sizzling asphalt, sun-drenched beaches. He could almost feel the beads of sweat start to roll. Damn the cold. He was, and always had been, a creature of summer. His mother's warnings were diluted in a flood of late-sprung, visceral patriotism.

For years he had dreamed of a return to Rio. He wanted to taste the salt on the sea breeze. And finally he was there, sweating and cuffed. But it didn't take long for his fantasies to die of heat-stroke. Within twenty-four hours of his arrival in a typical Rio holding prison, the pennies of reality started to drop. Among the glorious iniquities of old Rio was corruption. The informal solidarity of the authorities was always up for sale. The prison economy had a lot to offer the better-heeled prisoner, and in a microcosm prone to rioting and gang-related massacres, top of everyone's wish list was a place in a special cell. Tony managed to get himself into one, where he stayed, at a reasonably safe distance from the confines of civilization, between the months of May and August.

When he reached the transfer facility where he was to be held before moving on to one of the penitentiaries in the dreaded Bangu complex, he was told to hand in all his personal belongings but was spared the trip to the barber, where prisoners' heads were unceremoniously shaved with a few deft flicks of the wrist. He was addressed with the deference of 'senhor', the conventional Brazilian recognition of status or seniority, and he took that as a very good sign, though he wasn't sure of what. He found out soon enough: he was white and from a middle-class background. As such, he was a potential source of perks for the badly paid prison wardens. Before he'd even opened his mouth, the guards and *faxinas* (inmates who assist the guards) had already identified his strength and his weakness: money and fear. He was taken to a grossly overcrowded underground cell block. His chaperone led Tony through the place painfully slowly in order to fill him with unbearable dread. However welcome tropical heat had seemed when he was shivering his way through an English winter, it was hellish now, and all his romantic notions melted away. His mother had not been exaggerating: it must have been 50 degrees Celsius in there. Hundreds of half-naked, emaciated men were herded in together like cattle, spewing the language of hate and hanging from vertical nets like birds trapped in mid-flight. There wasn't enough floor space for everyone at once, so the nets were the only option. The stink of latrines and sulphur accosted the nose. The floor was alive with rodents visiting pools of blood and vomit amid rivulets of urine. As Tony made his way along the cell bars, the inmates stared and scowled. About 500 people were packed into that hell-hole. It was a brief re-introduction to a Rio that had slipped his mind.

Tony was terrified, much more so than on any stormy Atlantic night. The only episodes that could rival this for sheer fear were when his yacht was attacked by whales and the time he saw a shark stalk some of his travel buddies in the Red Sea. The only occasion he'd ever been more scared was when he found his spirit drifting above his body in that British courtroom.

He stopped, looked into the cell and tried to summon the courage to go inside, where he saw a tightly shuffling queue of bare-chested prisoners that moved but never shortened. He realized what they were queuing for: a shower. An oasis. The queue stood for a few seconds under the trickle of cold water, after which they'd get straight back in line for another round as the water dried on their skin.

Before terror overcame him altogether, his chaperone said:

'You don't have to stay here.'

It took Tony a second to compute. Maybe it was jet lag, the emotion, sensory overload, disorientation. His brain stalled. He turned to look at his chaperone. Had he heard him right?

'You're loaded, aren't ya? So . . .'

'You mean I can stay somewhere else?' 'If you can pay.' 'How much?'

'Depends.'

'How much do you want?' 'I don't set the price. There's a list. Things are organized round here.' 'How much?'

'The two special cells with separate beds and air conditioning are occupied at the moment, but there's a bigger cell, in the social wing. There's no air conditioning and no separate beds. Just bunks.'

'OK, OK. Anywhere but here.'

'There are eight beds in four bunks, but eight TV sets, a shower and a fridge.'

'How much?' 'Two thousand upfront and two hundred a week.' 'Deal.' The *faxina* quit the tour. Mission accomplished. Sale made. And the customer didn't even haggle. The tour was infallible. Even if the new arrival didn't have the money, he'd find some way to get it. Everyone did, just to get out of that cesspit. Well, nearly everyone. Hell was for the poor.

Love's Labours Lost on the Morning of Carnival

A few months after settling into the special cell at the transfer facility, still waiting for an opening at the Bangu penitentiary, where he would serve out his sentence, Tony received a surprise visit. The warden came up to the bars and called him. Someone was here to see him. Weird. It wasn't visiting day. Seven years incarcerated in England had stoked his propensity toward paranoia. The contrast with a decade on the open ocean had melted his psychological compass.

'Someone's here to see you. Let's go.' 'My lawyer?' Tony stuck his wrists through the hatch as the warden pulled out his cuffs.

'My daughter?'

'A cop.' Tony's head was spinning. He tried to calm his nerves. The guard added: 'From Bope.'

They marched down the corridor and turned into a large room he'd never been in before. The guard left immediately. The new surroundings mobilized Tony's persecutory imagination.

'Tony.'

In the unmistakable black uniform, with his gun hanging loudly on his belt, the skull-and-bones badge on his cap, the black Bope officer smiled at Tony from the doorway.

'Tony, let me see you, man.'

He stepped forward, arms wide, and enveloped Tony in a bear-hug. He could hardly believe it. It was Rogério Mendes, his one-time future son-in-law. Slapping Tony heavily on the back, Mendes welled with emotion so genuine it momentarily took the hieratic edge off his stormtrooper uniform:

'Man, you don't know how good it is to see you again.'

The soldier's warmth wilted Tony's defences, and all became clear when he took a step back and said:

'It wasn't racism. It wasn't racism. It was drugs. I get it. I get that now. Thank Christ.'

He pulled Tony into an another bear-hug:

'Drug-smuggling, it happens. That happens.'

He leant back again, hands on Tony's shoulders, a warm glow in his eyes:

'It wasn't racism.'

It all started back in the 1990s, when Rogério Mendes, a black kid from the favela, fell for the beautiful, precocious, assertive and active daughter of the white upper-middle-class economist Tony Lemos Bisneto. Mendes, a Bope cadet, was handsome, charming, athletic, honest, affectionate, hard-working and brave, and Ana swooned. The uniform alone was a walking gallery of symbols of virility. You could write a book about Rogério's life, so I did, and it was turned into the film *Elite Squad*. Mendes spent his nights raiding Rio's shanty towns to locate and eliminate drug lords. At daybreak he changed out of his uniform, showered, sprayed on some cologne, had a hearty breakfast and rode the bus out to Gávea, in the upmarket South Zone, to study law at the city's premier university. His classmates were the pampered rich kids who consumed the drugs peddled by his nightly prey. It didn't take him long to see the obvious: the rich kids were white; the poor kids were black. The whites, the users, were rarely accosted by the cops, but the blacks, the sellers, were hounded, tortured and summarily executed.

Tony was already up to his neck in the smuggling business when his daughter brought the dashing young cop home to meet the parents. It didn't strike Tony as a good idea to have a Bope officer under his roof, so he told his daughter not to bring the lad over any more. If she wanted to date him, they could meet elsewhere. No matter how polite the kid was, he didn't want a stranger in the house. He said no more. No more was needed. Ana had understood. She was the type who stood by her convictions and her choices, and was known among friends and acquaintances as a straight-talker, so straight she often came across as aggressive. When she told Mendes about her father's decision, the young cop took it hard. The hostility hurt because it was all too familiar. It replicated the paternal abandonment that lay beneath the topsoil of all Mendes' troubles, and found echo in Brazil's and Rio's specific brand of racism, cloaked by the empty rhetoric of racial democracy. Mendes' own father had rejected him too – not because of his colour, but he'd rejected him, and that was enough. That original wound had never healed and it was ripped open again and again by the claws of racial discrimination.

The relationship between Ana and Mendes grew more serious and became an engagement, but a single day can undo years of solid development. On Carnival Friday, February 1999, Ana woke up feeling sprightly. It was a beautiful morning. Rogério had proposed to her only two days earlier and they'd set the date for the second half of that same year. They were going to take Carnival as a dry run for the honeymoon; a romantic break. The future bride jumped out of bed. She wanted to get to the supermarket early so she could stock the fridge for her stepmother and seven-year-old brother. Rogério would pick her up in the car at ten. Just before eight, with the breakfast dishes still on the table, her stepmother watering the plants on the balcony and Michel already playing his video game, there was a loud knock on the door. Strange. The doorman always rang visitors through before letting them come up. Ana opened the door. A Federal Police officer flashed his ID and asked if this was the home of Tony Lemos Bisneto:

'Yes. I'm his daughter.'

The officer got straight to the point:

'Your father has been arrested in London on charges of conspiracy to smuggle two tonnes of cocaine.'

Her world crumbled. Nothing made sense. It had to be some terrible mistake – a huge misunderstanding. The officer handed her the search warrant as the other policemen filed into the apartment. She didn't want her little brother to witness the traumatic, mortifying spectacle, so she asked for permission to take him downstairs. Descending in the elevator, she held back the tears so as not to upset him. Luckily, the first Carnival revellers getting an early start at the bars of Ipanema were colourful and boisterous enough to distract young Michel from the fleet of police cars outside his building. Carnival was readying its attractions: scantily clad beachgoers, drums and tambourines, alcohol and bar choirs, bottles in hand. The whole hypnotic choreography was warming up, waiting for the trance of samba, the inebriating pheromones of sensuality, the bacchanal of rhythms and universal inversions.*

But Tony's daughter's world was falling apart. Images, feelings, words and hypotheses churned up without the anchor of logical connection as she wandered the shoreline promenade with her little brother. Her rational mind urged her to bring order to the chaos, arrange the fragments into sequences of cause and effect. Her father's arrest could signal Rogério's ruin, the end of a career he'd worked so hard to

---

*During Carnival, men can become women, and vice versa, poor people become kings.

build which had taken such energy and sacrifice. The Feds would quickly discover that Rogério Mendes was engaged to the daughter of an international drug smuggler. She couldn't let that happen. There was no guarantee that breaking off their relationship would keep Mendes out of the frame, but it was essential anyway. She would have to let him go, for the sake of his future, to prevent him from having to atone for the sins of her father—if indeed they were her father's sins, which she doubted. She believed in Tony's innocence. Walking among the revellers as the city raised the curtain on a parallel universe, a diabolical doubt took hold in the folds of Ana's mind and sent shockwaves to her heart: what if Rogério already knew about her dad's arrest? What if he was behind it? What if their relationship had just been cover for his infiltration? Those hypotheses wrestled in her thoughts, but they both led to the same conclusion: she had to end the relationship. Devastated by the self-mutilation forced upon her, she pulled out her cellphone and called her fiancé, telling him not to come, that her father had been arrested in London, and that they couldn't be together any longer.

They never saw each other again.

Ten years after his conviction and two years after his extradition, Tony was released from jail.* The life of an ex-con isn't easy. At the age of fifty-eight, carrying that kind of stigma, everything is hard: finding a job, shaking off a pro-

---

* A full biography is given in Luiz Eduardo Soares, *Tudo ou nada* (Nova Fronteira, 2012).

tracted adolescence, but he found milder seas to sail, and made a fresh start. His new life has been a happy one, with his kids, with his new wife, with the indestructible will to enjoy his restored liberty. Despite it all, he continues to believe that nothing on earth compares to the beauty of Rio de Janeiro.

ALLEN LANE
an imprint of
PENGUIN BOOKS

Recently Published

Peter H. Wilson, *The Holy Roman Empire: A Thousand Years of Europe's History*

Todd Rose, *The End of Average: How to Succeed in a World that Values Sameness*

Frank Trentmann, *Empire of Things: How We Became a World of Consumers, from the Fifteenth Century to the Twenty-First*

Laura Ashe, *Richard II: A Brittle Glory*

John Donvan and Caren Zucker, *In a Different Key: The Story of Autism*

Jack Shenker, *The Egyptians: A Radical Story*

Tim Judah, *In Wartime: Stories from Ukraine*

Serhii Plokhy, *The Gates of Europe: A History of Ukraine*

Robin Lane Fox, *Augustine: Conversions and Confessions*

Peter Hennessy and James Jinks, *The Silent Deep: The Royal Navy Submarine Service Since 1945*

Sean McMeekin, *The Ottoman Endgame: War, Revolution and the Making of the Modern Middle East, 1908–1923*

Charles Moore, *Margaret Thatcher: The Authorized Biography, Volume Two: Everything She Wants*

Dominic Sandbrook, *The Great British Dream Factory: The Strange History of Our National Imagination*

Larissa MacFarquhar, *Strangers Drowning: Voyages to the Brink of Moral Extremity*

Niall Ferguson, *Kissinger: 1923-1968: The Idealist*

Carlo Rovelli, *Seven Brief Lessons on Physics*

Tim Blanning, *Frederick the Great: King of Prussia*

Ian Kershaw, *To Hell and Back: Europe, 1914–1949*

Pedro Domingos, *The Master Algorithm: How the Quest for the Ultimate Learning Machine Will Remake Our World*

David Wootton, *The Invention of Science: A New History of the Scientific Revolution*

Christopher Tyerman, *How to Plan a Crusade: Reason and Religious War in the Middle Ages*

Andy Beckett, *Promised You A Miracle: UK 80–82*

Carl Watkins, *Stephen: The Reign of Anarchy*

Anne Curry, *Henry V: From Playboy Prince to Warrior King*

John Gillingham, *William II: The Red King*

Roger Knight, *William IV: A King at Sea*

Douglas Hurd, *Elizabeth II: The Steadfast*

Richard Nisbett, *Mindware: Tools for Smart Thinking*

Jochen Bleicken, *Augustus: The Biography*

Paul Mason, *PostCapitalism: A Guide to Our Future*

Frank Wilczek, *A Beautiful Question: Finding Nature's Deep Design*

Roberto Saviano, *Zero Zero Zero*

Owen Hatherley, *Landscapes of Communism: A History Through Buildings*

César Hidalgo, *Why Information Grows: The Evolution of Order, from Atoms to Economies*

Aziz Ansari and Eric Klinenberg, *Modern Romance: An Investigation*

Sudhir Hazareesingh, *How the French Think: An Affectionate Portrait of an Intellectual People*

Steven D. Levitt and Stephen J. Dubner, *When to Rob a Bank: A Rogue Economist's Guide to the World*

Leonard Mlodinow, *The Upright Thinkers: The Human Journey from Living in Trees to Understanding the Cosmos*

Hans Ulrich Obrist, *Lives of the Artists, Lives of the Architects*

Richard H. Thaler, *Misbehaving: The Making of Behavioural Economics*

Sheldon Solomon, Jeff Greenberg and Tom Pyszczynski, *Worm at the Core: On the Role of Death in Life*

Nathaniel Popper, *Digital Gold: The Untold Story of Bitcoin*

Dominic Lieven, *Towards the Flame: Empire, War and the End of Tsarist Russia*

Noel Malcolm, *Agents of Empire: Knights, Corsairs, Jesuits and Spies in the Sixteenth-Century Mediterranean World*

James Rebanks, *The Shepherd's Life: A Tale of the Lake District*

David Brooks, *The Road to Character*

Joseph Stiglitz, *The Great Divide*

Ken Robinson and Lou Aronica, *Creative Schools: Revolutionizing Education from the Ground Up*

Clotaire Rapaille and Andrés Roemer, *Move UP: Why Some Cultures Advances While Others Don't*

Jonathan Keates, *William III and Mary II: Partners in Revolution*

David Womersley, *James II: The Last Catholic King*

Richard Barber, *Henry II: A Prince Among Princes*

Jane Ridley, *Victoria: Queen, Matriarch, Empress*

John Gray, *The Soul of the Marionette: A Short Enquiry into Human Freedom*

Emily Wilson, *Seneca: A Life*

Michael Barber, *How to Run a Government: So That Citizens Benefit and Taxpayers Don't Go Crazy*

Dana Thomas, *Gods and Kings: The Rise and Fall of Alexander McQueen and John Galliano*

Steven Weinberg, *To Explain the World: The Discovery of Modern Science*

Jennifer Jacquet, *Is Shame Necessary?: New Uses for an Old Tool*

Eugene Rogan, *The Fall of the Ottomans: The Great War in the Middle East, 1914-1920*

Norman Doidge, *The Brain's Way of Healing: Stories of Remarkable Recoveries and Discoveries*

John Hooper, *The Italians*

Sven Beckert, *Empire of Cotton: A New History of Global Capitalism*

Mark Kishlansky, *Charles I: An Abbreviated Life*

Philip Ziegler, *George VI: The Dutiful King*

David Cannadine, *George V: The Unexpected King*

Stephen Alford, *Edward VI: The Last Boy King*

John Guy, *Henry VIII: The Quest for Fame*

Robert Tombs, *The English and their History: The First Thirteen Centuries*

Neil MacGregor, *Germany: The Memories of a Nation*

Uwe Tellkamp, *The Tower: A Novel*

Roberto Calasso, *Ardor*

Slavoj Žižek, *Trouble in Paradise: Communism After the End of History*

Francis Pryor, *Home: A Time Traveller's Tales from Britain's Prehistory*

R. F. Foster, *Vivid Faces: The Revolutionary Generation in Ireland, 1890-1923*

Andrew Roberts, *Napoleon the Great*

Shami Chakrabarti, *On Liberty*

Bessel van der Kolk, *The Body Keeps the Score: Mind, Brain and Body in the Transformation of Trauma*

Brendan Simms, *The Longest Afternoon: The 400 Men Who Decided the Battle of Waterloo*

Naomi Klein, *This Changes Everything: Capitalism vs the Climate*

Owen Jones, *The Establishment: And How They Get Away with It*

Caleb Scharf, *The Copernicus Complex: Our Cosmic Significance in a Universe of Planets and Probabilities*

Martin Wolf, *The Shifts and the Shocks: What We've Learned - and Have Still to Learn - from the Financial Crisis*

Steven Pinker, *The Sense of Style: The Thinking Person's Guide to Writing in the 21st Century*

Vincent Deary, *How We Are: Book One of the How to Live Trilogy*

Henry Kissinger, *World Order*